Praise **THE GENDER CRE**

"*The Gender Creative Child* is an invaluable resource for families and practitioners wanting to understand the complexity and beauty of gender development and the value of affirmative care. I'm struck that Dr. Ehrensaft's most revolutionary idea is also her most straightforward—if we really learn how to listen to our children, they will tell us what they need."—**Aron Janssen, MD,** director and founder of the Gender and Sexuality Service, NYU Langone Medical Center

"Dr. Ehrensaft has achieved the impossible: an easy-to-read, but hard-to-forget, handbook that speaks to parents, teachers, medical doctors, counselors, and policymakers alike. In an accessible and conversational manner, Ehrensaft tackles tough challenges such as how to help gender creative children who also struggle with autism; why some youth intentionally choose the middle of the gender spectrum instead of the binary; how to navigate the legal and financial barriers to cross-sex hormone treatments; and why we must analyze traditional gender-based research studies with a critical eye and the wisdom of experience. This book urges us to abandon the fantasy that gender is a simple either/or proposition, and embrace the reality that there are infinite manifestations of a person's identity. If we allow children to blaze the trail, however, then their path to self-actualization becomes clearer. A must-have for any professional who works with youth." —**Jessica Herthel,** coauthor of *I Am Jazz*

"*The Gender Creative Child* should be required reading for all therapists, pediatricians, and K–12 educators and for parents whose children express their gender differently from societal expectations. Diane Ehrensaft deftly shows that many trans and gender-nonconforming children can be identified from a young age and how critical it is to provide support to them."—**Genny Beemyn, PHD,** trans educator and coauthor of *The Lives of Transgender People*

THE EXPERIMENT

BECAUSE EVERY BOOK IS A TEST OF NEW IDEAS

"Diane Ehrensaft has written an exceptional book—smart, accessible, and beautifully written. Her work is fueled by empathy and compassion, apparent on each page, and informed by her unparalleled expertise as a gender expert, as well as her characteristic thoughtful intelligence. Her first book, *Gender Born, Gender Made*, presaged the more widespread recognition of gender diversity in children. In *The Gender Creative Child*, she elaborates on the forces that shape gender development, drawing on years of work with children and families. She entwines her dual clinical and scholarly perspectives into a clear and coherent framework of understanding. This book will serve as an education for those who are naive about gender diversity and as a refuge for individuals and families who are attempting to raise gender creative children on their developmental odyssey with sensitivity and love."

—**Amy C. Tishelman, PHD,** director of clinical research and senior staff psychologist, Gender Management Service, Boston Children's Hospital and Harvard Medical School

"*The Gender Creative Child* is a must-read for parents of transgender and gender-expansive children and the professionals who work with them. Dr. Ehrensaft, a leading authority on gender development, uses an inviting, engaging, and humble style to present the gender affirmative model and provide insight into achieving gender health for all people. Dr. Ehrensaft's concepts of gender webs, gender smoothies, gender ghosts, and gender angels, and her methods of distinguishing 'apples,' 'oranges,' and 'fruit salads,' are illuminated by her use of multiple real-life stories of families with gender creative children. There is no other resource like *The Gender Creative Child* and I am thrilled to recommend it to my clients."—**Colt Keo-Meier, PHD,** licensed psychologist and cofounder of Gender Infinity in Houston, Texas

"This book offers an accessible, engaging, and informative guide for families and therapists supporting transgender and gender creative youth. Dr. Ehrensaft's commitment to and empathy for the young people with whom she works as well as for their families is clear throughout the book."—**Heather Killelea McEntarfer, PHD,** author of *Navigating Gender and Sexuality in the Classroom*

"*The Gender Creative Child* lays out what we now know—or think we know—about gender and points out how much we still have to learn. Dr. Ehrensaft deftly illustrates that, despite our tenaciously held view to the contrary, gender never has been binary; we just couldn't or wouldn't see that clearly. She uses a multitude of case vignettes to help remove the blinders to gender complexity. Dr. Ehrensaft's young patients are wonderful guides on this journey—often pointing out things that we would rather not see, but also showing us the limitless vistas that lie ahead. This is essential reading for the mental health community."
—**Toni Heineman, DMH,** executive director and founder of A Home Within and author of *Relational Treatment of Trauma*

"An amazing book! It is a must-read for anyone whose daily life involves children, from parents and pediatricians to mental health providers and family court judges. *The Gender Creative Child* is a comprehensive, thorough, and accessible resource written by the preeminent expert in the field. The book holds the reader's hand as it takes them through basic concepts and complex issues, answering common questions and concerns."—**Asaf Orr, Esq.,** Transgender Youth Project Staff Attorney, National Center for Lesbian Rights

"Dr. Ehrensaft explains gender and children like no one can. She equips adults to understand and support gender-expansive children the way they deserve to be. This book is the newest must-have for every LGBTQ library and a must-read for every adult with a child in their life."
—**Lori Duron,** author of *Raising My Rainbow*

"In *The Gender Creative Child*, Diane Ehrensaft illuminates the tremendous variation in gender identity and expression that we find in children. With a depth of understanding that comes from years of experience, she shows parents, professionals, and the culture at large how to foster authenticity and psychological health. Dr. Ehrensaft's emphasis on the uniqueness of each child reminds us to be thoughtful, keep an open mind, and listen carefully. I highly recommend this book!"
—**Irwin Krieger,** author of *Helping Your Transgender Teen*

"Finally a book that appropriately reflects the great spectrum of gender diversity that young children and teens embody and envision. Dr. Ehrensaft has, once again, moved beyond the challenges of identity politics and academic controversies and meets parents, families, and young people where they live—exploring the edges of gender expression in rapidly changing times."

—**Arlene Istar Lev, LCSW-R, CASAC,** family therapist, gender specialist, and founder of Choices Counseling and Consulting

"*The Gender Creative Child* is a critical resource for anyone who loves or works with gender-nonconforming children and youth. In addition to providing an insightful overview of the medical and social context in which our misperceptions of gender have been passed down and the efforts underway to correct them, the author of *Gender Born, Gender Made* once again brings us into the room with a wide array of gender-nonconforming children to hear their struggles and wisdom as they communicate their experience of gender. True to her word as listener and translator, the author articulates what she has learned and faithfully guides families, professionals, educators, and communities to create safe, accepting environments that foster the full development of all."

—**Candace Waldron,** author of *My Daughter He: Transitioning with Our Transgender Children*, trans parent coach, and speaker

"Diane Ehrensaft's new book is a timely treatise on the ways families can best support the journeys of their gender creative children. As a pioneer in the care of transgender and gender-nonconforming kids, Dr. Ehrensaft continues to teach us important new concepts in the ever-evolving gender landscape. Parents, teachers, therapists, and medical practitioners, sit up and take note! Although society may still be riddled with the outdated gender ghosts of times past, Dr. Ehrensaft is here to safely steer us toward a day when all children will feel safe and assured in their authentic, affirmed gender."

—**Rachel Pepper, LMFT,** coauthor of *The Transgender Child: A Handbook for Families and Professionals*

"This exciting book from the author of *Gender Born, Gender Made* is an essential guide for any parent whose child goes against the grain of society's expectations about gender. Diane Ehrensaft has delved deeply into the hearts and minds of gender-nonconforming and transgender children and adolescents to bust a multitude of myths. In simple language, *The Gender Creative Child* explores and explains new ways of thinking about gender-nonconformity. It's an invaluable handbook, providing sensitive wisdom, helpful messages, and constructive advice for confused or anxious parents challenged by their child's gender creativity and complexity. It's a must for all parents, teachers, and pediatricians and should be in every public library. Riding the crest of the sea change of gender she describes, Dr. Ehrensaft is indeed a 'gender angel.' I only wish I'd had this book when my son was a toddler in the early '90s." —**Julie Tarney,** author of *My Son Wears Heels*

"Diane Ehrensaft's timely book offers parents, practitioners, and community members an invaluable road map for supporting children who are transgender or gender-nonconforming. Highly accessible, Dr. Ehrensaft offers the adults in the lives of transgender children a compelling analysis of the dangers of trying to change a child's gender expression and/or identity. Dr. Ehrensaft draws on her vast clinical experience and an emerging body of research to argue that we should instead strive to cultivate a child's gender health by 'listening and acting.' *The Gender Creative Child* should be required reading for anyone wanting to support the well-being of transgender and gender-nonconforming children."
—**Kimberley Ens Manning**, founding board member of Gender Creative
Kids Canada, and principal at the Simone de Beauvoir Institute,
Concordia University

"Without Dr. Ehrensaft's willingness to share her knowledge, our family's journey would have been unimaginable. Dr. Ehrensaft has crafted yet another remarkable tool for the world to understand gender creative children. Using her own professional experience with countless gender-nonconforming individuals, this book will undoubtedly guide more parents to see gender is not as simple as checking a box."
—**Hillary Whittington,** author of *Raising Ryland: Our Story of Parenting
a Transgender Child with No Strings Attached*

ALSO BY DIANE EHRENSAFT, PhD

*Gender Born, Gender Made: Raising Healthy
Gender-Nonconforming Children*

*Parenting Together: Men and Women
Sharing the Care of Their Children*

*Spoiling Childhood: How Well-Meaning Parents Are
Giving Children Too Much—But Not What They Need*

*Mommies, Daddies, Donors, Surrogates:
Answering Tough Questions and Building Strong Families*

WITH TONI VAUGHN HEINEMAN

*Building a Home Within: Meeting the Emotional
Needs of Children and Youth in Foster Care*

THE
GENDER
CREATIVE
CHILD

Pathways for Nurturing and Supporting
Children Who Live Outside Gender Boxes

DIANE EHRENSAFT, PhD

FOREWORD BY NORMAN SPACK, MD

THE EXPERIMENT
NEW YORK

The Experiment, LLC
220 East 23rd Street, Suite 301
New York, NY 10010-4674
www.theexperimentpublishing.com

The Experiment's books are available at special discounts when purchased in bulk for premiums and sales promotions as well as for fund-raising or educational use. For details, contact us at info@theexperimentpublishing.com.

Library of Congress Cataloging-in-Publication Data

Names: Ehrensaft, Diane, author.
Title: The gender creative child : pathways for nurturing and supporting
    children who live outside gender boxes / Diane Ehrensaft, PhD ; foreword
    by Norman Spack, MD.
Description: New York, NY : Experiment, 2016. | Includes bibliographical
    references and index.
Identifiers: LCCN 2015041549| ISBN 9781615193066 (pbk.) | ISBN 9781615193073
    (ebook)
Subjects: LCSH: Transgender children. | Transgender youth. | Gender
    identity--Psychological aspects. | Child rearing.
Classification: LCC HQ1075 .E363 2016 | DDC 649.1--dc23
LC record available at http://lccn.loc.gov/2015041549

ISBN 978-1-61519-306-6
Ebook ISBN 978-1-61519-307-3

Cover design by Sarah Smith
Cover photograph by Lindsay Morris/INSTITUTE
Author photograph by Jim Hawley
Text design by Sarah Schneider

Manufactured in the United States of America
Distributed by Workman Publishing Company, Inc.
Distributed simultaneously in Canada by Thomas Allen & Son Ltd.

First printing April 2016
10 9 8 7 6 5 4 3 2 1

*To my beloved parents, Edith Ehrensaft
and Morris Ehrensaft, ninety-six and
ninety-eight years old, and still going strong*

Contents

FOREWORD BY
NORMAN SPACK, MD

IN 1985, when I ran an adolescent medicine practice, a colleague asked me to provide testosterone treatment for a recent college graduate, my first transgender patient. Although the patient had been born anatomically female and had reached full female puberty, he went through college as a male with the support of his three male non-trans roommates, who kept his secret.

Treatment was simplistic and insufficient then, especially for patients transitioning from male to female. We only treated adolescents over the age of sixteen (post-puberty) who had been referred by highly experienced therapists, of whom there were few who worked closely with gender-nonconforming young people. No psychological tests were performed, no blockers given to suppress the hormones from the ovaries or testes.

The cross-sex hormonal protocols used for those patients transitioning from female to male were identical to those used for genetic males born without testes or with low levels of testosterone. Even patients who had undergone full puberty could cease menstruating with normal male replacement doses of testosterone. The patients emerged much the way they do now: bearded, with a male build, although often short for a male, and in need of mastectomy to flatten the chest. They looked so virilized that, when clothed, only someone with knowledge of their history would guess their anatomic birth sex.

In contrast, it took massive doses of estrogen to feminize anatomic males. It remained difficult to suppress undesired erections.

And it was nearly impossible to adequately suppress the testosterone levels in patients with functional gonads. Thus, breast development was usually suboptimal, causing many patients to bear the added expense of augmentation surgery. In sum, at the time, I felt that the available treatment for my patients, even those who arrived as young as sixteen, was inadequate. If born anatomically male, they had difficulty passing for female in society, which contributed to their depression. If born anatomically female, they arrived too late to have prevented unwanted breast development and menses.

The approach to understanding gender-nonconforming children, too, was insufficient. Criticized for supporting their children's transgender identity, parents were told by some prominent therapists to restrict access to toys and clothes of the opposite sex. Fortunately, that seemingly punitive attempt to redirect children from becoming transgender has been discredited. In her seminal book, *Gender Born, Gender Made* (2011), Dr. Diane Ehrensaft describes the more compassionate way for parents to support their children.

Approaches to early pubertal adolescents have also taken a sharp turn. In 1998, pediatric psychologists, psychiatrists, and endocrinologists at the Free University Medical Center in Amsterdam initiated treatment with reversible blocking drugs to suppress pubertal hormones at the inception of puberty. Their protocol was based on the hypothesis that, while prepubertal children of both sexes are similar in appearance, pubertal hormones cause permanent physical changes that interfere with the physical form they desire. In a state of pubertal arrest, patients gain time to be further evaluated, to come to terms with their gender identity, and to understand the medical consequences of taking irreversible hormones of the opposite sex, including infertility. Once patients reach the age of fifteen to sixteen, the Dutch add testosterone or estrogen treatment to the blockers in *normative doses*. In our clinic, virilizing breast removals are done at ages fourteen to sixteen, and feminizing genital surgeries are delayed until ages seventeen to eighteen.

In 2007, with the blessing of the chief of the endocrine division and the most senior administrative leadership at Boston Children's Hospital, I cofounded the Gender Management Service (GeMs), following the Amsterdam model. The research conducted in Amsterdam, published in 2014, has shown the efficacy, safety, and psychosocial well-being that results from this approach. The GeMs was the first pediatric academic center in North America to open a medical clinic for transgender adolescents. In 2008, Dr. Diane Ehrensaft cofounded the Child and Adolescent Gender Center at the University of California, San Francisco. They, too, treat children and teens with hormone blockers. And, most importantly, Dr. Ehrensaft and others like her promote the gender affirmative approach—an effort to aid children in affirming their authentic gender rather than influencing them to accept the gender that would match the sex assigned to them at birth.

In 2009, the Endocrine Society, the largest and most prestigious international association of endocrinologists, released the *Endocrine Treatment of Transsexual Persons*, which recommended pubertal suppression as the treatment of choice in earliest puberty. The American Psychiatric Association's fifth edition (2013) of the *Diagnostic and Statistic Manual of Mental Disorders (DSM V)* replaced its former term "gender identity disorder" with "gender dysphoria." In an instant, transgenderism was no longer an inherent psychiatric disease. As a result of these groundbreaking publications, insurance companies could no longer justify denial of medications and surgeries. Pediatric endocrine and adolescent medicine divisions were empowered to create medical clinics for transgender youth. By 2015, fifty such programs had sprung up in North America, and the numbers continue to grow.

The evolution of counseling and medical treatment for adolescents has not been so straightforward, however. It has been like opening one of those wooden Russian dolls and finding another smaller one inside. In focusing on adolescents, we were reminded that we had missed the opportunity to provide ongoing support for the parents of children with gender dysphoria who felt isolated and confused by the conflicting opinions of academic clinicians. Dr. Ehrensaft's guidance via her landmark interview on National Public Radio in 2008 and her book *Gender Born, Gender Made* was a balm for these families, who have literally been held together by this original work. Consistent with Dr. Ehrensaft's teachings, our clinic is now staffed to offer intensive support for such families.

Then another Russian doll appeared. Patients arrived with issues that were new to us, although not to Dr. Ehrensaft. Referring to themselves as "genderqueer" or "gender fluid" (the term I prefer), these teens rejected any permanent gender identity. Their parents were understandably at wit's end and in need of experienced advice. Fortunately, they can receive support in this newest book of Dr. Ehrensaft's, *The Gender Creative Child*. Her recommendations will ease the journey for even more families with gender creative children. Dr. Ehrensaft's wisdom is equally essential for and accessible to their therapists, physicians, evaluating psychologists, and teachers, as well as all of us who struggle to understand gender fluidity.

NORMAN SPACK, MD, is the director and cofounder of the Gender Management Service clinic at Boston Children's Hospital, the first US clinic to medically treat transgender children. Dr. Spack has helped pioneer the use of hormone blockers to delay puberty and of hormone replacement therapy in teens. He has received national attention for his 2014 TEDx Talk "How I Help Transgender Teens Become Who They Want to Be" (over one million views) and was featured in Diane Sawyer's landmark interview with Bruce (now Caitlyn) Jenner. Dr. Spack is associate professor of pediatrics at Harvard Medical School.

THE
GENDER
CREATIVE
CHILD

CHAPTER ONE

Who Is the Gender Creative Child?

Our genders are as unique as we are. No one's definition is the same, and compartmentalizing a person as either a boy or a girl based entirely on the appearance of genitalia at birth undercuts our complex life experiences.

—Janet Mock, *Redefining Realness*

SOME YEARS AGO, I began to see a little girl in therapy. Stephanie had been grumbling since she was three years old: "I think I might be a boy." Her parents thought it was just a stage that she'd grow out of. But she didn't, and for some time she lived as a boy-girl. Then she gradually moved in the direction of boy. Now, Stephanie is Stephen and goes to middle school. It is not always so easy, and some schoolmates who knew Stephen as a girl tease him and tell him he's not a "real" boy. That hurts his feelings, and his father tells him just to knock them flat, not such a great strategy for the smallest boy in the class. But Stephen marches forth to carve out a space to be the boy that he is now discovering himself to be. I hadn't seen Stephen for a while, but one day recently we had a check-in appointment. No sooner had we settled in when Stephen pronounced, with great aplomb, "You know, Dr. Ehrensaft, *Gender Born, Gender Made* was pretty good, but you should write another book. And this time it should be a book about me."

So, here I am, writing that book, not just about Stephen but about all the children and youth I have gotten to know since I crossed the last *t* and dotted the last *i* (virtually) on *Gender Born, Gender Made*. From the time I wrote *Gender Born, Gender Made*, so much has happened on the gender front in such a short number of years that I hardly know where to start. But let me try.

GENDER AND GEOLOGY

Gender-bedrock: two words that have been fused together for centuries in Western culture. Why else would the first question to a pregnant friend be, "Is it a boy or a girl? Do you know yet?" But suddenly in the last decade, the two words have been broken apart. Instead of gender as bedrock, we are now witnessing gender as moving boulders. I live in earthquake country, so I'm always a bit queasy about making references to the earth's moving under our feet, but I'd have to say that an earthshaking explosion has been happening when it comes to gender. No sooner do we think we have all the new terminology about gender clear in our heads than we discover we were all wrong, and that today's words are already passé. Moving from geological metaphor to human action, nothing less than a gender revolution is going on, with people taking to the streets to shout out, "No more gender boxes," and the trans community and its allies mobilizing to push the agenda so succinctly articulated by Janet Mock: "Our genders are as unique as we are." Who is leading this revolution? Children who are nimbly pushing the boulders around, creating an ever-shifting terrain as we try to grasp "What's your gender?"

Indeed, a new group of boys, the "pink boys," have made their voices heard. Actually, pink boys have been around for a long time, but now they have coalesced into a social entity with a message to deliver. Like the traditional tomboy, they wear clothes of the opposite gender but assert themselves as boys—"I like dresses; why shouldn't I get to wear them just because I'm a boy?" They are getting media attention. Such books as *My Princess Boy*, *Jacob's New Dress*, and *Raising My Rainbow*[1] are being written about them. Their celebratory gender freedom and people's uneasy reactions to it lay bare the sexist double standard that more freely allows girls to cross gender lines but stay girls, while policing or even punishing any boy who attempts to do the same. Rather than leaving us in question about their gender, they are demanding just the opposite: "No question. I'm a boy. I like dresses. So, get over it."

Right after *Gender Born, Gender Made* was published, a flurry of activity showed up in Toronto, Canada. Two parents, Kathy Witterick and David Stocker, had made the decision to keep private the assigned sex of their five-month-old baby. They then decided to go public with their story.[2] The genitals of that child, whose name is Storm, were known by only a select few. The parents did not want cultural pressures to intrude on Storm's freedom to discover their[3] own gender, and they wanted to give the child as much opportunity as possible to explore gender without being boxed into a category. And so we had the Storm about Storm. Within twenty-four hours the story, first published in the *Toronto Star*, went viral, with a flood of social media commentary mounting into the hundreds of thousands. And the majority of those comments were vitriolic in their condemnation of Storm's parents—they're turning their child into a freak; they're using their child for their own political ends; babies are not social experiments; Storm will grow up forever damaged, maybe even deranged. Many people looked at the photo of this blond-haired little baby and said definitively, "Oh, I know it's a boy. You can tell," or "Who are they trying to kid? Storm is obviously a girl." I received requests for comments on Storm from reporters and journalists all over the world. The most common question posed to me was: "If Storm isn't told what gender Storm is, won't Storm be confused?" My response: "Not as confused as we are." It makes us incredibly anxious when someone purposefully removes gender markers. How are we going to get our bearings and classify a person without them? Think about it—it's almost reflexive for us to scan a room we enter and take note: Who are the men, who are the women? And so, as bedrock crumbles and moving boulders rumble, it will be a challenge for all of us to unmoor ourselves from the constrictive and restrictive confines of gender-binary assumptive assuredness.

As I wrote *Gender Born, Gender Made*, I had an inkling that a sea change in gender was occurring, but I had no idea that in such a short time it would hit land and rock the earth as it has—at home, in our communities, in our society, and across the globe. In February 2014 Facebook changed its US profile options for gender, extending it from two to fifty categories, including transgender, cisgender, agender, gender fluid, intersex, neither, trans female, trans male, trans person, gender variant, gender questioning, bigender, androgynous, pangender, and transsexual. People creating a profile can choose as many categories as they want. In 2012 California passed legislation prohibiting mental health practitioners from engaging in practices that attempted to change a minor's gender behaviors (State Assembly Bill 1172). New Jersey soon followed suit, along with the District of Columbia, and as I sit here writing, fifteen other states have similar bills pending. Looking north across the border, Ontario passed a no-reparative-therapy bill in 2015, in the same year that President Obama and the White House issued a statement condemning the practice of reparative therapy. In 2013 California passed another piece of legislation ensuring that all students in public schools are allowed to use the facilities and engage in activities associated with their affirmed gender, rather than their natal sex (State Assembly Bill 1266). In 2013 gender identity disorder was removed from the *Diagnostic and Statistical Manual of Mental Disorders*, replaced by a more palatable (but still problematic) mental health diagnosis of gender dysphoria. In the fall of 2011, the World Professional Association of Transgender Health (WPATH) released its new standards of care, which state explicitly that it is unethical and harmful to engage in any form of therapy that attempts to change one's gender. The American Psychological Association followed suit and released a large volume of new guidelines for gender-supportive care. New gender clinics have begun to pop up across the United States and beyond, to aid children in affirming their authentic gender. The "gender affirmative" approach has emerged and has become an ascending international model for supporting children and youth's gender health, an effort that I am proud to be a part of. Simultaneously, therapeutic models aimed at altering children's gender to conform to cultural norms or influencing children to accept the gender that matches the sex on their birth certificate have been challenged, declared unethical, and evaluated as harmful to children's well-being. In 2007 Barbara Walters produced a *20/20* documentary on transgender kids. It was the first of its kind in TV broadcasts and a transformative turn of events in media history—with transgender children and their families from cities and small towns all over the United States (not just Berkeley, California) portrayed in a positive and empathic light. As I write this in 2015 it seems that a week does not go by without a new media account of gender-nonconforming or transgender children. I could go on, but suffice it to say that as these changes have rolled out in such a short band of time, we gender specialists, in partnership with the families who are raising the children, can hardly keep up. Every day we learn more and see how much more we have to learn about helping our children discover and fortify their true gender selves.

Upon completion of *Gender Born, Gender Made*, I received an email from a gay cousin of mine that meant more to me than any published book review or commentary. He wrote, "Having lived in San Francisco and West Hollywood I've seen the gamut on gender nonconformity and the 'work in progress' and end result of those who finally accept who they are, or are meant to be. If more parents would have had your book as a guide we would have a much more accepting world, and much more happy children and adults."

I can think of nothing better as my small contribution to making the world a better place than to create a more gender-accepting world and open the path for more happy children and adults. But I have come to realize that my work had only just begun when I put the final touches on *Gender Born, Gender Made*, and now it is time to continue that journey.

To that end, I'd like to zoom in on a particular poignant moment in our new "gender as moving boulders" world. On June 9, 2014, Laverne Cox, the transgender actress in the TV series *Orange Is the New Black*, appeared on the cover of *Time* magazine. Hers was the lead story in that issue. In it, the author, Kate Steinmetz, highlighted a moment when Cox appeared in San Francisco as part of the San Francisco Arts and Lectures series, a very popular Bay Area event. A note was passed up to her onstage, written in pencil in a child's handwriting on a piece of notebook paper. It read, "I'm Soleil. I'm 6 and I get bullied. Since I get teased in school, I go to the bathroom or to the office. What can I say to the kids who tease me? What if they don't listen to me?" Soleil was a transgender little girl. The audience cheered when they discovered Soleil was right there in the audience, and then Laverne Cox called her up to the stage and said these words to her: "You're beautiful. You're perfect just the way you are. I was bullied, too, and I was called all kinds of names, and now, I'm a big TV star. Don't let anything they say get to you. Just know that you're amazing."[4]

That will probably be an indelible event in Soleil's memory. Realistically, most gender-nonconforming children on the way to affirming their true gender are not going to have the opportunity to get up on a stage and shake hands with a transgender media celebrity. Yet contrast Soleil's uplifting experience with a time back in the 1950s when I was just a little girl and picked up a copy of my parents' *Life* magazine. I just stared and stared at the cover, transfixed. It was a picture of a woman who used to be a man—Christine Jorgensen. She was an ex-GI who became the first documented American to go through a "sex change" operation. I do not recall any 1950s stories about her having the opportunity to speak to an audience of sympathetic listeners and connect with a little girl just like her, proudly accompanied up to the stage by an older relative. Instead, we all reacted to the news about Christine Jorgensen with voyeuristic excitement or disbelief, as if it was a phenomenon as impossible as launching a rocket into space (which would happen only a few years later, when the Soviets sent Sputnik orbiting into the stratosphere).

Fast-forward to 2014 and we now have clinics around the world that provide a myriad of medical interventions to help not just adults but youth become the gender they know themselves to be, even if it is does not match the sex listed on their birth certificate. So, yes, we've come a long way, baby, but this time it is not about women's rights (although that, too), but about the expanded opportunities for children to go forward and declare they have a gender that is dictated neither by a medical assignment on their birth certificate nor by the social gender proscriptions and prescriptions of the culture around them. And we are not talking about the fantastic, as if these events are some sci-fi vision come true. We are zooming in on the everyday lives of present-day children and their parents as they follow a path that will allow their children's gender to bloom. And yet those lives are indeed fantastic—in their creativity, in their complexity, and in their challenge to our outmoded thinking about gender as an immutable given once you exit the womb and get an *M* or *F* printed on your birth certificate.

THE GENDER CREATIVE CHILD

While writing *Gender Born, Gender Made*, I conjured up the concept of the gender creative child—the child who weaves together nature, nurture, and culture in an infinite variety of ways to establish the gender that is "me." That "me" may be a boy, a girl, or a mélange of gender, and may not reflect the sex that was listed on the child's birth certificate—or it could. At the time, a suggestion was made by some of the staff at The Experiment that I name that book *The Gender Creative Child*. I brought that idea to a local group of gender specialists, asking them to brainstorm with me on book titles. *The Gender Creative Child* got nixed. Some trans activists in the group were concerned that without having read the book, seeing that as the title would make people think that I was promoting the idea that people invent or select their gender, rather than discovering what is simply there inside them. I deferred to their wisdom and landed on the title *Gender Born, Gender Made*, which I was quite happy with. But, as with any birth, you don't know what the baby is going to bring until it's born, and upon publishing *Gender Born, Gender Made*, what became one of the most popular concepts? That of the "gender creative child," adopted in conferences, workshops, lectures, and professional and community lexicon. So, with *Gender Born, Gender Made* as its parent, I now introduce you to the new baby, *The Gender Creative Child*.

TWO FATHERS, TWO SONS

Let me tell you two different stories about a father and a son to set the stage for the journey we will be going on together, a journey exploring the ins, outs, and sideways of following the path of gender creativity in a world that is becoming far more expansive in its acceptance of gender that lives outside binary boxes. The first story: It was 2012. Nils Pickert was the father of a five-year-old boy who liked to wear dresses. They live in Germany. Their family moved from Berlin to a small town, a town that might not take kindly to a boy in a dress. Nils contemplated what he would do for his son when they got to their new town: "I didn't want to talk my son into not wearing dresses and skirts. . . . He didn't make friends doing that in Berlin . . . so after a lot of contemplation I had only one option left: To broaden my shoulders for my little buddy and dress in a skirt myself."[5] Posted online was a picture of

Nils and his son, hand in hand, he in a red skirt, his son in a red dress, strolling down a cobblestone street in their new town. The story went viral, and, for his efforts on behalf of his son, Nils was hailed "Father of the Year" by Gawker Media and praised in parenting blogs all over the world. Nils' son is now feeling confident because Dad's got his back. When he's teased about his skirts and dresses now, he tells his classmates: "You don't dare to wear skirts and dresses because your dads don't dare to either."

The second story: 2014. Seth Menachem is the father of two children, a daughter, Sydney, age four, and a son, Asher, age two. Asher's favorite mode of attire: dresses, the sparklier the better. Seth described the negative reactions of his friends when Asher attended a party in his preferred garments: "Do you think this is funny? There are kids here. You want them to see this?" From another, "You want him to be gay?" How did Seth respond?

> I stayed calm. And I explained to them the best I could that there is no correlation between kids' cross-dressing and being gay. And if he is gay, it's not because of anything I did. It's because he's gay. And maybe it's a stage. And maybe it's not. But either way, I don't want him to ever feel like he wasn't able to express himself because his parents didn't support him.

Some of his friends still gave him grief, yet many were supportive. When people on the street would assume Asher was a girl and compliment him on his appearance, they would smile when corrected by Seth ("He's my son"), express appreciation for Asher, but then apologize for confusing Asher's gender. Seth's response: "Don't apologize. He's in a purple dress with sparkly shoes. How would you know?" And I think to myself, *yes, how can any of us know?* The old ground rules of boys will be boys and girls will be girls have been rightly challenged, primarily by the children themselves. A dress no longer equals girl; a buzz cut no longer equals boy. As one gender-nonconforming eight-year-old patient of mine said to me in exasperation about his own pink tops: "Don't people get it? They're not girls' shirts. They're just people shirts."

As an addendum, Seth followed in Nils Pickert's shoes. When his children suggested he wear a dress, too, he raided his wife's closet, found one loose enough to fit, and strolled down the street with his son and daughter, all in dresses. Along with laughing, the only comment to Seth from his wife as she pulled up to the house and saw Seth in her dress was: "Make sure you don't rip it."[6]

Going back to my eight-year-old patient in his pink tops, my wish for this book is that by the last sentence in the last chapter we will get it, even more than we think we do now. I invite you as the readers to be in a dialogue with me, understanding that I, too, will be learning as I write, and you may have some things to teach me as you read, underlining how much the progression toward gender creativity and gender expansiveness is an evolving journey with infinite pathways where the expert becomes the student and the student becomes the teacher. And in the end, every town and village will hopefully be a place where sons and fathers can stroll in their dresses . . . and mothers and daughters in tuxedos and bow ties, if that is what suits their gender fancy.

BEWARE SNAKES IN THE GRASS

Lest you think that the road is clear of ruts and obstacles in reaching that end, let me say a little about the hurdles we still have to jump to get to a gender-expansive world. Laura Ingraham, a conservative commentator, was hired in April 2014 as a radio talk show host for ABC. In the recent past she has taken it upon herself to hold forth, on the air, on the lives of gender-nonconforming children and their families. She has said some remarkable things:

> *On how putting kids on hormone blockers might have "long-term effects" that children will "regret":* The concern . . . that, look, these are children, right? They can't give informed consent for hormone-blocking drugs that are now being given

to children as young as, in California, this famous case from last fall, an eleven-year-old child of, I guess it was lesbian parents who decided to give this little boy hormone-blocking drugs that prevents him from going into puberty. These are children we wouldn't trust to pick what they want to eat for the day . . . we as parents guide them according to our own moral convictions about what's right and what's wrong.[7]

On how supporting transgender youth "push[es] kids into a box": It's got to be confusing for kids. . . . We are always pushing, pushing, pushing. And kids really can't be kids any longer. They have to be sexual beings at age six—five even. . . . And I am not saying some of these kids don't end up sexually in different places; I don't know. But I know when they're kids, their brains have not developed. You don't have your—your sexual being even if you can have sex, your sexual being, from everything I have read from all the accomplished psychotherapists and everyone who has examined this, your sexual, quote, identity is really not solidified until much later on.[8]

On how providing children with hormone therapy is "child abuse": These people are all about natural living and organic living, and "oh, I want organic food," are all too willing to shoot themselves up or their children up with hormone therapy before the child has even gone through puberty. Let the child go through puberty for goodness sakes. . . . Your child is suffering. I'm sure there are other strategies, other ways to work on this without at least shooting your kids up with hormones.[9]

On transgender kids' "wanting attention": Maybe some of them want, yeah, some of them want attention, I think, probably as well. I'm just guessing, I have no idea. But I would imagine, kids act out for a whole bunch of different ways and these are little children. These are children. Let children be children.[10]

These are just a sampling of the remarks she has made over a two-year period, 2012 to 2014. And it hasn't gotten better since then, so no sea change for Laura Ingraham when it comes to gender sensibilities. When I was asked by Luke Blinder of Media Matters to review and comment on what she has said, in an effort to censor her remarks and counteract their toxic effect on the listening public, I could not get to the computer fast enough to write the following:

> When one speaks from ignorance, there is a good chance that they will say ignorant things. This could be no more true than for Laura Ingraham. The only informed statement she made is, "I have no idea." She does not. So to help her out, a 101 lesson on gender-nonconforming children. Sex and gender are two different developmental tracks. They may cross, but how I know myself as male, female, or other is completely separate from my sexual identity—who I will find myself attracted to. Many children explore and experiment with gender over time, but among them is a small group of children who are insistent, persistent, and consistent from a very early age that the gender they know themselves to be does not match the sex listed on their birth certificate. And there are other children where it is not so clear until later in their childhood, but once it becomes clear, it is vibrantly apparent. If we do nothing for these children, just let them be children, as Ingraham suggests, we are actually doing something, and that something is not good: We put them at risk for anxiety, depression, poor school performance, and later drug abuse, self-harm, sexual acting out, and suicidal thoughts, attempts, or completions. If we listen to them when they tell us something very profound about their core being—"Hey, you've all got it wrong; I'm not the gender you think I am, and if you keep policing me on that I may go under"—those youth stand a good chance of coming out whole and healthy. Especially if they have the support of their families and highly skilled professional gender

specialists, along with the reeducation of misinformed citizens like Ingraham who in their ill-informed, off-the-cuff remarks add to the transphobic environment that makes it so hard for our gender creative youth to have a good go of it in their lives. Ingraham repeats what so many in my own field, mental health, have done to significantly harm gender-nonconforming youth: dismiss what they are trying to tell us, blame the parents who are trying to support them, and deny them adequate care in one fell swoop. Yes, attention is an important variable: These children are not attention-seeking; they are merely trying to get our attention so we can begin to be smart enough to start listening to what they are saying. As for medical interventions, puberty blockers are a completely reversible intervention, with no documented medical risks, when administered and monitored carefully by a trained medical professional. Their use is twofold: By temporarily turning off the biological spigot that gets puberty going when it starts releasing adult hormones into the body, a youth and the youth's parents are allotted more time to carefully explore what that child's authentic gender identity is before permanent body changes set in; secondly, the use of puberty blockers gives youths the chance to ward off unwanted physical body changes that can be quite traumatic to youths who know they are not the gender that would go along with those bodily changes. For some youth who are already clear about their gender identity (as being different from what's on their birth certificate, of which there are an increasing number of children, once we give them the chance to speak up), denying them this intervention, rather than offering it to them, is the action with the higher and very significant risk: that the child will be so despairing of ever being the person they know themselves to be with a harmony between body and mind that they would want to end their life, in the worst case scenario. We might even consider the denial of the service a form of child abuse—there's a life jacket right there, we're watching, and we're letting the child drown. What parent would want that for their child when they can offer them something better—an intervention that gives their child the opportunity for a better life?

I know I'm jumping ahead here into discussions of medical interventions for gender-nonconforming youth, which we will visit later in the book, but imagine for a moment that you are a parent of a gender-nonconforming child. You're confused about what that means and what you should do about it, and you trust media experts hired by reputable networks to help enlighten you. The Laura Ingrahams of the world not only speak untruths, they leave parents in confusion and shame. Hopefully, Ingraham will someday read this book, then recognize and put an end to the damage she may be inflicting—on children, on parents, on our communities—as she feeds the cancers of transphobia with her myths and accusations. In the meantime, it is important for all of us to remember that in our efforts to create a gender creative life for all of us, the Laura Ingrahams of the world need to be either silenced or reeducated if we are to stop the flow of toxic messages to children that their gender expression is just foolish child's play or attention-getting behavior. Even more important, we need to get the message across to parents that any efforts to not meet their child's gender needs is what would count as negligence, lax discipline, or outright abuse.

THE GENDER AFFIRMATIVE MODEL

In 2008, I was interviewed by Alix Spiegel for an NPR radio broadcast on transgender children. The other psychologist featured was Dr. Ken Zucker, who until recently was the head of the child and adolescent gender identity clinic at Toronto's Centre for Addiction and Mental Health. I spoke of the importance of listening to children and following their lead about their gender identity—it is not for us to say, but for them to tell. Dr. Zucker presented a model for helping young children accept the sex they were assigned at birth, by shaping their behavior in that direction in the hopes of getting them to live comfortably in their own skin (i.e., the skin associated with their genitals). When asked by Spiegel at that time which model was more prevalent among mental health practitioners, I sighed, breathed out a nervous laugh, but responded without a moment's hesitation, "Oh, his." If Spiegel were to come back to me now and ask the same question, I am happy to say that I would smile, no sigh, no nervous laugh, and respond without a moment's hesitation, "Oh, ours." What do I mean by "ours"?

Many of us have banded across disciplines and across countries to shape what is now known as the gender affirmative model. We have also organized an international gender affirmative consortium under the auspices of Gender Spectrum, open to professionals of all disciplines who work with or advocate for gender-nonconforming and transgender children and youth and share our basic philosophy. Our model stretches and grows as we grow, but the basic premises remain in place:

- Gender variations are not disorders; they are not pathological.
- Gender variations are healthy expressions of infinite possibilities of human gender.
- Gender presentations are diverse and varied across cultures, requiring cultural sensitivity to those variations.
- Gender involves an interweaving of nature, nurture, and culture—no one of these stands alone in shaping gender.
- A person's gender may be binary; a person's gender may be fluid or multiple.
- If people suffer from any kind of emotional or psychiatric problem connected to their gender, this is most likely because of negative reactions to them from the outside world.
- If there is gender pathology, we will find it not in the child but in the culture (otherwise known as transphobia).[11]

In outmoded models of gender treatment, gender health has been understood to be the ability for children to accept their core gender identity (the sex assigned to them on their birth certificate) and conform to the expectations for gender in their culture. In the gender affirmative model, gender health is defined as the opportunity for children to live in the gender that feels most real and/or comfortable. Alternatively, we understand gender health as the ability for children to express gender without experiencing restriction, criticism, or ostracism.

In the gender affirmative model, we say, as I did in my 2008 radio interview, that children are the experts of their own gender self, and, at most, we adults are their translators—striving to understand what they are telling us about their gender in words, actions, feelings, thoughts, and relationships. When it comes to considering medical interventions for youth who desire a gender transition, we measure in stages, not ages. In other words, we do not say that children have to be a minimum of twelve years old to receive puberty blockers that will put a pause on forthcoming body changes; we do not say that youth have to be at least sixteen years old to be considered for cross-sex hormones or hormone replacement therapy (HRT), a term more recently preferred by many, to affirm their transgender self.[12] We rely on the concept of readiness—when children reach Tanner stage II of puberty, when their incipient body changes are in evidence, they are ready to be considered for puberty blockers, whether they are nine or fifteen. When children have been on puberty blockers for four years, are clear about their affirmed gender identity, and are sure they want to go on hormones to complete their gender affirmation, they are ready, whether they are thirteen, fifteen, or eighteen. Age norms, although ostensibly set in concordance with children's emotional or cognitive maturity, often turn out to be dictated by a particular country's legal statutes regarding youths' medical decision-making rights rather than an individual child's emotional readiness. We also endorse social transitions for prepubertal children who are clear about their gender and communicate to us in no uncertain terms that a happy life for them will be a life in their affirmed gender, not later, but now. They could be ten years old; they could be four years old.

I lay this all out to you in advance, before going into detail about any one of these things, so you can be clear about where I am coming from as I flesh out the full profile of the gender creative child and the world that surrounds that child. I am neither an essentialist—one who says that gender is a given and set at birth or before—nor am I a social constructivist—one who says that gender is just a people-made concept that fluctuates over time. Rather, I am a transactionalist—one who says that nature and nurture crisscross over time in a myriad of ways in the context of each particular culture to create gender as we know it. No doubt some of what we will look at about gender is heavily weighted on the nature end—having to do with the biology of the child. And some of it is heavily weighted on the nurture end—having to do with the social mores of gender and family practices. But like a well-built mobile, every weighted piece is carefully balanced in relationship to every other piece to make the suspended, gracefully flowing gender sculpture that is unique to each person on earth.

THE JOURNEY WE WILL TAKE

Since I completed *Gender Born, Gender Made*, I've traveled many miles in my journey as a gender specialist. I became the director of mental health at the Child and Adolescent Gender Center (CAGC), the attending psychologist at the CAGC gender clinic at the University of California, San Francisco, Benioff Children's Hospital, and the ever-evolving therapist of an ever-growing group of gender creative children and their families. I continue to lecture, train, write, advocate, build a professional community, and conduct research on the lives of these people who have been my greatest teachers. Using composite portraits of the children and families I have had the honor to work with, each of the following chapters in *The Gender Creative Child* is designed to be its own independent learning module about psychological, social, and community issues as we get in clearer focus the infinite variety and rapidly growing population of gender creative children across the globe. And at the end, we will ask what more we need to learn.

In Chapter 2, "What's Your Gender?," I will lay out a framework for thinking about the evolution of each child's gender, an evolution that can result, like snowflakes, in an infinite variety of shapes and forms, with no two exactly alike. Chapter 3, "The Gender Spread: Apples, Oranges, and Fruit Salad," will then organize those infinite shapes into some identifiable groupings—the children who are clear that the sex listed on their birth certificate does not match the gender they know themselves to be; the children whose gender matches that assigned sex but who do not express their gender in ways that conform to social norms, expectations, prescriptions, or proscriptions; and the children who either are a mix, live in the middle, or repudiate any categories of gender altogether. Chapter 4, "When It's Gender *and* Something Else *or* Something Else," looks at the accompanying psychological factors that often show up alongside gender creativity and then differentiates them from the psychological factors in situations where gender variance may be a symptom or solution to some underlying nongender stressor rather than a core expression of a gender self. In Chapter 5, "It Takes a Gender Creative Parent to Negotiate the Gender Maze," we both honor and lay bare the rugged terrain of raising a gender-nonconforming child, both when social supports are there, and when they are not. Chapter 6, "If Gender Is Expansive, Wherefore a Shrink?," maps out the mental health field as we know it now, with particular attention to the gender affirmative model of clinical practice that is advocated in this book. In Chapter 7, "Do We Want a Doctor in the House?," we explore medical options for gender-nonconforming youth, paying close attention to the cultural context, the psychological complexities, and the quality-of-life implications for both children and parents with each of these interventions. Chapter 8, "Into the Streets/Onto the Screens," addresses the mobilization of gender activist forces in schools and in communities coupled with the profound impact of the Internet and social media on gender-nonconforming youth across the globe. Even in the most remote of places where they might believe themselves to be the only one in the world, social media affords them the opportunity to experience a mirror of themselves, to find each other in a virtual community, and to discover a name and discourse for what they are experiencing. In Chapter 9, "What's Left to Learn?," I share the unexpected epiphanies I had while writing this book, highlighting what I learned along the way, and shining a light on the transformations in the making or yet to come in solidifying gender infinity in our society.

Just as I was finishing writing the first draft of this chapter, I got a call from a gynecologist in my area, someone I did not know. She got my name from another local doctor. Distraught, she sounded close to tears. A father had just brought in his eighteen-year-old to see her. This young person was assigned female at birth but knew from age seven that he was a boy, and had only recently announced to his family that he was transgender. The father wanted the gynecologist to fix him—discover the medical problem and make him be a girl. If he didn't get fixed, he was not going to be allowed to go to the prestigious university he was scheduled to leave for in four weeks. He would have to stay home and go to a local community college until he was cured. The gynecologist handled the situation beautifully, refusing to do a medical exam and allowing the youth to meet privately with her to express himself about his gender, offering an accepting and empathic ear. I and the gynecologist shared our grief that this young person, eager to start his university studies in his newly affirmed gender, had to suffer this setback. We came up with some possible solutions to support him and to work with his family. We both had fleeting fantasies of paying his college tuition so he could attend. As we spoke to each other on the phone, I could only wish that I was at the end rather than the beginning of this book when the call came in, so that this father might have a resource to help him recognize that his child was in no way gender disordered; rather, gender creative. Yet, I hope that there will be many other mothers and fathers who will benefit from hearing the possibilities for gender creativity and the tremendous gift we can give all of our children if we just let them be who they are. So to that end, I now invite you to travel with me through the pages of *The Gender Creative Child*.

CHAPTER TWO

What's Your Gender? From Boxes to Spectrums to Webs to Gender Infinity

*There's tremendous untapped creative power in
children's diversification of the gender landscape.*
—Kathy Witterick, mother of Storm

ON AUGUST 24, 2014, the "Women's Fashion" edition of *T: The
New York Times Style Magazine* came out. Because of either their
extreme prices or outlandish styles, it is hard to imagine anyone
dressing for everyday life in any of the clothes. But what struck
me was the gender fluidity. Men wore scoop-neck tops and flowing scarves historically the purview of French ingenues or 1950s
bombshells. Women wore baggy overcoats and men's trousers, the
elegant kind my grandfather the tailor would sew for my brothers
and my boy cousins. And really, who knew whether any of these
models were men or women, or just posing as such?

Four days before that, the *San Francisco Chronicle* published a
front-page article about Mills College, one of the few remaining
women's colleges in the United States. The headline. MILLS COL-
LEGE SPELLS OUT WHAT IT MEANS TO BE FEMALE. *Well,* I thought,
I'm glad somebody's *figured it out.* What did I learn? Mills College is
the only single-sex college campus that allows applicants to identify themselves by their affirmed gender on the application, with

no reference to their natal sex—if it is female, they're a candidate. Included as eligible undergraduate applicants to the all-women's college: those not assigned a female sex at birth but who identify as female, as well as those assigned a female sex at birth but who do not fit into the gender binary. Excluded as applicants: people assigned a female sex at birth but who have become legally male before applying, or those assigned male sex at birth but who are questioning. Allowed to stay and complete their undergraduate studies: students who enrolled as female but transitioned to male after entrance. In fact, the incoming student body president is a transgender man. Some still object to the new written gender policy as too binary, given the requirement that only women need apply, either by birth assignment or affirmed identity, leaving no room for gender-neutral applicants who are assigned males.[13] But it is still a monumental shift toward gender inclusiveness and a far cry from the 1990 eruption on the Mills College campus when trustees voted to include men in the college to increase revenue, setting off an uproar "Better Dead than Coed" that resulted in the rescinding of that vote and reinstatement as an all-women's college. As the female students protested, no one in that decade could have had any inkling of the effects of the next twenty-five years on Mills College's gender sensitivities, as the bedrock of gender morphed into moving boulders.

Two weeks before the 2014 announcement of Mills College's new gender policies, *The New Yorker* published an article titled "What Is a Woman?" So, now a second person was going to enlighten me. Its author, Michelle Goldberg, focused on the conflict between radical feminism and transgenderism. I remember when radical feminism was first surfacing in the 1960s, usually to the tune of "We don't need the men." At the time it was overall a separatist movement where men need not apply. But a half-century later, the radical feminists must now deal with an ever-expanding social movement composed of gender-challenging people: transgender women. Astonishingly, rather than being welcomed into the fold for their repudiation of manhood and celebration of their womanhood, transgender women are shunned among certain proponents of radical feminism. Like the Mills College constituency, radical feminists have found themselves tangled up in the discourse of who qualifies as a woman. For them, gender is not about how you identify, it is who you were when you were born. Once born female, you will suffer the social prescriptions, proscriptions, and discrimination that qualify women as an oppressed group. Once born male, you will reap the benefits of male privilege and never truly comprehend the depths of female oppression. Opposing the idea that cisborn women (those whose affirmed gender identity is the same as the female sex assigned to them at birth) should accept trans women into the fold, these radical feminists perceive trans women as simply imposing their male privilege, one that allows them to believe that they are entitled to go where they want and get what they want.[14] I need hardly say what a farfetched concept this is—just ask any trans woman who has suffered dysphoria or discrimination, or lived in fear of violence for most of her adult life, if not her childhood as well. And what about a four-year-old transgender girl who would hardly have had enough time to reap the benefits of male privilege? When Sojourner Truth delivered her speech "Ain't I a Woman?" at the Women's Convention in Akron, Ohio, on May 29, 1851, she had no idea that her outcry about her rights as a former black slave from the South would resonate a century and a half later among another group of women—those who were born with an *M* on their birth certificate. Who would ever have imagined that the contemporary trans cry for recognition, "Ain't I a Woman?" would be directed at another group of women, self-identified feminists, who are supposed to be representing the release of gender from the grips of oppression?

The finale came on October 10, 2014, with the cover story of *The New York Times Magazine*, SISTERHOOD IS COMPLICATED, with the subhead, "Men of Wellesley: Can Women's Colleges Survive the

Transgender Movement?" What was Wellesley College to do with their incoming women students who were exiting as men? How will it be able to retain its status as a women's college when gender is no longer considered binary?[15] This is the dilemma facing the administration of the college, an institution whose very roots were tied to the mission of educating women in a single-sex environment. When single turns to swishy, that mission will definitely have its challenges.

What does this have to with the little people we are talking about in this book? The fashion spread, the college gender policy, the feminist treatise and its pushback all fall under the umbrella of gender as moving boulders rather than bedrock, leaving us with the question "Who are the genders in your neighborhood?" This is no neutral query, but one that is clearly fraught with a high level of emotion and unease, as seen in the disruption in colleges and storefront social movements. It is in the midst of this historical gender tumult that we struggle to get our gender creative children into focus. And that gender tumult filters into the air those gender creative children are breathing as they work to get their own gender in focus. Yet they are not only the recipients of history, they are also its shapers; and as they call out to us, they are forever our teachers, educating us on: (1) What is gender? and (2) What's *my* gender?

FROM BOXES TO WEBS

As people have grown more aware that gender comes in more than two boxes, the gender binary has been replaced by the notion of the gender spectrum, the gender rainbow, and, my creation, the gender web.[16] In each of these, gender is asserted to come in an infinite variety of shapes, sizes, and hues, rather than in just two sizes that fit either one or the other, boy or girl, and too often fit neither. The gender web proposes that gender is a three-dimensional construction and that all children weave their own gender web—based on three major threads: nature, nurture, and culture—to arrive at the gender that is "me." *Nature* includes chromosomes, hormones, hormone receptors, gonads, primary sex characteristics, secondary sex characteristics, brain, and mind. *Nurture* includes socialization practices and intimate relationships, and is usually housed in the family, the school, peer relations, and religious and community institutions. *Culture* includes a particular society's values, ethics, laws, theories, and practices. Like fingerprints, no two children's gender webs will be alike. The same is true for any adult's gender web as well. But unlike fingerprints, the gender web can alter in myriad ways from birth to death. Gender is not set in stone by age six, as I was taught in my training as a psychologist many decades ago, but can change over the course of a lifetime; so we all, you and I and everyone around us, will always be tweaking our gender webs until the day we die. That is where the fourth dimension of the gender web comes in—time. Gender is not static; it changes over time.

Who should be in control of the gender web? While we are little, to promote our individual gender health—defined as freedom to explore and live in the gender that feels most authentic to us— the only person who should be doing that tweaking is us. If our parents grab the thread of the web from us as we are spinning it, and tell us what our gender has to be, rather than listening to us as we spell out our gender, or rather than watching us do our own creative work, we are at risk of ending up with a tangled knot of threads, rather than a beautifully spun web that shimmers and glows.

Let us take a look at one of these gender webs as it is being spun. Antonio is five years old and lives in a small town in the Midwest. He is an only child. His mother, Satya, is from India;

his father, Alfonso, emigrated from Sicily. Ever since Antonio was eighteen months old, he has been pulling Mom's scarves out of her drawers and wrapping them around his head to make long, flowing hair like Satya's. As soon as he developed enough language to make sentences, he announced, "Me girl." (Well, that counts for a sentence in the toddler world.) Alfonso and Satya didn't make much of Antonio's antics and thought it was just cute. But in the back of her mind Satya wondered whether the fertility drugs she took while trying to get pregnant might have had some effect on Antonio's little brain while he was growing inside her. She had also just heard from a relative back in India that one of her cousins had moved to Thailand and was in the process of transitioning from male to female at age thirty-two, soon to have gender affirmation surgery. Could there be some genetic loading?

As Antonio grew a little older, his declarations became more insistent: "I am a girl, and you made a mistake. You gave me a boy's name." Satya and Alfonso now took notice. They are very warm and giving parents, both of them equally involved in Antonio's rearing, and they themselves never bought into the prescribed rigid gender norms of their respective families of origin. It was very important to them that Antonio learn that boys and girls are equal and that there was no such thing as boy or girl toys, just people toys. But growing up in Italy, Alfonso only knew of two genders—male and female. Satya, on the other hand, had had familiarity in her childhood with the Hijra, the third-gender people of India, and had recently gone online to discover that India's Supreme Court had just recognized transgender people as a third gender, in a landmark ruling. In the words of the court, "It is the right of every human being to choose their gender," as it granted full legal rights to those who identify themselves as neither male nor female.[17] Yet the small Midwestern town they now lived in did not abide by a court ruling from far away and had little tolerance for children who overstepped their boundaries in adopting the dress, play, or activities that were prescribed for "the other gender."

How does little Antonio, just entering kindergarten in this small town, spin a gender web? His brain and mind are telling him he is a girl—that constitutes the nature part of his web, albeit both brain and mind are profoundly influenced by the culture in which they grow. His socialization has some gender web threads that don't match so well: Satya nurtures his right to choose his own gender, just as her homeland's Supreme Court has asserted. Alfonso is okay with Antonio's expressing his gender—how he presents himself in the world in clothes, activities, friendship choices, body movements—any way he wants, but when it comes to his child's gender identity—"Who am I—boy, girl, or other?"— Dad gets a little squeamish. Antonio came into the world as Alfonso's son, and his father wants to keep it that way. Antonio's culture threads are as complicated as his parents': When visiting India, his mother's country of origin, laws and social movements protect his desire to be the gender he knows himself to be—male, female, or other. When visiting his father's homeland, Sicily, it is as foreign to them that a boy would be a girl as that a child could identify as a Martian. And at home in the United States, the cultural messages are really very confusing. Antonio and his mom went on the Internet and watched the YouTube video about Ryland, the child who transitioned at age six to his affirmed male identity and received, with his family, the Inspiration Award at the annual Harvey Milk Diversity Breakfast in San Diego, before an audience of one thousand people. That told Antonio that the country he lived in was on board with his becoming the girl he knew himself to be—my goodness, he might even get an award for it. But he also learned that the state he lived in had ruled that boys who said they were girls or girls who said they were boys still had to play on the sports teams that matched the sex assigned to them on their birth certificate. Likewise, the public school Antonio will be attending is gender conservative—organizing many activities by binary gender (boys over here, girls over there). No exceptions allowed.

With all that tangle of threads, here is how five-year-old Antonio wove together his gender web—for now: "I will be a girl at home and a boy at school. I am kind of both, you know. I like wearing dresses, and those will be my weekend clothes, and at school I'll just wear my skinny jeans and sparkly T-shirts, and people can think I'm whatever they think I am, and if they ask, I'll say, 'Boy-girl for now.' And for pronouns—Just say 'Antonio' or 'Antonio's,' don't say *he*, don't say *she*, don't say *him*, don't say *her*. I'll tell my mom that the real truth is that I know I'm all girl, but I'm keeping the boy part for now—it's just easier. But my dad— well, I'll just keep to the boy-girl story, because I don't think he quite gets it yet that boys can really be girls and you can be a girl with a penis." If we revisit Antonio at age eight, my prediction is that his gender web might look quite different, as he explores and further solidifies both gender identity and gender expression, or alternatively, as Antonio's gender desires get run underground in the face of social disapproval or rejection.

Now let's bring in the cousin to the gender web—the true gender self. This is another one of my own inventions, borrowed from the ideas of D. W. Winnicott, a British pediatrician and psychoanalyst who wrote about the three parts of personality development—the true self, the false self, and individual creativity.[18] The true self is the essence and core of our personality; its first kernels are already present at birth, typically known to us as the baby's temperament. The false self is the coating we put around our true self to comply with the demands of the social environment and to protect the true self from harm. Individual creativity involves the impulse within us to weave together an authentic self, calling both on what comes from within us and what comes toward us from the outside world. Winnicott, always one of my favorite writers and thinkers, guiding me through my clinical work, posthumously offered me a wonderful gift when one day I thought, *By golly, I've* got it. *If I take those ideas and transfer them over to the arena of gender, I think I might have a perfect model for understanding how the gender web comes together over time:* We have the true gender self, the base of which is evident at birth, but which then goes in so many directions depending on how, in our infancy, we meet up with the social environment and how the social environment meets up with us. In the earliest months and years of life, that social environment will be the mommies, daddies, and primary caregivers of the child, with other family members in a close second place. Then we have the false gender self; that is the protective coating we wrap around our core gender as we meet up with the world and gauge how safe or unsafe it is for the true gender self to come out. Last, we have gender creativity, our endeavors to weave together and hold on to our very own unique and authentic gender self, based on core feelings of identity and chosen gender expressions.

Now, let's tie together how gender creativity relates to the true gender self and the gender web. Gender creativity is children's use of fanciful thinking, perseverance, fortitude, and finesse to incorporate the world around them into their inner psyche and their gender as they know it and want it to be. This creativity that allows them to navigate within the gender web and the greater world to discover and be their authentic self is the crux of the true gender self. The job of the adults is to allow a wide berth for this spinning and weaving, mirroring the children's artistic creations— their gender self—back to them, rather than controlling the motion of the threads and imposing their own gender images on the child. Now that more and more parents and other adults in children's lives have gotten caught up in the waves of the sea change in gender that swirls all around us, gender creative children have a greater opportunity to come out into the light of day, rather than remaining shrouded in their false gender self while their gender creativity gasps for air. Having read Genny Beemyn and Susan Rankin's book *The Lives of Transgender People*, which came out the same year as *Gender Born, Gender Made*, what moved me most was the repeated story across the nearly 3,500 adults they interviewed.[19] The story went something like this: "If only I had the supports and green light that some of the young children have today, I would have had such a better life. I always knew since I was little that my gender was not what people thought, but there was no place to go with it. So, I had to wait, and wait, with many years of pain and suffering until I could get to the place that was 'me.'" I both envy and applaud our youngest transgender children. They don't have to wait to be who they are.

WHAT DO WE KNOW ABOUT THE WHY OF GENDER?

As we read about the gender web and merge that model with the concept of the true gender self, we can begin to get a sense of the complicated interplay between nature, nurture, and culture for children as they reach for the gender "that is me." We no longer take it for granted that this is an effortless task, defined simply as learning what it means to be the gender that reflects the sex listed on one's birth certificate. Since completing *Gender Born, Gender Made*, I have observed ever-growing attention being given to the biology of gender—what is it in our physiological systems that can create a specific "gender loading"? A recent study of the effects of in utero virilization (exposure to high levels of androgens while in the womb) on girls diagnosed with congenital adrenal hyperplasia (CAH) found, remarkably, that female fetuses exposed to those high levels of androgens and diagnosed with CAH showed higher levels of both cross-gender identifications and cross-gender behaviors than a control group of girls not having had such exposure. The significance of this study is that it suggests, not only for babies diagnosed with CAH, but for all children, that levels of hormone exposure and their absorption by hormone receptors could play a strong role in the gender identity development of a child.[20] In other words, a male fetus receiving high levels of estrogen or a female fetus receiving high levels of androgens may so be tilted toward a gender-nonconforming self in childhood. We could consider this the earliest of environmental effects, but it also settles in as part of the constitutional physiological makeup of the child. Other studies of people diagnosed with disorders of sexual development (DSD) have also found higher levels of gender dysphoria or gender-expansive or transgender identity in these individuals than in the population at large, again suggesting that prenatal and postnatal hormone exposure and absorption have an effect on gender identity.[21] For some time we have been talking about gender not being located between our legs, but between our ears—in our brain and mind. These studies suggest that the particular balance of prenatal "male" and "female" hormone bathing on those little brains and minds, with the nature set of threads strong and center, may very much influence those little children in the spinning of their gender web. I am not saying that there are girl brains and boy brains, but that there are messages sent from the brain about one's gender that may create a discordance between chromosomes and genitalia, on the one side, and the mental sense of oneself as boy, girl, or other on the other.

I will come back to what we are learning about the biology of gender, but for now suffice it to say that nature clearly plays its hand, although we're still not exactly sure how and why. Even in the girls with CAH, not all of them showed up later as gender-nonconforming or with cross-gender identifications; it was just more likely that they would. So, as we go along, we have to be humble enough to admit to knowing much more about the "what" of gender (how each of us puts our gender together, how it looks in a particular culture, and so forth) than the "why" of gender (the actual determinants that may make, for example, one twin transgender, but not the other, as well as, more generally speaking, cause only some people to be transgender). Throughout these pages I will be concentrating on the whats and hows—what gender is, how we put it together, how we help promote gender health. Over a century ago, to paraphrase the father of psycho-analysis, when Freud was asked to reflect on women's develop-ment, he pretty much said, "If you want to understand women, ask the stars." I'm not suggesting we turn to astrology to answer our questions about why one twin is trans and the other is not, why only a small minority of people will turn out to be transgen-der, and so forth; rather, I'm suggesting we be humble enough to admit, like Freud, that we really don't know yet.

Some people get anxious when they hear someone like myself say about our youngest gender-nonconforming children, "These children just come to us that way." They hear us as saying that gender is a fixed phenomenon and we are born with it, and that means it is set in nature's stone rather than flowing with the rivers of time and experience. Au contraire; it simply means that nature has a hand to play in contributing to whether children will know themselves to be a boy, girl, or other, or embrace gender expres-sions that do not fit neatly into boy-girl boxes. In addition to the findings about CAH girls who have had high levels of prenatal androgens, identical twin studies have shown a higher incidence of transgender identities among monozygotic twins than among fraternal twins or nontwin siblings, suggesting a genetic link to the gender webs our children spin. Brain-imaging studies sug-gest that transgender women's brains look similar to cisgender women's brains, and the same is true for males as well, suggest-ing indeed that gender lies between our ears rather than between our legs. I find it particularly interesting that transgender men and women are more likely to be left-handed than the public at large, given that I always use the analogy that being left-handed as a variation on human functioning (one available to only about 10 percent of the world population) is comparable to gender non-conformity, particularly transgender identity (which also occurs in only a small percentage of the population). And now I discover a possible crossover between the two, only highlighting my belief in the creativity of both left-handedness (confession: I am one) and transgenderness, and the possibility that they may be linked in the brain in some way. To find out the particulars of these research studies, I refer you to the work on the biology of gender by my colleague Dr. Stephen Rosenthal, who provides an excellent summary of the research in the *Journal of Clinical Endocrinology and Metabolism*. Based on the studies he reviewed, Dr. Rosenthal proposes that the concept of gender identity is not simply a psychosocial construct, but "likely reflects a complex interplay of biologic, environmental, and cultural factors."[22] Pre- and postnatal hormonal exposure and absorption, genetics, and brain formation appear to be leading candidates in the biological category.

Noticing what appears to be a sudden proliferation of trans and gender-expansive children and adults, some people are scratching their heads and asking, "What's the deal here? Is there something in the drinking water?" Some who oppose gender outside of two boxes—male/female—argue that gender is a choice, and so you can choose not to be transgender, just as gay people are told that they can choose to be heterosexual if they want to. From those gender creative people who experience it from the inside and those allies who know it from the outside comes an outcry: "It is not a choice, it is who we are—male, female, or other. It just is." Informed by all the children who have taught me what I know, I would say that there is no better answer than that: It just is. Yet to say it is not a choice does not mean that it is completely constitutional, determined by nature. It simply means that before we were born and then along our journey through life, a confluence of influences met, some flowing from nature, some from nurture, and some from the culture surrounding both the nature and the nurture. That is why I counsel gender specialists in training, along with parents of gender-nonconforming children, "Don't bother asking children *why* they want to be a boy or girl or other, or *why* they think they are a boy or girl or other. They'll just dodge the question or look at you as if you're suffering from dementia. They can't answer the question any more than you can about your own gender. It just is. That does not mean that our gender is innate—just that gender is our subjective experience, the results of our gender web–spinning at any cross-section of time. It may have looked different three years ago; it may look different three years from now. In most instances, our gender identity will be more stable over time, whereas our gender expressions may be as expansive and changing as the day is long. To embrace our gender creative children is to situate ourselves neither as an essentialist (things are a given in nature) nor an environmentalist (all that we are and know our genders to be is socially constructed), but as a transactionalist (we are an ever-evolving interweaving of biology and environment over the course of time). So, now let's come back to the question at hand, "What's your gender?"

BACK TO BOXES

Some years ago, I discovered that no matter what language and terminology we struggle to develop that will both reflect and be respectful of the multiple ways gender can present itself, the children will lead the way in carving out their own self-descriptions, categorizations, and assignations of gender. So, I began to make a list, given my propensity for list-making. The list consists of all the ways I have heard gender described by the children and youth who have come to see me, along with some items borrowed from social media, other people's writing, and word on the street. By the time *Gender Born, Gender Made* was released, I had come up with quite an extensive list, shared in the pages of that book. But yet more have come my way since then, along with responses to the list itself. I'm recalling the words of a mother at a keynote address I gave at the Gender Creative Kids Workshop in Montreal. In the keynote I had presented my slide with my list of "Gender Beyond the Binary" categories. This woman strode up to the audience microphone and irately challenged me, "Aren't you just creating more boxes to squeeze kids into?" I defensively answered that these categories were just schemas, always a work in progress, as I had already said in my talk, and that any child could traverse from one category to another without ever having to feel boxed in. But later, in the quiet of my hotel room, with time to reflect, I wondered whether she was right. Maybe I should really think about that. I try to be humble enough to admit to myself and others that there's so much more to learn and we're definitely going to make mistakes as we move toward making a better world for all our genders. Was I in error? Should I dispense with all my obsessive list-making? Is it oppressing rather than supporting the gender creative kids? I thought for a while; a few years later I am still thinking, and I've come up with a working response: The concept of gender expansiveness, which I fully embrace, promotes a concept of gender that has no borders or boundaries—it is infinite in its possibilities. And so I've continued to let the children lead the way in teaching me the ever-evolving set of terms they apply to themselves and to other people's gender, albeit aware of the trap of falling back on binary boy-girl as our gender divining rods.

I'd like to revisit and update that list for you. Interestingly, nothing from the original list has become obsolete during this recent and seemingly sudden sea change in gender sensibilities. Instead, it has simply grown. As an umbrella, we have all of our gender creative children, those who declare in word and action that the gender they are does not match the sex marker on their birth certificate and those who are our gender bandits—transgressing the culturally prescribed norms for "gender appropriateness." In other words, the list includes all children and youth who challenge and explore both gender identity and gender expressions. Under the umbrella we have:

Transgender Children: Children who declare their gender as other than reflected by the sex marker on their birth certificate. This can include male to female, female to male, male to other, and female to other, and can show up at any age.

Gender Fluid Children: Children who flow between the female and male poles of gender, either at a point in time or over time.

Gender Hybrids: Children who combine or alternate between genders, often in a binary way. Among gender hybrids we have:

Gender Priuses—Half Girl/Half Boy: This gender label was taught to me by a school-age child who, from the front, looked like any third grade boy in basketball shorts, tank top, and basketball sneakers, and, from the back, had a long blond braid tied at the end with a bright pink bow. As this little person explained to me, "You see—I'm a Prius." And then, in response to my puzzled look, "I'm a boy in the front, a girl in the back. A hybrid."

Gender Minotaurs: Riffing on the notion of the Prius and the minotaur in Greek mythology—half-bull/half-man—I came up with my own label for all the children who were explaining to me that they were one gender on the top, one on the bottom, this usually to account for genitals that were at odds with the gender they knew themselves to be. Prior to puberty, everyone's top is the same, so one can facilely claim their top as being either male or female. But bottoms are another story, particularly in a culture like ours where penis = boy (rather than a penis-bodied person) and vagina = girl (rather than a vagina-bodied person). So, these children live like minotaurs, but rather than bull on the bottom, human on the top, they are typically sex assigned at birth on the bottom and affirmed gender—the one that is "me"—on the top. Not surprisingly, these children, particularly the female-identified natal males, are enamored with the mermaids in my office, on the big screen, and in their toy boxes: a girl on the top, a fish on the bottom, who can morph into a whole girl under the right circumstances. Indeed, my Ariel (Little Mermaid) figures are the number one choice for many of the younger gender minotaurs who come for an office visit.

Gender-by-Season Children: In spinning their gender webs, many children scout the territory around them, or their parents do it for them, and they assess that school, where they spend much of their time during the year, will not be a comfortable place to either explore or live in their authentic gender. They may also feel they have a history that follows them: Everyone at school has always known them as a boy or a girl, so they'll just keep it that way and wait until the summer, when they're off to a summer camp or to a different part of the country where they can shed their false gender self. A remove from the everyday setting allows their true gender to come out, at least to try it on for size, if not to declare it. So, we might have Sally during the academic year who enrolls in camp as Sam, or Joey at school who lives as Joelle in the summer when it's time to be a helper at Mother's family day care. Sometimes it's the opposite—a youth whose true gender self is forbidden at home but who goes to a school that is gender inclusive and accepting, transforming school into a gender underground for the youth, a place where the school personnel try to make up for the lack of acceptance that the child is meeting up with at home. I learned the gender-by-season category from a nine-year-old who explained to me, "I would die if anyone at school knew, but I stay with my grandma and grandpa in New York in the summer and they say I can be any gender I want. So, I'm like Clark Kent/Superman—a plain old boy at school, but the most beautiful girl at my grandma's. Better than having tights, a cape, and flying."

Gender-by-Location Children: A close cousin to gender by season, many boys come to my office explaining how they tear home to put on their favorite dress, and will even wear it to the park, but they leave it in the closet when they go to Aunt Susie's, or to school, because it just doesn't feel good to have to answer all the questions. Or because it wouldn't even be allowed in their school. Or they go over to their friend Tommy's and put on dresses there, because Tommy's parents understand and let him wear dresses all the time, not like at home.

Gender-Ambidextrous Children: This is a different category than gender hybrids because, like gender fluid children, who do not live as a gender hybrid, they are puzzled by all our efforts to pin them down as one thing. Here is the story of the child who brought this category to light: I was meeting with two moms to talk about their child, a natal male. It turns out that six-year-old Tony changes gender not only by setting but by relationship. What Tony never changes is what is worn every day—dresses over leggings. Tony is angry if Tony's brother Marklin refers to Tony as a sister, but fine if Tony's neighbor across the street thinks Tony is a girl. Tony is both a girl and a boy right now. In talking to the moms, who have been puzzling for years now, urgently wanting to pin down Tony's gender, whatever it might be, I spontaneously came up with the term *gender ambidextrous.* Again, I was learning from the children who they knew themselves to be, simply finding my own words to describe what they were telling me—in Tony's case, "I'm just me. Why does everyone keep asking?" As soon as I threw out the idea of gender ambidexterity, both moms completely relaxed and one of them said, "Yes, this makes so much sense. And this is what we can tell people—Tony is gender ambidextrous." Finally they could pin something down, a way to place their child in the gender scroll of life. If children can use both their left and right hand on par with each other, so, too, can they use their female and their male part of self, not to mention all the parts in between and beyond those two genders; ergo, we have the gender-ambidextrous child.

Gender Teslas: The gender Tesla is the state some children reach after a stint being a gender hybrid or gender ambidextrous. Some simply go from zero to sixty to get there, meaning from the sex assigned to them at birth to their affirmed cross-gender identity. Some go more slowly. Let me explain. One day I was meeting with a patient of mine at the gender clinic, a child I had been following for several years. Shannon was still exploring gender, not sure where it would land, but by all observations moving from girl (natal sex) to boy. Prior to this clinic visit, Dr. Rosenthal, our medical director, had been using a gender scale (1 = girl, 10 = boy for children assigned female at birth; 1 = boy, 10 = girl for children assigned male at birth) and asked all children who were gender exploring to give themselves a number along the scale, with an idea of measuring movement versus stability over time. At a clinic meeting we decided to dispense with the scale as being too binary and suggesting there were only two options—toward boy or toward girl. Some of us who were feminists also didn't like the idea that girls got a 1 while boys got a 10 for the birth-assigned females (with the implication that 10 is a higher score than 1). However, Shannon had always counted on that scale and was looking forward to reporting some new ratings to us. So, when I walked in the room, Shannon said to me, with some innuendoes of accusation, "You know, Dr. Rosenthal forgot to give me the scale today." Without telling him the news that we had discarded the scale, I simply asked, "What is it that you wanted to tell Dr. Rosenthal?" "Well, I've moved from a 4 to a 6." I took this opportunity to share the idea of the gender Prius, a hybrid, half-electric/half-gas. Shannon loved this idea and mulled it over for a while, then looked up pensively and shared, "Well, then, I think I'm moving toward being a Tesla—all electric." So now we have the gender Tesla, all boy or all girl, no half and half. We could say that any child in the transgender category would count as a Tesla, as would any cisgender child, but I like to preserve this term for children who are in motion toward an all-one-gender status.

Gender Smoothies: Gender smoothies are just a variation on the theme of gender fluid, but the imagery is so vibrant that I like to keep it as a separate category. Again, I was taught this label by a patient of mine, a teenager who reveled in mixing the cultural idioms of male and female in both looks and dress so no one could possibly pin down a gender for this youth. Sitting at the edge of his seat (he was using male pronouns then), he explained to me, "You see, you take everything about gender, throw it in the blender, press the button, and you've got me—a gender smoothie." And so that label has stuck for me to describe our gender blenders.

Genderqueer Youth: This is not only a category of gender, but also a social movement of young people who look at people like me and ask, "Why do you even bother? We are so beyond gender." They are any and all, never either/or, and they challenge our thinking and carve a new path in which they invite us all to both imagine and embody a world where gender is no longer a defining category.

Agender Youth: Agender youth are a close cousin if not the same as genderqueer youth. We can play with the word *agender*, seeing its double entendres—"I'm a gender, but not any particular gender," or "I'm devoid of gender [as in asexual]," which is the more common referent to the meaning of *agender*. But I like to think of it both ways. These are youth who, like their genderqueer compatriots, are also pushing beyond the limits of constricting gender confines to say, "You can't catch me" if it means pinning down a particular gender or any sense of gender at all as being relevant to living a life. Indeed, many youth who self-identify as agender also reference themselves as genderqueer.

Protogay Children: These are the children who start out exploring and pushing the margins of gender on the way to discovering their sexual identity. They are typically exploring their gender expressions rather than gender identity, though not always. Although gender development and sexual identity formation are two different developmental tracks, they do sometimes cross, as they do for these children, and it should also be remembered that in early life gender is taking shape well before sexual identity appears on the developmental stage floor. Some of these children will maintain their gender fluidity/expansiveness throughout life; some will move toward more gender conformity; and regrettably, some, particularly if they are little boys, will end up entrapped early in life by unsympathetic parties who will attempt to make these children more gender conforming, often with the overt or implicit intent of warding off a "homosexual" outcome.

Prototransgender Youth: These are children who travel in the exact opposite direction from the protogay children. In the process of exploring their sexual identity, usually in adolescence or young adulthood, they discover, often through their romantic or sexual liaisons, that it is not actually their sexuality but their gender that is in question. We see this particularly in young females who have always been "masculine" in presentation and find a welcome reception in the lesbian community as "butch females" only to discover that they are actually butch males. As one teenager I worked with explained to me, "I really thought I was a girl who liked girls, but every time I was making out with my girlfriend I realized that in my head I was not a girl making out with her, but a boy. And then I realized that my head was sending me a message—I am a *boy* who likes girls." Five years later, this teen, now a young adult, has gone through a full transition from female to male, including hormones, and top and bottom surgery. The prototransgender youth are the ones challenging the same-sex colleges, particularly the ones who enter a women's college as a lesbian and exit as a trans man. Often it takes leaving home for either college or post–high school life for some prototransgender youth to get themselves in focus, as these days it still remains easier to declare a gay identity than a trans identity in the confines of home and high school.

Gender Tootsie Roll Pops: These are the children who exhibit one gender on the outside but experience another gender on the inside. In the spirit of the true gender self and false gender self, the crunchy outside is often the gender that accommodates to the expectations of the surrounding world, while the soft, gooey inside is the stuff of authenticity and realness. So, the hard candy is in place to protect or shield the inside chewiness from an unaccepting world or an internalized unaccepting part of one's own self. It is the gender Tootsie Roll Pops, if not provided with resilience building, who can buckle under the weight of hiding their true insides from the world, putting them at risk for psychological stress and distress.

What about the concern that such categories simply make new boxes to bind children in, rather than giving them open space to wander and explore all the possibilities of gender? Let me try to answer that question with a story from my practice. Recently I met with a mother whose six-year-old child, assigned male, wears dresses and has informed the family, "Just use my name, Justin, instead of pronouns, because I'm not a boy and I'm not a girl so *he* doesn't work and *she* doesn't, either." As we talked, Meredith, the mom, mused that there were no books for a child like hers, a child who was letting the world know, "Right now I am neither female nor male." Meredith then went on to explain, "Justin really wants to find a box that Justin fits in. And so far Justin couldn't find one that was right." My first thought: *Was this really Justin's need or Meredith's, given the training, both implicit and explicit, that all of us who are adults in Western culture have gotten that gender comes in two boxes, male and female?* I gently suggested this possibility, and Meredith was not in the least bit defensive in admitting that maybe this was her need, too. But then she gave me numerous examples that convinced me that six-year-old Justin was truly struggling with this need for a box independent of Meredith's wish for an accurate label. Justin would come home from school holding back tears, distraught that someone had cornered Justin on the playground, shouting in Justin's face, "Wait a second, wait a second. Your name's Justin. That's a boy's name. But you always wear dresses. That's a girl's thing. So, what are you? Boy or girl? You have to be one or the other."

Obviously Justin needs help building a "gender toolbox" to equip Justin to answer such questions in a way that feels authentic. And Justin's school needs to get on board to make sure that Justin is treated with respect and sensitivity and that all the children are exposed to the expanded idea that gender comes in many flavors, not just two. Yet as soon as Meredith left the office, I had an urge to run to my computer and begin writing a children's book about gender hybrids, gender fluid children, and gender-ambidextrous children. Instead of doing that (I'm not sure I have the talents to write a children's book), I began thinking about other kinds of boxes, rather than toolboxes. So, I pulled out my old developmental psych texts and brushed up on the childhood stages of cognitive-emotional development.[23] By toddler age, babies are sorting out shapes into different boxes. Preschool is probably the freest of "in a box" stages, as children engage in magical thinking and fantastic fantasies, such as people turning into frogs, and beasts into elegant royalty. Yet they still like to categorize things to make sense of them, as when a little three-year-old informed her mother, who was just stepping out of the shower, "Mommies have breasts, and daddies read a lot of books" (this particular daddy was a college professor). School age is all about developing increasingly sophisticated skills in categorizing discrete items into larger entities, being able to discern what is the same and what is different and why certain things should go in one pile rather than another. Indeed, all intelligence tests for children involve investigating their ability for sorting and grouping under a common label. Then we get to adolescence, where, if Erik Erikson was on the mark, youth are dead set on forging their own identity, continuously applying labels to themselves to try them on for size. From toddlerhood to young adulthood, our children are in the market for boxes—both for themselves and for others.

The lesson to be learned: Beware taking away boxes from children. They like boxes; they just don't want to be boxed into one that's a bad fit. And when it comes to gender, they do best with an ever-expanding variety of them, with fluid boundaries around each. So, we have to wonder if we are doing our children a disservice by hailing, "Down with boxes." Children at different ages and stages, like Justin, seem to love outlines to live in, be it the dark lines around an image in the coloring book where the color is supposed to go, or a label they can give themselves that acknowledges who they are. It may just be in their organic makeup, rather than socially constructed by a rule-bound regimented culture. We may think such boxes are constrictive or countercreative as we visualize the gender web with all its infinite possibilities, but let's take it from the child's developmental perspective. How about an image of a rainbow of boxes or a big Lego construction with boxes upon boxes all interwoven together and borrowing from each other's interlocking blocks? This would take care of dispensing with the rigid notion of two boxes only (check male or female), but bow to children's need for some system of gender categorization, if that is what children need to organize themselves. If they did not have that need, how would I have come up with all the schematic categories of gender I've described, the majority of them creatively invented by the children themselves? In reaching to be gender affirmative, is it possible that we are confined by our own limitations in thinking beyond two to many, many gender boxes?

Justin has taught us that even the child who does not want to be pegged as fitting into one of two binary gender boxes still may yearn for a discrete definition of the gender self, be it ambidextrous, Prius, Tesla, minotaur, smoothie, and so forth. Using these categories still leaves room for expansiveness and individual interpretation. Let's take the natal boy in a dress who says, "I'm a gender hybrid." Is this a child who is telling us by gender expression "I'm a girl" but by core gender identity "I'm a boy—just a boy who likes to wear dresses"? Or is this a child who fully lives in a middle place between boy and girl, more girl in expressions but synthesizing male and female and/or some other combination in gender identity? Or is this a child who is moving toward girl in both identity and expressions but doesn't know what to do with the trailing, perhaps leftover boy in the psyche? How about children who embrace the self-label of agender? Are they saying that they have no gender, or just not a particular gender, or certainly not one of the two, boy or girl? You can see how one category is still open to so many possibilities, and as long as we keep it that way, let's make sure the children still get to have gender boxes. Facebook offered them fifty-plus such boxes; maybe they'll want many more. And we can count on them to keep generating their own.

Let us return to the mother in the audience in Montreal who objected to my list of gender categories. Before we stop ourselves from throwing out the baby with the bathwater, how about if we take a moment to contemplate why we can have such a knee-jerk reaction to the boxes that the children long for. Is it because we've been retrained to be politically correct about binary gender boxes? If we just communicate to the children that there are an infinite number of gender box possibilities, including "all and any," "I don't know," and "why do you ask?" I think we can continue to reinforce gender creativity and allow all the genders in our neighborhood to come out and announce themselves. Genderqueer youth may be beyond gender, but that is a label in itself. And my own observations tell me that our genderqueer little ones haven't gotten to the place of "beyond gender" yet. Pulling in the culture threads of the gender web, perhaps there will be a time when gender is an obsolete defining characteristic, superseded by "people" as the primary category of humanity, but there is no such culture on this planet yet. So, until that time, let us think of gender infinity as an endless terrain with tumbleweed boxes rolling across the plains.

TO INFINITY AND BEYOND

The gender creative child defies nature. The gender creative child defies nurture. When we think of the social prescriptions and proscriptions for gender in a gender-binary world, we can even think of the gender creative child as a gender outlaw, breaking all the rules to make a better life. Some people think that the gender creative child resides only in radical hotspots like the San Francisco Bay Area or New York City. But the fact of the matter is that these children are showing up everywhere, not just in the fifty states of the United States but across continents. To quote my granddaughter's first favorite avatar, Buzz Lightyear, we are all preparing ourselves for infinity and beyond, only we hope that when it comes to gender it will not be light years away.

We still don't know the *why* of gender, although I believe we are getting closer. We find ourselves having to devote a good deal of time to unlearning the gender theories and beliefs we cut our teeth on, because they are not fitting the realities of our gender creative children. From the children, we are learning new things every day about the expansive possibilities of gender. Yet the central mantra, "If you want to know a child's gender, listen to the child and the child will tell you," and its corollary, "It is not for us to tell, but for the children to say," while sounding so simple, are only deceptively so. The complexity comes in deciphering what the children are trying to tell us in both word and action about their true gender self and about the intricacies of the gender web they are spinning from the multiple threads of nature, nurture, and culture, over time. And what makes such a seemingly simple question—"What's your gender?"—so difficult to answer? Here is an alert to all of us— parents, siblings, grandparents, relatives, professionals: If we want to learn the answer to that question, we're going to have to learn to speak the children's language, or at least translate it into words we can understand. So, let us begin by listening to the children to see whether we can separate the apples from the oranges and from the fruit salad, the focus of our next chapter.

CHAPTER THREE

The Gender Spread: Apples, Oranges, and Fruit Salad

To put it simply, I feel like a girl trapped in a boy's body, and I've felt that way ever since I was 4.

—Leelah Alcorn, 2015

LEELAH NEVER MADE IT to her eighteenth birthday—she committed suicide in late December 2014—and her own words, written in a suicide note posted on Tumblr after she died, are profoundly poignant; they tell us how early Leelah knew her true gender self. In her note, Leelah let us know how difficult it was to transform that self-knowledge into action, to be the girl she knew herself to be, to the point where she did not want to live. I begin with this tragic story both so Leelah will not be forgotten, and also to emphatically insist that we pay attention to a controversy in the new world of gender as moving boulders: Can children really know their gender at an early age? Should we let young children transition from one gender to another or ask them to wait until they're older? Within the gender affirmative model of care, I am not even considering the other stance—that they should never transition at all—a position taken by the therapists treating Leelah that by self-report contributed to her tragic death by suicide.

The controversy about young children's ability to have a secure hold on their own gender stems from the findings of research studies to date: The majority of children who show up at gender clinics as "gender dysphoric" in early childhood do not grow up to be transgender. So, what does it mean for families or professionals to promote the social transition of "gender dysphoric" children who have not yet reached the age of puberty, since, according to existing research, most of those children will not be in the same place at age twelve, thirteen, or fourteen? *Social transition* is defined as a child's movement from one gender, typically the one matching the sex assigned on the birth certificate, to either the "other" gender or to another gender that the child affirms to be the authentic one. The transition is typically accompanied by a change in name, gender pronoun, gender marker on legal documents, and gender presentation.

The question of young children socially transitioning or not all started with the robust research studies coming out of the gender clinic at the Vrije Universiteit (VU) University Medical Center in Amsterdam, under the leadership of Peggy Cohen-Kettenis, followed by the work of Dr. Ken Zucker at the Centre for Addiction and Mental Health in Toronto. The first group to offer puberty blockers as a method for stalling the advance of puberty in gender-questioning youth, Dr. Cohen-Kettenis and her associates collected massive amounts of data on the children who came through their clinic starting in their early childhood. They discovered that the majority of children they served in their clinic qualified as "desisters," meaning that by adolescence their earlier assessed gender dysphoria would drop by the wayside. A minority of the children would carry that gender dysphoria with them throughout their childhood and into adolescence, and those would be the children, the "persisters," who would be good candidates for puberty blockers and then later for hormones. In the meantime, it was viewed as precipitous if not potentially harmful to indulge young children in their wishes to alter their gender identity, given the good probability that a child who longed to be a girl at age six, for example, would have lost that longing as puberty rolled around.

The data on persisters and desisters were readily available in 2011 when the World Professional Association for Transgender Health (WPATH) released its new standards of care for gender-nonconforming children. While it took the stance that each family, possibly with the help of a mental health professional, will make its own decision as to whether a child should socially transition from one gender to another, WPATH also tacked on a cautionary message. In the association's own words:

> Mental health professionals can help families to make decisions regarding the timing and process of any gender role changes [social transitions] for their young children. They should provide information and help parents to weigh the potential benefits and challenges of particular choices. Relevant in this respect are the previously described relatively low persistence rates of childhood gender dysphoria (Drummond et al., 2008; Wallien & Cohen-Kettenis, 2008). A change back to the original gender role [assigned sex] can be highly distressing and even result in postponement of this second social transition on the child's part (Steensma & Cohen-Kettenis, 2011). For reasons such as these, parents may want to present this role change [social transition] as an exploration of living in another gender role, rather than an irreversible situation. Mental health professionals can assist parents in identifying potential in-between solutions or compromises (e.g., only when on vacation). It is also important that parents explicitly let the child know that there is a way back.[24]

The concern was that children given a green light to change their gender early in life may have a hard time turning back, and given that the bulk of young children do not continue on a path that would involve a gender change, it would be best to think twice before you go ahead and let a child transition in advance of even knowing if it's true blue or not. As a member of WPATH, I very much rely on the organization's wisdom and guidance in my work as a gender specialist. Yet this cautionary message just didn't ring true. When I probed further into the study of the early adolescents by Steensma and Cohen-Kettenis that the WPATH guidelines relied on in crafting its cautionary message about social transitions, I discovered that this qualitative research study, ostensibly demonstrating the distress of a second social transition back to the natal sex after an initial cross-gender social transition, was based on an investigation of only three pubescent girls, each of whom presented in a masculine way until middle school and then went back to a more socially defined feminine presentation. The cause of their distress: the unwillingness of their peers to accept them in their new early adolescent "fem" selves. I thought, *If their schoolmates had been "chill" about their gender flow from butch to fem, all might have been fine for these three young women in switching to a more feminine presentation.* Furthermore, it was never clear that they had actually socially transitioned earlier, rather than simply presenting as "masculine" and allowing others to perceive them as such. This seemed more of an excursion in gender expressions than a transition of gender identity, and regardless of which it was, the cause of distress seemed to be far more the reactions to gender fluidity by an unaccepting social world rather than internal turmoil or gender confusion. So, why not just fix the social world rather than send out a warning about the potential dangers of social transitions?

The cautionary words in the WPATH standards of care are actually quite temperate in comparison to the strong reactions of some other folks toward young children's transitioning from one gender to another. At its worst, I have received vitriolic messages from critics accusing me of child abuse, sin, loss of Christian values (quite ironic, as I am Jewish), and pacts with the devil for allowing children to change their gender (either through social transitions or later with the aid of medical interventions). These gender watchdogs, typically with conservative political leanings and the Bible as their guide, carry on about pushing drugs and surgeries on unsuspecting, innocent young children, even though no child will ever receive any such interventions before reaching puberty.

Then there are others who are not so vehement in their objections but seem befuddled by the whole concept of young children's shedding the gender the adults around them "know" them to be and declaring another. For example, I have experienced the following interchanges, not just once, but several times in my community presentations about gender-nonconforming children. From the audience: "Dr. Ehrensaft, you've said that it is not up to us to say, but for the children to tell what their gender is. And you say it's okay for a five-year-old to transition from one gender to another and their parents should listen to the child. But you're the one who wrote the book *Spoiling Childhood*, and there you said that parents give their kids way too much power and control, listen to them too much, and that we should just learn to say 'No,' 'Stop,' and 'Why not? Because I'm the parent and you're the kid.' Now you're turning around and saying that children should be allowed to be the boss of something as monumental as their gender, and we should let them call the shots. How could this be?" I have been asked this same question many times, so I had plenty of practice polishing up my response. Here it is: "Well, I think we're talking about apples and oranges here. Letting a five-year-old declare their own bedtime, let's say midnight, is a totally different phenomenon than listening to a little one who is pleading with you to take seriously what they're trying to tell you—'You got it wrong. I'm not the gender you think I am. Here's who I am.' It's up to parents to determine their children's appropriate bedtime. But it's up to children to declare their own gender. Campaigning for a midnight bedtime calls for setting limits; sending out a plea for gender affirmation calls for carefully attending to something that is at the very core of that child's being. If we let a five-year-old determine their own bedtime, we do them a great disservice, and maybe even impair their health. If we let a five-year-old have a say about their gender, we do them a great service and maybe even improve their health by giving them a chance to live a true gender rather than a false gender life."

But are young children really capable of making that kind of affirmation? "Apples and oranges" kept running through my head, not just about bedtimes versus gender affirmations, but about all the different ways children can be gender-nonconforming and what the different gender creative children need from us. Let's go back to persisters and desisters. Is it possible that they are another example of apples and oranges? The persisters might be a completely different group of children than the desisters, from very early on. If they are, we ought to be able to sort out the desisters from the persisters, rather than lumping them all together, just like we can sort out apples and oranges into different bushel baskets.

If we fail to do this sorting and instead ask all the children to wait until much later so we can be absolutely sure who they are, we might be asking a whole cohort of children (the apples, the persisters, perhaps our youngest transgender people) to put a brake on their gender explorations because another group of children (the oranges, the desisters, in large part made up of our protogay children) are headed in another direction. This hardly seems fair to the persisters, not to mention potentially detrimental to their mental health, as we know that children who are restricted, constricted, or policed in their efforts to let their true gender self come out are at risk for psychological stress, distress, and suffering. To be able to sort out the apples from the oranges is not just an academic exercise. For a particular child, it could make the difference between gender effervescence versus gender despair, gender expansiveness versus gender deflation. So, let me share with you my musings about apples, oranges, and yes, even fruit salad in the gender orchard.

Over the past five years I've pored over the research, followed the social critiques, and watched with my own eyes as more and more children parade before us in their full gender regalia. I've listened to the arguments about the instability of gender stress, distress, and dysphoria among our younger cohort of gender-nonconforming people. I have examined the statistical arguments that the majority of children identified at gender clinics early in life as gender dysphoric (or until the recent past, showing signs of the erstwhile "gender identity disorder") will outgrow these "symptoms" and cease to be dysphoric by the time they reach puberty. These data have led others to the conclusion that without early litmus tests, we should just wait and see how a child's gender unfolds before leaping to globally change a child's name, pronouns, and gender identity, the key ingredients of social transitions.

No doubt, we watch our children carve out an infinite variety of gender paths. Otherwise, the gender web would be a useless tool. Yet when I step back with a wide-angle lens on the ever-expanding variety of gender webs spun by the children, I can see a pattern of three types of webs, or, to switch metaphors, I can locate three major roads the gender creative children travel on, albeit with the opportunity for lane switches, merges, and highway changes at any point along the way. I know that, based on the extant research of persisters and desisters, many experts espouse that in early childhood we cannot yet tell which road a particular child will end up on. For those of us who have now had years of experience gazing at the children through a gender affirmative lens, we say, to borrow from the slogan of President Obama's first presidential campaign, "Yes, we can."

To recap, those who say we cannot know a child's affirmed gender identity early in life—because so many young children who are "gender dysphoric" stop being so when they reach adolescence—conclude that it would be precipitous to allow any of these children to socially transition when they are little: Since the young children stand a good chance of growing out of their gender dysphoria later, why not wait until adolescence to make any moves? If the children still feel they are in the wrong gender, then we can talk about helping them switch to the gender they know themselves to be. But my own clinical sensibilities and experience tell me, "That's not how it is. Once again, you're talking apples and oranges, and we can tell the apples (the transgender children) from the oranges (the gender-nonconforming but not trans kids), sometimes as early as when they are three years old. So, why hold the apples back if they already know who they are?" Oh, and by the way, besides the apples and the oranges, each of whom need different things from us, we've run across the fruit salads—children and youth with a mélange of gender expressions and identities that are more than just gender-nonconforming but different from transgender. So, let's see if we can sketch the outlines of each of these three groups—apples, oranges, and fruit salad—and talk about how they are both alike and different.

APPLES

"Now you will be quiet, you horrid frog!"
But as he fell, he ceased to be a frog, and became all at once a
prince with beautiful blue eyes.
—The Brothers Grimm, "The Frog Prince"[25]

This is the allegory of the apple: not a frog who turns into a prince, but a boy who turns into a girl, a girl who turns into a boy, or a child who constructs some other gender identity that is neither one nor the other but all and any or some gender.

Apples are the children who often show up in child gender research as cross-gender in their identifications early in life and who continue on the same track into and beyond puberty (the persisters). We use a motto of "insistent, persistent, and consistent" to identify them. I am recalling a child, Aline, whom I had the great pleasure of meeting at our gender clinic. This child was then eight years old and had been diagnosed as being on the autism spectrum. Assigned female at birth, Aline was now insistent that she was a boy. Actually, according to her parents' report, Aline was headed in that direction from the time she was three. The parents were at a loss for what to do. Aline demanded a short haircut like her brother's and would wear only clothes from the boys' department. Possessing very limited language, most of Aline's time at the clinic visit was taken up with humming—until she would hear one of the parents say something like, "When she was younger . . ." Immediately Aline would come to attention and yell out, "Don't say *she*. Say *he*," and then go back to humming. Consistency was evident from the parents' report of five years of cross-gender identifications, and nothing could have been more insistent and persistent than this little person's protests and her attempts at gender correction when feeling misgendered, even more poignant in a child with very little language to call on. "Don't say *she*" was the only sentence, indeed the only string of words, that I heard this child say (repeatedly) during the entire session.

"Persistent, insistent, and consistent" is typically preceded by a very early onset of gender-nonconforming behaviors. Parents often marvel that as early as their child's second year of life, even the end of the first year, they saw signs of "gender transgression"—a son with a towel wrapped around his head to look like long flowing hair; a daughter throwing a tantrum about wearing dresses; a little boy throwing toy trucks out of the crib and grabbing at an older sister's baby dolls; a little girl pretending to shave or standing up to pee like Daddy. These actions are often accompanied by early verbal declarations—from a little girl, "Me boy"; from a little boy, "Me girl"—said not just once in passing but over and over.

These children's parents often present their child's gender history with a look of confusion or wonder—"I didn't do anything to make this happen. This child just came to me that way, before she could hardly talk. I have three other children and not one of them is like this." Listen to Candace Waldron's description of her transgender son's early life, poignantly described in her book *My Daughter, He*:

> As Kendra grew, there were signs she was on a path all her own. Almost as soon as she could walk she enjoyed toddling around in Tony's [her dad's] high top sneakers. Never did she put on my [her mom's] shoes. My encouragement for her to dress up for photos and family gatherings if for no other reason than to show off a dress from a relative, was usually met with tears and tantrums. Kendra made her contempt for dresses clear by the age of two when I put her in a dress her grandma gave her for a formal photo.[26]

My psychoanalytic training always pipes in an inner voice that says, "Well, maybe someone was already encouraging this behavior, or maybe one or both of Kendra's parents had some inner conflicts or earlier traumas that caused them to be ambivalent about little girls or little girls' gender expressions. Having never met Kendra and her parents, how could I really know?" What leads me to conclude otherwise, in addition to reading more about Kendra's life in *My Daughter, He*, is my evaluation of the aggregate clinical data I have been compiling: Parents are the bystanders. They watch the unfolding of their child's insistent, persistent, and consistent cross-gender identifications with the exact parental feelings that Andrew Solomon describes so poignantly in *Far from the Tree*: Presented with a child who is not the one they expected and may be so different from them and from their dreams for their child that they are flummoxed, they don't know how to make sense of this child; they only know that this child came to them that way. It is their job to then figure out how to meet the child.

In that way, the little apples are to their parents as Stuart Little was to his parents. For those who are not familiar with Stuart Little, he was the fictional mouse created by E. B. White in his book of that title, a mouse unexpectedly born into a nice middle-class family. Like the parents of a gender "apple," "Mr. and Mrs. Little often discussed Stuart quietly between themselves when he wasn't around, for they had never quite recovered from the shock and surprise of having a mouse in the family."[27] Constitutionally, Stuart Little was a mouse. Constitutionally, the gender apples appear to be transgender—they have a strong "nature" component to their gender selves, something in their brain that sends cross-gender or other-gender signals, suggesting that for them those nature threads will be a strong determinant of their woven gender web, which we can expect to be a transgender one.

One simple verb will also be one of the signposts that can differentiate a young transgender child from other gender creative children. It is the verb to be. Children who are communicating to us their transgender self will often say, "I am a . . . (fill in opposite gender or some other gender)" rather than "I wish I were a . . ." or "I want to be a . . ." This is not universally true, and indeed, some transgender children, as early as their third year of life, will pick up from the confused or disapproving responses of those around them that it will be shocking or unacceptable to say, "I am a . . . ," and so they might soften it to, "Well, sometimes maybe I might want to be a . . ." But for those children who feel no necessity to hedge their bets to appease others or who have met with no such confused or disapproving responses, the simple sentence "I am a . . ." is a very clear signpost identifying a child who is not the gender people think they are, and is indeed one of our apples.

Accompanying the early onset is the early sense of know-ing, which makes sense in light of the declaration, "I am a . . ." In reading Genny Beemyn and Susan Rankin's study *The Lives of Transgender People*,[28] I was struck by the number of respondents in this massive study of over three thousand transgender adults who reported knowing at a very early age that their gender was not what other people thought it was. The main problems they had were that they either didn't have words to express this or knew that it would not be well received by the people around them if they were to disclose what they were discovering about their gender. The main differences we have today are both the new narratives that are available and the space that adults are providing to allow the youngest of our transgender children to speak up about who they are—which they appear to be doing earlier and earlier, much to the admiration or envy of their older transgender compatriots, who only wish they had had the same opportunities rather than having had to wait and suffer until far later in life to be able to declare their transgender selves.

Then we come to bodies. Little gender apples, our youngest transgender people, may express distress, disappointment, or frustration about the bodies they have. You might hear a child sobbing, "Why do I have a penis if I'm a girl?" or "Where's my penis if I'm a boy?" Some children will beg their parents to put them back in the tummy they came out of and let them come out with the right body next time, or ask them to write God a letter to say God got it wrong last time and should start over and make the right body. These laments fall in the category of body dysphoria, from which some, but not all, young transgender children suf-fer pretty poignantly: the anguish that their body doesn't match the gender they know themselves to be. I'm recalling one little four-year-old who desperately tried to saw off his penis with a bar of soap, so that he could get to the vagina underneath and become the girl he knew he was. At older ages, if not attended to, this body dysphoria can escalate to dangerous levels, with some youth attempting to or succeeding in mutilating their bodies, as if to say to their assigned sex, "Out, out, damned spot." Some may refuse to look at their bodies in the mirror, or they bathe with their clothes on to avoid contact with body parts they repudiate. All this in the hopes of someday having a body that will be a better gender match, a wish that can come true these days with the advent of medical interventions to bring bodies in better sync with psyches.

Now we come to what I call the ex post facto test as a way to confirm that you have a gender apple in your hand. Let's start with children who say, "I am not the gender you think I am," and who go on to ask, "Can you please let me be the gender I am?" Before that request is granted, many of these young children will show signs of anxiety, stress, agitation, or anger. They may become reclusive or lethargic, or alternatively, wild and hard to manage. If, after careful consideration and preparation, the request is granted and the child then begins living in their affirmed gender, there can be an immediate and, in some instances, dramatic shift in the child. Like a caterpillar morphing into a butterfly, we see a vibrant, soaring little person—with confidence, joie de vivre, and a general sense of psychological well-being replacing any or all of the aforementioned symptoms of discomfort or distress. This transformation does not negate the reality that this child may still have a challenging road to travel in acclimating their transgender self to the world around them, but they do so with a new sense of equanimity and joy. The ex post facto test is often what allows us to fully see who the children are—happy, transgender little people.

I should mention that our young apples are often quite binary in their gender identity, but not necessarily in their gender expressions. They often carry with them the past experience, albeit brief, of living in another gender, with all the gender activities aligned with that gender. So, we may have our transgender little girl who still explodes bombs with army tankers in sand tray play, much to the consternation of the observing therapist or parents who jump to the conclusion, "Oh, my God, we must have gotten it wrong. She really is a little boy, not a girl." No, she is just being a gender-expansive little girl, who understands full well what *gender-nonconforming* means, in every sense of the term.

Other little apples go in a different direction with their gender expressions. They are as binary as any cisgender child might be, maybe even more so, in their gender expressions of appearance, preferring only the frilliest of dresses and the most feminine of shoes, or only the most combat-style T-shirts matched with camouflage pants. For some of these children, before transitioning, their cross-gender activities don't just appear as joyful excursions. Their play can also exude an element of serious business—"I play with these toys not just because they're fun and what I like to play with; I play with them as part of my communication to you that this is who I am and this is how I want to be," such as Barbie dolls on the one hand, or GI Joes on the other. In a world that would dispense with gender-labeled toys and activities, the gender apple's play might revert to simply fun and games; but as long as such play serves as a stamp on or declaration of one's gender status, it may continue to contain serious if not urgent gender communications. In some cases, the child's gender expressions of appearance and play may take on an exaggerated, even almost hysterical timbre, which can quiet down remarkably once the child feels heard and seen in their gender declarations.

Now recall the data about the persisters and the desisters. At the end of those five years of me scratching my head and saying surely we can find ways to differentiate the persisters and desisters early in life, and realizing all the ways I seemed to be able to identify the persisters in my clinical work, I opened my email to find an article written by the group at the Amsterdam clinic, in which the researchers reanalyzed their data on persisters and desisters and found that there were more persisters than they'd originally calculated and that they were able to delineate features from their early profiles that indeed differentiated the persisters from the desisters.[29] Those features—saying "I am" rather than "I want to be," showing signs of body dysphoria and showing early onset of cross-gender identifications, and being persistent— exactly matched the profile that I've just laid out to you. All arrows are pointing in the same direction regarding the possibility of identifying our youngest transgender people. I think it is now safe to say, "Yes, we can," not with 100 percent accuracy, but with some assurance that we have guidelines in place that can help us determine who the little apples are. I think it is also safe to say we can feel confident that facilitating a social transition will do no harm. In fact, it might do more harm if we *don't* allow it to happen, causing unnecessary suspension in an unauthentic gender life. And just in case we should identify a little apple who later changes their mind—because, as I said earlier, gender is a lifelong unfolding, not set in stone by age six—I can find no evidence that would suggest that another gender transition would create psychological harm. It just may be challenging to the people around that child, particularly if they adhere to the belief that gender is bedrock. As long as there are social supports around children to facilitate a later transition either back to the gender aligned with the sex on their birth certificate or on to something else, there is no reason that these children cannot thrive. We should also remember that although many of the apples show up early in life, this is not a necessary criterion to be counted as an apple. Some transgender youth do not discover their transgender identity until much later (especially when puberty rolls around), some not even until adulthood, and the rubric will always be the same—once you learn that a child is an apple, honor them as such.

Apples

- ▶ Children who often show up in child gender research as the "persisters"
- ▶ Cross-gender in identifications early in life that continue on the same track into and beyond puberty (consistent, persistent, and insistent)
- ▶ Typically they say, "I am a . . ." rather than "I wish I was a . . ."
- ▶ Many express body dysphoria.
- ▶ Gender explorations typically present not as child's play but as serious work.
- ▶ The nature thread of their gender web is often quite strong.
- ▶ Our youngest cohort of transgender people

Recently, when I was preparing slides for a presentation on gender-nonconforming children, I searched on the Internet for a compelling picture of an apple—a young child who had fully transitioned from one gender to another. I came upon a picture of a little girl standing in front of a ballet practice barre, vixenlike in her pink leotard and tights and wispy blond curls. I investigated further and discovered that she was a young transgender girl from the Netherlands. As I probed further, I discovered that in the Netherlands, where the professional stance at the renowned gender clinic started by Dr. Cohen-Kettenis has until recently been to hold back on early social transitions, a growing number of families are not waiting for professionals to give them a green light. They are allowing their sons or daughters to transition to their affirmed gender well before puberty and well before they may ever seek out the services of a gender specialist. We could say that these families are acting precipitously or irresponsibly. Alternatively, I will posit that these mothers and fathers know an apple when they see one—because of the gender messages from their own child to which they have learned to listen, their exposure to the ever-expanding fount of literature on the subject, changing social mores about gender beyond the assigned binary, and most important, their participation in a now-existent international community of parents who have come together to support one another in reinforcing the children's gender creativity and giving the children the opportunity to live in the gender that feels most authentic. And we can also pay attention to the children themselves, pushing the agenda forward. I am reminded of one little five-year-old, held back from transitioning because of the condemning attitudes in the community in which he lived, climbing to the top of the slide at his neighborhood park, throwing out his arms, and yelling for all to hear (much to his mother's astonishment), "Everybody—someday I'm going to be a beautiful woman."

ORANGES

Jacob pulled on his witch's dress and twirled. He loved the way the black lace swirled around him.
"I want to wear my dress to school!"
—Sarah and Ian Hoffman, *Jacob's New Dress*[30]

An orange might be a boy who signs up for ballet and wears a tutu to class but who otherwise identifies as a boy. It might be a girl who likes to wear boxer shorts instead of frilly underpants, yet who still considers herself a girl. It might be a child who persists with this way of being into adolescence or beyond. It might be a child who moves on to be more "gender normative" by cultural standards. What the category of oranges will include are all children who would have fallen into the category of "desisters" in the gender clinic studies. They will not go on to want to change their gender identity and live full-time in the other gender. They will be increasingly satisfied with the sex assignment on their birth certificate as time goes on. So, who are these children who might be pegged as "desisters" in the research studies?

A good number of them will fall into the category of protogay youth—children who explore their gender on the way to identifying and consolidating their gay or queer sexual identity. I am recalling many years ago sitting in bed with the flu reading Richard Green's 1987 book *The "Sissy Boy Syndrome" and the Development of Homosexuality*[31] from cover to cover. Fuzzy-headed as I was, still the end of the book hit me with a startling revelation. The vast majority of these little boys who were put through a regime of therapy to repair their inappropriate gender behaviors and desires grew up many years later to become—gay. If we work backward, we can understand that these particular gay men were once identified, most likely first by their parents, as "effeminate" little boys, clamoring for dolls, gravitating to the princess dresses and tiaras in the dress-up corner, preferring girls to boys as friends, retreating from competitive sports and rough-and-tumble play. By every definition of the term, they were gender dysphoric, or in that era referred to as having a gender identity disorder. As these boys reached adolescence or beyond, some of this dysphoria dissipated or disappeared completely. In other words, they were desisters. By the time they reached adulthood, some had no memory of their early cross-gender behaviors. What they did know is that they were gay. As children, they were part of the cohort I have dubbed the oranges, the children who explore gender expressions far beyond the boundaries of binary gender boxes, play with the idea of being the other gender, but never actually repudiate their assigned sex. In fact, over time some of them may grow to embrace and celebrate it, as a woman who loves women, or a man who loves men. And other of our little oranges will grow to be gender-nonconforming cisgender heterosexuals; still others will shed their gender nonconformity by adolescence, regardless of what path they follow in their sexual identity formation.

Sometimes the oranges confuse us, because we can't tell if they might be low-key apples, just not stating their case about their gender identity vociferously with persistence, insistence, and consistency. But if you listen carefully, you can tell that their cross-gender excursions are in fantasy rather than a statement of fact. Their mainstay is that they do not comply with the rules for gender behavior—in their movements, their play activities, their dress, their appearance, their choice of playmates. We might think of them as the proverbial tomboy or sissy, but better to think of them as our gender creative playing-outside-the-box little people who celebrate their expansive gender expressions but sit tight with their cisgender identity.

Sadly, they are also the people who get targeted most as being "gender offensive." They are the boys who get teased for throwing like a girl; the girl who gets teased for playing football with the boys. In fact, if you look closely at the statistics of harassment and violence against LGBT youth, you will find that the main trigger is not their sexual orientation or their switch in gender but how their gender looks—if they don't fit the stereotype of what a boy or girl should look like or do, and they transgress, they are at risk for being stigmatized and cast out by those who cannot tolerate difference and those who grow anxious when gender does not remain bedrock. We worry about the safety of our little apples, our transgender children, but here is where they find themselves side by side with our little oranges—gender-expansive children who stand out in their appearance or activities and must wend their way through a potentially gender-restrictive, unfriendly, if not hostile world.

Oranges, too, like apples, typically show up early in life. How else would we have so many young desisters in the gender clinic studies? I am recalling my own son, at age three, donning his sister's ballet tutus and headbands; at age two, spurning trucks and beginning his porcelain doll collection; and even earlier than age one showing a preference for soft and cuddly things rather than fast and active things. By my measures today, he would count as an orange, one who would later grow into his gay self. By standard measures of the 1970s, when his gender creativity was unfolding, he could easily have been diagnosed with a gender disorder and, with a different set of parents, might have been sent off to a therapist to help him learn how to be a boy's boy and embrace his masculine self, rather than encouraged to be his own true self. So, how did we as his parents know he was an orange not an apple?

Recall, the difference between an apple and an orange is that a little apple will say, "I am a . . . ," whereas the little orange will more likely say, "I wish I were a . . ." or "Sometimes I want to be a . . ." That would have been my son. And wish and want oranges will do to the nth degree in their fantasy play, in their drawings, in their dress-up, and so forth. But at the root of their gender explorations, their core gender identity remains a match with the sex marker on their birth certificate. They typically do not lament their fate, curse the gods, or accuse their parents of getting it wrong. They may play with body transformations, such as stuffing socks into their thrift store prom dress to acquire a buxom bosom or "packing" their pants to pretend they have a penis, but they do not hate their bodies or suffer from the body dysphoria that the apples endure. And they usually bathe naked (instead of trying to avoid seeing their bodies).

Recall the rubric that, if we want to know a child's gender, it is not for us to say but for the child to tell. So, with our little oranges, by listening and observing, we discover over time that their explorations are in the realm of gender expressions rather than core gender identity. There is no need for these children to transition to another gender, but every necessity to open up a path to more expansive gender expressions and to challenge any social policing of those expressions. Typically, their gender webs are a true medley of nature, nurture, and culture, but for those oranges who are our protogay children, we also have to consider the strong nature loading for sexual identity that might in turn influence both their early gender explorations and desire to live outside any kind of prescribed and restrictive binary box, whether it be gender or sexuality.

Tiffany is nine. She has two moms. When she was seven, she gave away all her dresses and gave herself a haircut—shearing her long, flowing hair and transforming it into a spiky 'do resembling the protruding quills of a porcupine on high alert. One of her moms worked in the medical field and brought home boxes of surgical gloves. Tiffany swiped some of the gloves and converted them into homemade penises. She stuffed one in her pants and wore it to school. When her girlfriends found out, they all wanted one, too. So she made penises for all her friends and they all packed together, with squeals and giggles. Tiffany hates all things feminine, but also hates boys. "Girls rule," she says, and she dreams of someday becoming an astronaut and going on an all-women trip to the moon. Her favorite activity is basketball. Her biggest nemesis: kids who think she's a boy just because she doesn't dress like a girl (anyone seeing her on the street could easily misgender her as male). What would she change in the world? She would de-gender all toys, all activities, all clothes, so they would just be people things rather than male or female things. Tiffany is an orange.

Oranges

- ▸ Are gender-nonconforming but do not repudiate their assigned natal sex
- ▸ A large number of these children will become gay or queer, exploring gender on the way to discovering their sexual identity.
- ▸ Do not tend to repudiate their bodies but can engage in fantasy play or ruminations about life in another body
- ▸ Explorations are in the realm of gender expressions rather than core gender identities.
- ▸ Nature, nurture, and culture are all strong threads.

FRUIT SALADS

Have you ever felt . . .
Like M, F, or even FTM and MTF aren't enough? And certainly
not "gay," "straight," or "queer"?
Or that your gender changes by the minute, hour, day, or
season?
That maybe you were meant to have more than one gender?
Ever feel that your gender isn't so clear cut? (Or that it falls
right off the map?)

—GenderQueer Revolution[32]

If you have, you would qualify as a fruit salad.[33] They are the gender weavers who make a tapestry of self that is neither male nor female but their own creative understanding of gender, both in identity and expressions. These children are not necessarily beyond gender but are immersed in all of it. Many around them want to capture their spirit in one of two boxes—male or female— but the children, if fortified with enough gender resilience, will resist. As one nine-year-old explained to me, "Look, I'm a boy-girl. And that's all I can tell you about me right now." Or as another little six-year-old, equipped with a penis and wearing pink leggings, a long skirt, and a Spiderman sweatshirt, exploded in my office, "My moms are always asking me what I am—a boy or a girl. Would they just stop asking and let me keep playing with my Legos? I'm just me." It is so hard for us adults to comprehend a child who is neither one nor the other gender, but any and all or a hybrid, like our gender minotaurs or our gender Priuses or our gender-ambidextrous children. But comprehend we must, for such children and youth are indeed showing up in larger and larger numbers, and I dub them fruit salads because they are a combination of apple and orange and are not genetically but socially altered gender fruits. They may question both their gender identity and gender expressions simultaneously or in sequence.

When it comes to their bodies, their feelings may typically fall somewhere in the middle of the apples' and the oranges' somatic experiences. Because they are not binary in their thinking, they are not as distressed by the notion of being feminine-identified with a penis or male-identified with a vagina. This does not mean that their bodies cause no trouble at all, since some of the children struggle to put together their mosaic of being a boy with a penis who is also a girl, or a girl with a vagina who is also a boy, or genderqueer, or agender, particularly in a culture where penis = male and vagina = female. But not to the extent of the body dysphoria witnessed in the apples, because the fruit salads have an easier time with this than the apples, as they embrace middle ground where there is no either/or but all and any, and the concept of the penis- or vagina-bodied person more deftly replaces the equation of male = penis, girl = vagina. Yet they may not have the freedom from angst granted to the oranges, who love to play at gender in all its forms but at the end of the day come back to the natal-sexed-body they live in with comfort and acceptance, if not joy and celebration. I am recalling the youth who coined the term *gender smoothie*. When it came to body parts, this same youth gave a self-description as a "chick with a dick" or a guy with a vagina in the rear. This was not fun and games, but a strenuous attempt to make sense of a bodied self as a gender smoothie, or, if I might say, a gender blender.

In recent months many of us have experienced an explosion in the number of children and youth coming to us with a mélange of gender, our fruit salads. One colleague of mine described it as a tsunami. Some of them are little, like our six- and nine-year-olds discussed earlier, and some of them are big, like our gender smoothie. It is my observation that, for all of them, big and little, the culture thread of the gender web is vibrantly present, if not dominant, as they explore or question their gender and evolve into their true gender self. In a very short period of time, new social understandings of gender outside two boxes have literally gone viral, with a dissemination of information, personal stories, and sociopolitical tracts in books, in blogs, in YouTube videos, in Internet chat rooms. Just for fun, a minute ago I went to the Internet and Googled "gender fluid." I got 4,660,000 results. I'd say that counts for a lot going on in the rapidly flowing cultural current promoting gender infinity as a replacement for gender duality.

I am going to call on the words of someone a bit beyond youth status to shed light on this new social experience of exploring "What's my gender?" outside the two traditional boxes. This is a twenty-nine-year-old person who identifies as "genderqueer." First, let's start with definitions. According to Wikipedia, *genderqueer* "is a catchall category for gender identities other than man and woman, thus outside the gender binary and cisnormativity. Genderqueer people may identify as one or more of the following:

- having an overlap of, or indefinite lines between, gender identity and sexual and romantic orientation;
- two or more genders (bigender, trigender, pangender);
- without a gender (nongendered, genderless, agender; neutrois);
- moving between genders or with a fluctuating gender identity (genderfluid);
- third gender or other-gendered; includes those who do not place a name to their gender."[34]

In that context, let's listen to the words of this genderqueer person, spoken in 2014: "'It was like someone had opened a door in a previously unbroken wall. It had never occurred to me that gender might be a spectrum or something beyond the binary might exist. It was a huge formative moment in my life.'"[35] The door carved into the previously unbroken wall is simply our new social concepts of gender that challenge the old ones, not just in gender identity, but also in gender expressions. For this person at the end of the third decade of life in 2014, the reason "it had never occurred to me" was not because of ignorance or lack of imagination, but because of lack of existing information. Searching as a young child, there would have been nothing to bounce off of, no positive mirror of gender expansiveness from which to gain a reflection of self, because the concept wasn't yet in existence in Western culture, except as a form of pathology. So, the new reflective mirror of gender expansiveness then morphs into the door through which this young person now enters, culminating in a huge transformative moment in that person's life.

Our young fruit salads are breathing the same social air as their twenty-nine-year-old compatriot, a breath of fresh air that expands their own gender creative lungs. As they consolidate their true gender self, they discover that gender exists not only in their bodies and their minds but in the context of a social world that demonstrates revolutionizing realities and possibilities. This new social world of gender expansiveness appears to be playing a strong hand in suggesting to all the children that they are truly free to be you and me, not just in gender roles but in the full gamut of gender expressions and gender identity. With the proliferation of electronic devices and information sharing across the globe, the children and youth have complete access to these new gender possibilities, potentialities that fit the rumblings from their inner selves. The cultural threads of the gender web in turn stimulate the working threads of nature and nurture, as the fruit salads compose themselves in all their complexity of gender identity and gender expressions, not to mention accompanying variegated sexual identity and expressions. As these fruit salads step through that door that used to be an unbroken wall, they have a whole political movement to support them. In 2001 a group was founded in Southern California, GenderQueer Revolution, defined as a "national organization dedicated to empowering people of all genders, helping people to embrace the gift of gender in their own lives and in the lives of others, supporting and cultivating genderqueer, gender-gifted individuals and communities, uniquely gender-gifted art, spirituality, research, and academics, and educating and building bridges across trans, gendered, queer, and non-queer communities and beyond."[36] With GenderQueer Revolution as their predecessor and political guide, the next half-generation of genderqueer youth, our fruit salads, now rely less on any specific organization, but rather congregate on blogs and social media sites that allow them to connect across the globe and continue to educate and build bridges. So, culture also plays its hand through its political stirrings, activism that both gives definition and meaning to gender fluid lives and advocates for their rightful place in society.

What this means is that more and more youth (ages eleven to eighteen) are walking into my office, saying something like, "You know, I'm just not sure what my gender is—maybe I'm trans, maybe I'm not, maybe I'm somewhere in between, but I'm wondering." After a while, a lightbulb went on for me, powered by my training as a developmental psychologist. If Erik Erikson was right about the stages of life, adolescence is defined as "Identity vs. Role Confusion."[37] During this time, youth sort out who they are, who they identify with, how they want to compose their nascent adult selves. In essence, everything they have known may be up for grabs as they question and explore possibilities for redefining themselves and preparing for their future. When gender was considered bedrock, that part of their identity just wasn't a location of questioning; it was taken for granted, and, for heaven's sake, there were enough other things to have to attend to. And with gender as bedrock, there were no green lights encouraging youth to explore that part of their identity. In fact, then, you might get dragged to a therapist to be fixed if someone found out you were questioning your male or female self. But now that it is becoming more normative in our culture to accept that gender comes in infinite varieties, why wouldn't youth throw gender into the mix within the larger gestalt of exploring and consolidating their overall identity in preparation for stepping into grown-up life? With a multitude of models and reflections from social media to stir their imagination, what I am observing is a growing number of youth playing with their gender webs—imaginatively, creatively, albeit certainly not without angst and discomfort, two common ingredients in so many adolescent identity explorations. So, we can consider the possibility that fruit salads are showing up more and more because gender has now been added to the mix of more general identity explorations among all youth.

Think of a salad bar—the fruit salads are always more complex than simple fruits. That couldn't be more true for our gender salad bar—sometimes the most complexity comes in our struggles to get a child in focus who is neither male nor female, perhaps all and every, and not always staying in the same place over time. Our challenge is to facilitate these children living an authentic gender life without prematurely pushing them into one box or another. We have to liberate ourselves from our own binary mind-set and learn to live in a state of rich gender ambiguity, allowing our young fruit salads, along with the apples and oranges, to lead us into this expanding world of gender infinity.

Fruit Salads

- A tapestry of self that is neither male nor female but a creative understanding of gender, both in identities and expressions
- These children resist gender boxes.
- They often live in gender middle ground, with no either/or, but instead all and any.
- These are our agender, gender fluid, genderqueer children and youth.
- For these youth, the culture thread of the gender web is strong, showing up in the new, rapidly expanding social concept of gender beyond two boxes.

AM I AN APPLE, ORANGE, OR FRUIT SALAD?

I'd like to introduce you to a child of my acquaintance. From what I share with you, would you think that Casey is an apple, orange, or fruit salad?

Casey is seven years old. When Casey was born, Casey's parents, Meg and Jonathan, were excited to have a handsome little boy, perfect in every way. Casey, however, did not seem to share their excitement. By his second year of life, Casey was not so big on "boy stuff." He tottered around in his mother's high heels. He rocked his toy elephant in a cradle he fashioned from a shoe box and painted his nails red with a marking pen. One day, when Casey was three, he looked up at Meg and announced, "I'm a girl. When am I going to get a vagina?" Meg and Jonathan were stumped and decided to consult a therapist. So, they brought Casey to see a psychologist. The psychologist, having read child development texts well, told Meg that she was overbonded with Casey and it was time for her to step back. The psychologist then turned to Jonathan and instructed him to step forward, to get more engaged with Casey and go out and do "boy" things with him. The therapist directed both parents to remove Casey's "girl" toys (a therapeutic intervention, I might interject, that is now illegal in the state of California and four other states).

The psychologist's recommendations made no sense to Meg and Jonathan. They were both equally involved in Casey's life — there was no evidence of Jonathan's being absent or Meg's being overly present. They didn't come to a therapist to be told to strip Casey of his toys and passions; they just wanted to understand who he was and how to support him. So, they left this therapist and sought out another, this time a psychiatrist in their community who was known to specialize in gender issues. He listened to their account of life with Casey and invited Casey into his office for a play observation. After a few such sessions, the psychiatrist had the following to offer: We don't know who Casey is yet, so just stay neutral. Don't take away Casey's "girl" things, just try to limit them. Try to get Casey interested in cowboy stuff (revealing the psychiatrist's advanced age). This made more sense to them than the first therapist's approach, so they tried this for the next two years, along with the recommended message to Casey that he was a boy because he was born with a penis. By Jonathan and Meg's report, overall Casey seemed relatively happy during this time, yet Meg and Jonathan still felt that this second approach just didn't seem quite right, either.

It was now time for Casey to enter kindergarten. The parents made a decision to move to a new community with a public school that was more supportive of gender-nonconforming children than the community they left behind. Casey was now a child who was doing gender by location. In his kindergarten classroom, Casey showed no evidence of gender nonconformity. But at home he "let the good times roll." Out came the dress-up box, the nail polish, plus elaborate song-and-dance routines. Boy by day, girl by night and weekend continued into the fall of Casey's first grade year. Then one day in October, the school introduced a new "Crazy Day." For one day the students could dress any silly way they wanted. Casey chose a dress and silver tights for his Crazy Day. He was ecstatic, and this triggered a whole new routine for Casey. From now on he was going to extend his home-based gender expressions to school. He started wearing dresses every day and insisted on buying all his clothes from the girls' department at Macy's. Later that fall came Casey's sixth birthday. As a present, Meg and Jonathan gave him an elaborate American Girl doll. Now Casey was beyond ecstatic. Jumping up and down, he screeched, "This is the first time I got exactly the present I wanted. It's my favoritest ever." For months, that doll was never out of his sight.

With no mental health professional to cramp their style, Meg and Jonathan decided it was time to be much more proactive in opening up discussions about gender in all its shades and shapes. Enter Michael, Casey's brother, two years older than Casey. Michael hated any talk about Casey's gender expressions and would cover his ears and scream, "Why do we have to talk about this?" Meg and Jonathan took note of Michael's distress and made private time for him to talk about what it was like for him to have a brother who wore dresses to school and who was starting to look more like a sister than a brother.

Then comes second grade. Casey is now turning seven. He has decided to let his hair grow out—he would like it to reach the middle of his back. He wears "girl" clothes to school on a daily basis. He's completely enamored with the book *Be Who You Are*. He particularly likes one of the opening lines of the book, "He knew that his body looked like a boy, but it just didn't fit the way he felt inside."[38] Whereas Casey used to describe himself as a boy who liked girl things, or a boy who wanted to be a girl, by second grade he has changed his tune. Now he describes himself as a half-and-half—"I'm a girl on the inside, a boy on the outside." He has learned (perhaps too much information for a child so young) that medical interventions exist that would allow him to live as a girl, even get a vagina. Being a scientifically minded child, Casey is very interested in getting more information about these procedures. Thinking of his future, Casey imagines being a bride in a long, flowing white dress and veil. He becomes quite despondent when his parents explain that he would never be able to be pregnant and carry a baby in his own tummy (truth be told, with the advent of the first successful uterine transplant that resulted in the birth of a healthy baby, this may in reality become a possibility for transgender women in the future). In the meantime, he really wants to be a parent someday but is very worried that an adopted child would never love him (this worry might have stemmed from his older brother, who, in a moment of frustration and anger, made up a story that Casey was adopted and that's why nobody loved him).

Now when Casey is out in the world, people see a little girl. In his ballet class, everyone assumes Casey is female. Casey wears a pink leotard, pink tights, pint ballet shoes, and a pink ballet skirt. Casey is very happy with this and enjoys being perceived as a girl. If people he doesn't know refer to him as a girl, he does not want anyone to correct them. Yet with those who know him personally, he prefers male pronouns. All of his primary playmates are girls.

Moving the focus off gender, Casey is somewhat introverted and has never liked drawing attention to himself. Unlike his older brother, who easily spills out his thoughts and feelings to family and friends, Casey is more taciturn and prefers not to go into detail about his inner life. Both Meg and Jonathan describe Casey as quite mature for his age, both emotionally and intellectually.

Although a child of few words, Casey does have this to say: He reports that people tease him in the bathroom. He would use the boys' bathroom, and kids, especially the older boys, would yell at him, "What are *you* doing here? You're a girl." As a result, he avoided using bathrooms altogether and ended up with a wetting accident at school, which embarrassed him immensely. Now he uses the nurse's bathroom at school. In public places, he always chooses the women's bathroom.

Meg now sees Casey as "more girl." Jonathan is on the fence; he's not sure what to make of Casey, stalwart in his dresses yet perseverant with male pronouns. Jonathan has also done a fair amount of reading and has deep concerns about the difficulties in life confronting a transgender person. He would much rather not have that for Casey. Yet he also recognizes it is not up to him to legislate Casey's gender identity. Casey's gender just seems so murky right now, especially as Jonathan holds in mind all the times that Casey and Michael are as wild and woolly as any two scrappy boys could be together, according to our scripts for "boy" behaviors. At the same time, Jonathan is well aware that whenever Casey is asked to draw a self-portrait, it is always of a person who looks just like a little girl. So, is Casey an apple, orange, or fruit salad?

The answer: At the end of second grade, Casey announced, "I'm all girl now." Casey made a full social transition and entered third grade as a girl, still with the name Casey, which is conveniently gender neutral, but with female pronouns and a change in school records from *M* to *F*. As with so many other children, the ex post facto test after the social transition demonstrated a marked increase in happiness and well-being, as well as a greater willingness to engage in the world. For a while, Casey was living as a fruit salad, which we might consider for some children as a stepping stone on their way to emerging as an apple. Or, calling on another analogy from nature, the pupa as the stage in a butterfly's life when it is encased in a chrysalis and undergoing metamorphosis to its mature winged self is as the gender fluid stage might be while a child morphs into their full transgender status. For Casey, what were the signposts that pointed to the likelihood of this transformation? The early onset of cross-gender behaviors; the declaration "I am a girl" at age three; the dissatisfaction with his male body and desire to have a female one; the persistence of cross-gender identifications and behaviors; the pleasure in being gendered as a girl by those not in the know, that is, strangers; the ex post facto test.

THE FUTURE OF GENDER ORCHARDS

I dream of a world where pronouns are self-chosen, where every person's gender identity is acknowledged without necessitating physical transition, where fashion is not defined by gender, and where a book is not judged by its cover.
—Mx. Nathan Tamar Pautz, "On Not Judging a Book by Its Cover"[39]

What Pautz envisions is a world beyond apples, oranges, and fruit salad. We're not there yet. And maybe we never will be, as some children will grow up wanting that physical transition if they know it's available to them, and some may want to locate themselves somewhere on a gender spectrum of appearance and activities. But our metaphor of fruit orchard is a step in the right direction, recognizing that gender comes in different combinations of gender identity and gender expressions, and it is our job to provide fertilizer for each of the different kinds of fruit—apples, oranges, and fruit salad.

CHAPTER FOUR

When It's Gender *and* Something Else *or* Something Else

There are the fairy and the witch, the blond-haired princess and the women in black with murderous stiletto heels, whom a child might even call the black widow by association with the spider of that name. Perhaps one way of escaping a mother who is suffocating you with her loving care is to become a woman yourself—but an idealized woman and not one like your mother.

—Colette Chiland, *Transsexualism*

OVERBEARING MOTHER, entrapped little boy—the erstwhile standard explanation for the boy who wants to be a girl is emblematic of a long-standing belief that a child's gender nonconformity isn't about their authentic self but an unfortunate consequence of bad parenting or a reflection of some other troublesome event. In other words, if a child is being unconventional about their gender or in distress about their gender, it was traditionally believed to really be about something else. It could be a narcissistic mother. It could be a wimpy father. It could be a signal of a crazy mind, maybe even schizophrenia. It could be an attention getter. It could be a knee-jerk reaction to a traumatic situation, especially if the trauma was of a sexual nature. It could be a by-product of autism, because the child just never had a chance to develop accurate readings of social cues and social categories, including gender categories. Yes, any of these could be possibilities. But really—how often?

I hope I have now made a cogent argument for the ability to sort out apples, oranges, and fruit salad. If the complexity stopped there, we would have enough to fill our plates for years to come. So, now add the other conundrum: How do we know that gender is really at the root of it? The question comes from critics of our gender affirmative model, from professionals who are asked to make assessments of a child's gender status, and from parents who just want to get to the root of things but can see only a tangle of tendrils.

Not long ago I sat with a mother whose child, T.J., has been questioning, exploring, agonizing, and celebrating alternate gender possibilities for going on ten years now, landing most recently and consistently on a trans female identity with a fairly androgynous presentation. T.J., just turning twelve, is presently on puberty blockers and demanding, quite vociferously, "Give me hormones. I want boobs." Seems like an apple, yes? And yet . . . Mom wondered, and invited me to wonder with her. Perched at the end of the couch across from me, she revealed to me that she still had doubts if this was for real. T.J.'s gender protests started only after a sister was born, a girl who continued to be a thorn in T.J.'s side. T.J. still just seemed, well, "boy." Mom's question was particularly pressing because T.J. was now on a campaign for hormones, an only partially reversible intervention, unlike the puberty blockers that could be turned off at any time should T.J. go down a different gender path than the one lined with apples.

If a child wants to make alterations to their gender, or demands that the world see them as the gender they know themselves to be, how can you know it's for real? What if you make a mistake? What if it's really about something else, such as the uninvited entrance of a baby sister? What if they change their mind later and want to go back to their old gender? These are the questions that come up again and again. We could even say these questions are persistent, insistent, and consistent—again, from people who doubt our sanity in promoting children's messing around with their gender, from professionals who in good conscience do not want to make errors with negative repercussions for mental or medical health, from parents desperately trying to get their child in focus when that child shows up as a gender upstart.

Recently I had an epiphany while being interviewed by a host for a BBC production on gender-nonconforming children. He and his filming crew had just spent time with four of the families who come to our gender clinic, two with young children, two with teens. Regardless of their age, all four of the children/youth attending the clinic that day were clear that they were not the gender that matched the sex listed on their birth certificate but, rather, the opposite one. At the end of the afternoon, standing out in the hall of the shiny new University of California, San Francisco, Medical Center where our gender clinic is now housed, the BBC host directed this question to me (paraphrasing): "But what about the risks if these kids should change their minds later and want to go back to their natal sex?" His tone—not lighthearted or merely curious, but pensive and concerned. His facial expression—wrinkled brow, pursed lips. I'd had this question asked of me so many times before, and my standard response typically started with, "Well, the chances are slim and the risks are small . . ." But this time an inner voice shot up to the surface, shouting "Wait a minute!" and, like a spontaneous combustion, catapulted me into saying something quite different: "Well, if this happened, I would like to consider it not a risk but a possibility. So, let's just consider this possibility . . ."

Risk never means anything good—you risk losing your friends, you risk losing your job, you risk sliding into a deep depression, and so forth. But *possibility* is a neutral word—it's possible the ending will be bad, it's also possible the ending will be good, or neither good nor bad but simply there. So, as we think about situations when a child's story to us is about gender and something else, I am inviting us all, parents and professionals alike, to dispense with risks and associated dangers or fallout and instead think about all the different possibilities that might come from the situation when it's gender and something else or the gender ends up being about something else.

Before the new guidelines for standards of care were released by the World Professional Association for Transgender Health (WPATH) in 2011, it was understood that a child or youth (or adult, for that matter) who was expressing gender dysphoria in accompaniment with a "comorbid" psychiatric condition should have that condition attended to before considering any gender services. It was also assumed by many, and still is, that gender nonconformity itself was a symptom of other ills that needed to be cured, ills believed to be caused primarily by faulty parenting or psychotic thinking. We now see that gender variations are perfectly normal and healthy iterations of human development, and good parents are associated with gender-nonconforming children, with no faulty parenting to be seen, no witch mothers lurking in the background. And we know that putting up a red light to gender affirmation until nongender psychological ills are addressed (and presumably cured or managed) makes no sense at all, since many of those problems are not a cause of gender stress but, rather, a result of being held back from gender affirmation. We've also observed with amazement how these problems miraculously either disappear or shrink to minor proportions once a true gender self has the opportunity to see the light of day. And, yes, there are also other psychological problems that may run parallel to gender and not go away when gender issues are resolved, and that's to be expected and accepted. It doesn't mean that therefore these children should be prohibited from living in their true gender self. That would be as nonsensical as asking a child to wait to go to the orthodontist to get their teeth straightened until they correct their pigeon-toed gait.

The WPATH standards of care recognized the importance of dispensing with such gatekeeping in their guidelines for both youth and adults: "The presence of co-existing mental health concerns does not necessarily preclude possible changes in gender role or access to feminizing/masculinizing hormones or surgery; rather, these concerns need to be optimally managed prior to or concurrent with treatment of gender dysphoria."[40] I might take issue with the "prior to" part, as this still runs the risk of holding people back and exacerbating their symptoms, rather than giving them an opportunity to be soothed in anticipation of the gender affirmation, but the main gist of the message is clear and correct—let gender run free. Yet we are still left with the questions: "But what do we do if the gender nonconformity, at root, is about something else?" "What do we do if it's gender *and* something else?" We do the same thing we always do—find out what's going on and make sure the children get what they need to grow healthy and strong. In no way does that equate with barring children from living in their authentic gender because there's other stuff going on as well.

What might that other stuff be? It has already been documented so many times that children who are constricted in their gender suffer because of it. They get depressed; they get anxious; they get angry; they withdraw from life; they fail where they ought to be succeeding; they hurt themselves; they contemplate dying or try to put an end to their lives, sometimes successfully. These psychological ills are the result, not the cause, of the children's gender nonconformity in a world that is not ready to accept them or in a body that seems to be so wrong. So, I am not going to belabor that point. Instead, I want to talk about the fact that some children and youth do come along with gender on their minds as well as some other psychological things going on, and the question is, "So what?" Our biggest mistake: playing gender police just in case it's not about gender. Our wisest strategy: Stay open and curious, and listen for the pulsing beat of gender.

GENDER AS A SYMPTOM, SOLUTION, OR SOCIAL OPPORTUNITY

Occasionally, children will come to us distressed, distraught, or confused about their gender. As we sit with and listen to those children, we start to feel as if we've been thrown inside a washing machine on the spin cycle—it all seems to move so fast that we can't think straight. Today Johnny says he is Judy. But the day before he said he was a candy bar. And the day before that he just wanted to crawl back into the earth and become a flower. And tomorrow he might say he's Johnny again. With another child, we might start to feel as if we're locked in a stalled car—nothing's moving, the motor seems dead. Gretchen lies listlessly on the floor. She says she lost her brain, but a voice stayed back and is whispering in her ear, "Your name is really Gregory. Someday you will become a boy." She has no feelings about it. It's just that way. She doesn't care; she just wants to close her eyes. She has another voice that tells her to just sleep and sleep and sleep, and then she nods off. It's a fixed story; it never changes; Gretchen can't tell you anything more than that. The same story just keeps looping round and round.

If this sounds anything like your child, it will most likely take a mental health professional to help you decipher what is going on. We know this much: We are seeing a child who is in turmoil—about life, about how their mind is working, about where they fit in the world. Some children may be suffering from a general confusion of their whole self—they have no idea who they are, and gender is just one piece in the mix, rather than the root of their problems. Others may be caught up in the maelstrom of family chaos—where nothing seems stable, even their own gender. In rare cases, a child might be suffering from a psychotic experience in which hallucinations and delusions dominate—an inner world of fun house mirrors where anything can turn into something else. In each of these cases, gender gets thrown into the hopper as one more part of the psyche that has no core, no roots, no stability. These children need help to quiet down the clanging and churning of their minds, always watching for where the dust will settle. If it turns out that gender stress was merely a symptom of the more generic chaos, that stress should subside as the chaos dissipates. If it turns out that the gender stress was standing on its own as an independent issue, the stress will still be there after the dust settles and the chaos subsides—back to "insistent, persistent, and consistent" as our guideline.

Then there are the children who exhibit gender nonconformity not as a symptom of an underlying psychological ill but as a solution to an imposing social ill. It may be the girl who has been repeatedly molested by her male cousin and in both self-protection and despair about her life as a girl who is abused, comes upon the solution of becoming a boy—a tough boy at that. In her thinking, if she's a boy, no one will mess with her and no one will lust after her body anymore. It may be yet another girl who has been molested by her father, who wants to become a boy to keep her father out of her bed and also to protect her shattered mother from the accompanying domestic violence to which her mother is victim. It may be the boy who longs for friends and notices that girls are better at making friends and make better friends. Ergo: Become a girl. For most of these children, their gender presentations will actually be a false gender self—a gender shell that protects their more vulnerable underlying true gender from harm or from hurt. For a few of these children and youth, the social experience of living in the chosen self-protective gender evolves into an authentic sense of self, and if so, it will morph into a consistent, persistent, and insistent bona fide gender web, formed not so strongly from the nature but from the nurture and social threads in the web.

Let's think a little more about the relationship between trauma and the gender self. If gender is a mix of nature, nurture, and culture, and we have a child who has been repeatedly abused, sexually, to the point that the child would prefer to repudiate the gender that caused all that harm and enter life in another gender, is that any less authentic than the child who is persistent, consistent, and insistent since toddlerhood about their cross-gender identity? To test this out, we can help this child heal from the trauma of the abuse and pay attention to whether gender as a solution to those ills goes by the wayside as the child works through the horrors of what happened. This process is best guided by a trusted adult (or hopefully, more than one—parent, caregiver, therapist, teacher, support group leader) and should be accompanied by a revisit to the gender issue if it's still there. But supposing that child will then feel that along the way, no one ever took the gender identity issue seriously. So, here's a question for all of us: If a child composes a unique gender web in a way that also serves as a salve for past injuries, why would we want to take that away from that child?

Some children will be drawn to gender nonconformity not as a solution to life's ills, but as a social opportunity. In the concluding chapter of *Gender Born, Gender Made* I told the story of young girls in Afghanistan who are instructed by their parents to switch their gender, usually in situations where there is no boy in the family and it is advantageous to have one. This switch generally comes as a gender-by-location situation (girl in the privacy of home, boy out in the world where males can move freely and females are prohibited). The motivation is often economic and pragmatic—boys can get paid jobs to help the family income, they can run errands for their mothers; girls cannot. At adolescence, those girls cum boys are then instructed to go back to their female gender—

their "maleness" is no longer needed and it is time to grow into a woman and prepare for marriage and family. Yet some of the girls cum boys resist and say, "No way. I'm staying male." They have discovered life as a boy, and they like it. If you look at them in a group photo, there would be no way to differentiate them from any of the cisgender males lined up for the picture. Pushed into a cross-gender life by their parents at a young age, they now claim it as their own. Even with the potential social risks of being exposed as a natal female while living as male, for these youth coming of age, it feels so much better to be male in their culture; female no longer feels like a good fit. Would we want to take that away from them if male fits better and is a reflection of their authentic gender web, strongly influenced by the culture threads?

For some children, cross-gender presentation as social opportunity will only be a temporary strategy. I am reminded of the protagonist in Isaac Bashevis Singer's short story "Yentl the Yeshiva Boy," made famous by Barbra Streisand in her role as Yentl in the 1980s movie of the same name. Yentl is an orthodox Jewish girl in early-twentieth-century Poland who decides to pose as a young man so that she can continue to receive a Talmudic education after her father, who had been teaching her privately, dies. Talmudic education was forbidden to girls, open only to boys. Yentl's father rebelled against those gender laws; but with him gone, she would be forced to forgo her education— unless she became a male. And so she did, but only as a disguise. Her cross-gender excursion is strategic, so she can study the Talmud, and never morphs into an authentic sense of self, like with some of the cross-gender youth in Afghanistan. Instead, over time, she forgoes her male self; in other words, she desists, solving her education problem by immigrating to America where women can receive an education and reclaiming her female self full-time. Temporarily, Yentl's gender web included a strong cultural thread—the thread that said girls could not be yeshiva students, which, in her fervor to continue her intellectual studies, led to her "countercultural" adaptation—"Then, I'll present as a boy." But her web changed again as she repositioned herself in another country where the cultural threads were different—girls could study, not just boys, so she could return to girl, and did.

Willow came to me to talk about his desire to leave his boy self behind and live full-time as a girl. He had always been drawn to things "girl" starting from when he was about four years old. Now he was fifteen, and the prospect of spending the rest of his life as a male seemed bleak. He had adopted the mode of dress and style that was popular among the emo crowd at that time—heavy black eye makeup, nail polish to match, long wispy hair, skinny jeans, tight T-shirts, earrings, Dr. Martens boots. He hated that the world was so sexist and that women were treated so badly. He had always wondered if he was a boy or a girl, and now, years later, it was all becoming clear to him. Having just finished a class on gender, class, and race, he was shaken upon discovering the level of oppression of women. As Willow explained it to me, "Look, the world is so sexist. If I become a girl, I can fight the cause for women so much better than if I stay a boy." Cross-gender affirmation as a strategy to fight social ills—do we dismiss Willow's narrative about his female gender affirmation as faulty logic, as a solution to systemic sexism that has disturbed him so deeply—an oppression he believes he can not only attack more effectively as a female but also bow out of if he is no longer the male oppressor? I wouldn't say *dismiss*, but I have to say it definitely gave me pause, and led to the recommendation that we go slower and do more exploration before recommending hormones, surgeries, or legal gender marker changes for Willow. No matter where those explorations might lead (a work in progress at the moment), I have to hold the possibility that the cultural thread of sexism embedded in a social world that has simultaneously opened up the possibilities of gender infinity will influence the direction of Willow's already gender fluid web—toward a female design.

I said this before, and I will say it again—yes, it is always possible that gender nonconformity will be a symptom of or solution to a separate problem, be it psychiatric or social, and in those cases it may be wise to attend to the root problem to better see where the gender cards fall. This cautious approach opens up alternative possibilities for ensuring a good life, but it is not risk-free. The risk here, and I do say *risk* rather than *possibility*, is that a child's genuine gender woes will be dismissed as a facsimile of the "real" psychological or social problems, leaving the child suspended in a state of gender stress or distress, where it feels as if nobody is listening and there is no real. From there we run the even bigger risk of all the psychological fallout trailing that suspended state—anxiety, anger, depression, self-harm. So, let's get real and never forget that the gender web is not just about nature, but also about nurture and culture—and those threads are as real as it gets when it comes to a child or youth weaving together the gender that is most "me."

THE TEMPEST OF TEMPERAMENT

I had to unlearn everything I learned in school about gender, but one thing I did learn in my developmental psychology training that has been invaluable in my work as a gender specialist is temperament. Through the work of Thomas, Chess, and Birch, three mid-twentieth-century researchers, I was taught about nine categories of behavior that reflected our temperament: (1) how physically active or inactive we are (activity level); (2) how regular or irregular we are in our daily functioning (rhythmicity); (3) whether we tend to enter head on or shrink from situations (approach or withdrawal); (4) how flexible or inflexible we are (adaptability); (5) how much it takes to get a response from us (threshold of responsiveness); (6) how intense our responses are (intensity of reaction); (7) whether our moods tend toward positive or negative (quality of mood); (8) how focused or distractible we are (distractibility); and (9) how well we can attend to and keep going on something (attention span and persistence). From those nine categories, Thomas, Chess, and Birch identified three clusters of children: Easy, Difficult, and Slow to Warm Up.[41] Both then and now, the culturally laden values and prejudices that would label one child easy and another difficult based on said behaviors were not lost on me, but nonetheless, I have found Thomas, Chess, and Birch's constructs of temperament tremendously useful in my work with parents and children over the years, both in bringing to light good or not-as-good matches between parents and children, depending on their temperamental styles, and in underlining to parents, "Look, don't worry. You're child just came to you that way. Your challenge is to embrace this child that is yours." Now where have you heard that line before? Hint: The answer starts with a G.

We can think of temperament as the "how" of behavior. It's the way we meet the world—in a rush or cautiously, with a feeling of the glass half full or the glass half empty, with an irritable or a sunny disposition. Our temperament can be measured in the earliest months of life. Why? Because we come into the world with it. Not that it is immune to environmental tweaking, as much of the research has demonstrated. It just has a very strong constitutional and genetically inherited core—a given of personality, if you will. It is one factor that contributes to the amazement of identical twins separated at birth and reared apart who find each other only in adulthood. Despite incredibly different environments in the homes they grew up in, and despite being utter strangers before their adult encounters, they discover that their respective romantic partners, if they have them, complain about the same exact irritating traits they have, that they cry in the same parts of movies, that they never go to a party unless it's already been going on for at least an hour, and so forth. Yes, it is their identical genes that account for this, but only as their genes are transmitted to their personalities—through their temperaments.

So, what's temperament got to do with gender? Do not get me wrong—I am not saying that temperament shapes gender or is a "something else" that should give us caution about the authenticity of gender. What has struck me most poignantly is the way temperament plays its hand as children negotiate their gender creative self with the world around them. So, let's talk about temperament as one of the "something elses" that both accompanies and affects a child's gender journey, for better and for worse. Since every child comes with a temperament, and all children have the task of constructing their unique gender self, it goes without saying that the two will coexist throughout your child's life. But this particular "something else" can definitely influence whether your child's gender path will be rocky or smooth. It can make for the most gender resilient child on the block; it can send a gender creative child into hiding. It can even make people doubt whether gender is really what it's about.

Let's create two composite pictures. First, take Lauren. When Lauren was born, the take on Lauren was unanimous: This is one kick-ass baby. Lauren smiled as soon as it was humanly possible to smile. Lauren adapted easily to any place, person, or thing. Lauren plowed into any new situation with verve and excitement, confident it was going to be okay. At the same time, Lauren was mellow—it took a lot for Lauren to get riled up about anything. Lauren could zero in on a stuffed animal or even a piece of thread hanging from the bumpers in the crib and spend hours entranced. And when Lauren was born, everyone thought Lauren was a boy. Until—at about two Lauren started draping himself in diaphanous scarves he found in the dress-up corner at preschool. By age four Lauren started asking when he would grow breasts like his mommy and be a girl. By kindergarten he announced that he would be wearing boy dresses to school. By first grade he wasn't happy with that idea. He wanted his new dresses to be girl dresses. By second grade he confided to his parents that "boy" was all wrong, that Lauren was a girl. His parents listened, thought, and told Lauren that made a lot of sense, but where they lived and where he went to school, people might not understand, and they might not be so nice about it. Lauren, with his positive mood, bring-it-on approach to life, mellow disposition, focus, and perseverance, replied, "Well, I don't care. I have friends who like me, and I like me so it will all be good. And I just won't pay attention to the gender meanies." And off Lauren went to second grade, confident and buoyant in her affirmed girl self. No psychological bugaboos seemed to be getting in the way.

Now let's take Toby. As soon as Toby's family gathered around to see the new arrival, they all commented on how quiet he seemed. Whenever there was a loud noise, Toby started. When Toby's parents bundled him up to go to a big family Christmas party, Toby began crying as soon as they entered the room. Toby calmed down only when one of his parents carried him upstairs to a quiet alcove. Toby had a fear of strangers, was hesitant to make eye contact when someone entered the room, and took a long time to warm up to anyone he hadn't seen in a while. Toby was a serious baby, and his parents seldom found him laughing. Toby was somewhat distracted by everything going on around him and relied on a fixed routine to keep life on an even keel. As with Lauren, when Toby was born, everyone thought Toby was a boy. But at about age three, Toby began cowering in the corner of his day care center. He didn't like all the rough-and-tumble play. He liked the girls, and he liked to play house. He always wanted to be the mommy, but he was too shy to ask. At home he would play quietly in his room with his favorite stuffed animals; he gave all of them girls' names. But he kept that a secret. When he was four, his mom heard him whimpering in his bed. When she went to check on him, he mumbled into his pajama top, "I don't like being a boy." From then on, Toby's parents made sure he had lots of opportunities to express his gender the way he wanted, which he delighted in doing at home, but never anywhere else. This persisted all the way through second grade. By that time he had a favorite blue dress that his parents had bought for him. He put it on every day when he got home from school, but changed right out of it when he left the house. Toby's parents became more and more aware of his gender distress. They felt fortunate that Toby attended a very progressive, gender accepting school, with a director who would do anything possible to make Toby comfortable at school if he wanted to wear his blue dress to school, or if he decided to transition from he to she. But Toby would have none of it and just ran to his room when his parents tried to talk to him about it.

Was Toby less "gender sure" than Lauren? Was Toby more confused than Lauren about an affirmed gender identity? Was Toby's reach toward a girl self simply a strategy of a shy boy dodging the pushing and shoving of boy culture? I would say, none of the above. Toby simply came into his gender journey with a temperament that left him more vulnerable and less buoyant than Lauren in coming out as a girl. If Toby could slip in quietly with no one making a fuss about it, if he could be reassured that there were no gender meanies lurking, if no one would even take notice, he might be okay celebrating his true gender self. For a slow-to-warm-up child, that celebration might be a long time in coming, with quite a few painful patches along the way for a boy who is exquisitely self-conscious, not because of his gender nonconformity, but because of his temperament. Going against the gender grain only fuels that anxious self-consciousness, as, in case you haven't noticed, it's quite a noteworthy if not newsworthy event in our culture when a boy announces he's actually a girl, a brouhaha Toby would do anything to avoid. Toby does not need to have his authentic gender self questioned. He just needs protected time and space to come into his, most probably her, own.

To recap: Every gender-nonconforming child also comes with a temperament, so it will always be gender *and* temperament. Depending on the makeup of that temperament, gender creative children will have an easier or harder time letting their gender creativity come out and building gender resilience, particularly in a world that is not always kind to gender-nonconforming children. So, a shy, cautious boy, like Toby, might be like a deer in headlights at the very thought of wearing his dress to school, cringing at the idea that someone might look at him funny even for a nanosecond, whereas an outgoing, exuberant boy, like Lauren, might say, "Yes, I want to wear my dress. What do I care what anyone thinks? And people like me anyway." Sometimes we mistake the gender creative child who is more introverted for the child who really isn't sure about their gender or has some other inner trouble that is driving their gender stress, when nothing could be further from the truth. It is just that child's temperament meeting up with gender: wanting privacy for a very sensitive part of themselves.

Sometimes we err in the opposite direction—we mistake the child who has had to hide in a shell as being shy, when that particular gender creative child is actually just scared—living in fear of an environment hostile to their gender identity or expression. For that child, withdrawal is not a function of temperament but a reaction to perceived social danger. When they are given a chance to safely come out of their shell, with acceptance and protection to buoy them up, the so-called shyness evaporates, sometimes dramatically so. And that's how we know that it's not temperament, because temperament is not as flexible or removable. A simple rule of thumb: When considering a child's gender experience and responses, the best way to sort out basic temperamental factors from reactive retreat is to go back to infancy and try to remember how this particular child always was, before gender took its course. If it's the same now as then, temperament is at play. If it's radically different, this child may be cloaked in a false gender self to protect the true self from harm. Each is a something else we want to attend to: to either acknowledge the kind of child we have or remove the impediments that keep that child from being who they are.

GENDER AS FICTION

Back in the day when witch mothers or shadow fathers were seen as the cause of a child's gender ills, it was also typically thought that "gender disorders" should be suspect as "factitious disorders," defined as mental disturbances where the person intentionally acts mentally ill without obvious benefits. A close cousin to factitious disorder is Munchausen syndrome, where a person feigns an illness to garner the attention of medical professionals, or a parent fabricates disorders of their child for the same purpose. All three of these diagnoses have been improperly hurled at parents who were simply trying to support their gender creative children or at children who were simply trying to be their authentic gender self. And they still are today, in the painful and sometimes tragic cases where children are removed from the custody of their parent or parents, following the accusation that the parents are perversely contorting their children by forcing their sons to be daughters or their daughters to be sons—for their own ends, or because they irresponsibly allow their children to do that. And the children themselves may find themselves plopped into a psychiatric facility because they are not behaving as they should and ought to around their gender, when they could if they wanted to.

These are horrible crimes against children and families that we are doing our best to remedy as advocates and affirmative gender specialists. Yet we cannot throw the baby out with the bathwater by excluding from our consideration the rare cases when gender can indeed be a factitious or Munchausen situation. I have said repeatedly that one litmus test for authentic gender identity is the ex post facto measure—if a child is given the opportunity to live in the gender affirmed by the child, and it is authentic, we see symptoms of stress and distress go down markedly, if not disappear altogether. But what if they don't? Well, one possibility is that we got it wrong and this wasn't the child's affirmed gender.

Francisco, a fifteen-year-old teen living in a university town in New England, loved computers more than anything in the world, hiding in his room behind a screen whenever possible. He was always seen by both his family and his peers as a shy science geek. Then one day his body started to change—he was growing peach fuzz and his voice started to crack. Rather than celebrating his late entry into puberty, Francisco retreated even further into himself. Finally, he confessed to his mother, Dana, that he didn't want to grow into a man, because he was pretty sure he was a woman. Afterward, he sobbed in his mother's arms. Dana and her husband, Marco, discussed this turn of events and decided to seek out the services of a gender specialist. This gender specialist did a thorough evaluation and sent the family on for a second opinion, just to be sure. Both specialists concurred that Francisco was suffering from significant gender dysphoria and showed all the signs of being a transgender teen, with female as Francisco's authentic gender identity. A subsequent evaluation by a pediatric endocrinologist with a specialty in transgender care matched the two mental health professionals' conclusions—Francisco was a transgender teen and a good candidate for hormone blockers, fol-lowed soon after by hormones. Over a Christmas break Francisco transitioned to Frannie and returned to school the next semester with a change in both name and gender. But rather than calming down and feeling more comfortable in life, Frannie became more obstinate and resistant, refusing to do homework, consider col-lege applications, or complete household chores. While delighted to be the transgender poster child for the local newspaper, Frannie herself wanted nothing to do with the transgender community—unless she could teach them what she knew as the now expert. She did befriend one transgender youth on the Internet, but then fell apart when she got news that this youth had been abducted, raped, and buried alive, left to die. All of this was actually a cyber-ruse, but Frannie took it for real.

Frannie regained her composure and traveled with her family to Hawaii, where for the first time she could wear a bikini and show off her female body, except for the bulge at her crotch. It became clear to Frannie that the only path forward was to complete her gender affirmation with genital surgery. Close to age eighteen, Frannie was now able to arrange with the local surgeon, an expert in the field, to have this surgery around her eighteenth birthday. All the professionals—her therapist, her psychiatrist, her endocrinologist—were on board, supporting Frannie in pushing forward in her life as a young woman. Her parents were on board, as well, perhaps too eagerly so. The surgery went forward, and rather than appearing happy and more in sync with herself, Frannie began to develop other somatic complaints. First it was her stomach; then it was vertigo; then it became an eating disorder. With each disorder came a visit to yet another medical professional. All during this time Frannie refused to comply with the daily dilations that were to be an annoying but necessary part of achieving good results in the functioning of her newly acquired vagina. She began to get in trouble at school, which had never happened before. She made no efforts to complete college applications and simply believed that she would get into a fine school when the admissions officers learned about all her fantastic inventions sprawled out across a table in her basement lab at home. Things got so out of control that Frannie ended up in a psychiatric facility, where she continued to get in trouble and continued to introduce new physical ailments and body complaints.

Everybody, even the most trained, careful professionals, missed it. Her parents missed it, too. Frannie was a Munchausen patient. She spent hours secretly researching physical conditions on the Internet, conditions that would necessarily require medical attention. Gender was a perfect candidate. Once she had exhausted her gender options, she moved on to other conditions, now as a female. Frannie was not only suffering from Munchausen syndrome; she also had a healthy dose of sociopathic tendencies, and she was smart. So, she could fool the best of them. And she did. Will Frannie someday lament her physical transition from male to female? Maybe, maybe not. But is her gender most probably a symptom of some other disorder? Most definitely so, or rather we could say it was a convenient tool to provide her with the medical attention she craved but with which she could never be satiated. So, was this a risk—a gender transformation that never should have occurred— or a possibility—that Frannie chose a gender transformation for other reasons but now accepts her female gender self?

Occasionally, parents will come along who will show an unusually intense investment in their child's gender explorations, confusion, or distress. They may be hot to trot, expressing an urgency and intensity about moving forward with interventions for their child to acquire all the accoutrements of an authentic gender self—be it social transitions, hormones, top surgery, and so forth. Often parents are clearer and more adamant than the child in the request for services and become more spokespersons than listeners. Indeed, this dynamic can become the something else that precludes the parents from seeing the child before them, instead leading them to act on the basis of their own anxieties and agenda. Sometimes the agenda is to find relief from the excruciating position of living without knowing—"Is my child a son, a daughter, something else altogether? Let's just settle this ASAP so I can stop feeling so off-kilter and I can know what to tell people." Sometimes the desire is to have a longed-for daughter or son who did not show up at birth and is now offered as a possibility—so the gender fluid child is suddenly catapulted into the position of a transgender child, but not by their own doing. Sometimes a parent is seduced by the cameras and bright lights—getting to be the onstage heroic mother or father of the day in highlighted media tales of transgender children and their families. Sometimes a parent is lonely and looking for community—and a support group for parents of transgender children fits the bill. Without ever resorting to blame-the-parent, it is still important to always pay heed to parents' or caregivers' own inner motivations and psychological issues triggered by gender—not theirs but their child's.

At the risk of striking alarm bells about this "something else" that might influence a child's gender presentation and expressed gender desires, I still felt it necessary to acknowledge this rare phenomenon of factitious disease and Munchausen attached to gender so that we can recognize it if it comes our way. And if it does, the work is still the same—to listen as carefully as we can and do our best as parents and professionals to get the child's gender in focus while weeding out other life issues that color or bend that gender out of shape.

TWO SPECTRUMS CONVERGING: GENDER AND AUTISM

I cannot tell you the number of calls I get from other mental health providers who say something to the effect of, "I'm seeing this kid in therapy who insists he is a girl. But the thing of it is, he has [some form of an autism spectrum disorder (ASD)] so I really don't think it's about gender." I chuckle and respond, "Well, you see, it may very well be." Much of my early training involved assessing and doing therapy with children and youth on the autism spectrum. These are children who typically have trouble in social situations, lacking social skills and suffering from a surfeit of social anxiety. They are acutely sensitive to noises and human touch. They are well known for their persistent obsessions, which can be fickle over time but are always embraced with a fervor that goes well beyond enthusiasm. They can be inflexible and inpatient. They see the world in idiosyncratic ways. They are often quite concrete in their thinking, and expressing their feelings in words or having insight into what they are feeling is not typically their forte. Their IQs can sometimes far exceed those of everyone around them. And if you want to get to know them, you have to be willing to enter their world. They won't hop into yours.

I have always loved my work with children and youth who have been assessed as being on the autism spectrum, and I have continued to keep that work as part of my practice. And then lo and behold, I became a gender specialist and two paths converged—I was seeing more and more children who were neurodiverse, as the present language goes in describing children on the spectrum, but this time that's not why they were coming. Their parents were bringing them because of their gender.

We now have research data demonstrating that the incidence of gender-nonconforming children diagnosed with some form of autism spectrum disorder is significantly higher than one would expect by chance. It has been noticed enough by child gender specialists that researchers at Children's National Medical Center in Washington, DC, have recently launched a study to canvas mental health professionals' experience with gender-nonconforming children with ASD, and two studies have already been released by the Amsterdam group and by the group at the Gender Identity Service and Child, Youth and Family Services at the Centre for Addiction and Mental Health in Toronto, each demonstrating a statistically higher incidence of children diagnosed with ASD in their clinical patients than is found in the population at large.[42] Specifically, the Netherlands study found that the incidence of autism spectrum disorders was ten times higher at their gender clinic (7.8 percent of the patients) than in the general population (0.6 to 1 percent of children in the general population).

Certainly, for some of these children and youth, gender does become a solution to other life problems, as when a boy diagnosed with Asperger's syndrome explained to me that, like the child mentioned earlier, he wanted to become a girl because he had no friends and noticed that girls at his specialized high school had an easier time making friends than boys; ergo, becoming a girl was the key to acquiring a friend. But overwhelmingly, what we observe is an incidence of gender nonconformity *and* ASD, rather than gender as a symptom of something else—in this case, autism. We in the field are trying to make sense of why this is so: Is it a shared location on the brain? Is it caused by the same intra-uterine experiences that influence both? Does it have to do with weaknesses in reading social cues and therefore greater freedom to do gender as you like rather than how the culture tells you? Whatever the cause, it is critical that we stop and find out what is going on, because more and more children and youth are walking through our clinic doors presenting with both gender dysphoria and some type of autism spectrum disorder.

Recall Aline, the child from Chapter 3 who came to our gender clinic, a nine-year-old natal female with an early diagnosis of autism and speaking only one sentence: "Don't say *she*, say *he*." Nine months later Aline returned to the clinic. During that time Aline had been put on puberty blockers to forestall a fairly early onset of puberty that would have been very unwanted, not just because of gender dysphoria but because Aline was deathly afraid of blood, even from a minor cut, and the onset of menses with the accom-panying flow of blood would have been a traumatic experience for Aline on all counts. During this same period the family began to use male pronouns and acknowledge their child as a boy. The boy who walked into our clinic these nine months later displayed as dramatic a transformation as the before-after makeovers ad-vertised in popular magazines. Aline made eye contact, spoke in full sentences, and smiled every time he heard one of his parents or one of us refer to him as *he*. And I thought to myself: *Yes, this is a child who is both autistic and transgender. But not only that; facilitating a gender transition from female to male has actually increased his social skills and expressive language capacities while simultaneously reducing his symptoms of autism, if you will.* Which means, not only should we make sure that gender affirmation is allowed to go forward despite a diagnosis of autism, but also that gender affirmation can actually serve as a *treatment* for autism. When you think about it, there is an internal logic to this equa-tion: Autism renders a child feeling anxious and avoidant in social situations. How much worse it must be if that child is also forced to live in a gender that does not feel real. Given a chance to be "the gender that is me," the child then gets a booster for living in the world with its social challenges, since now we've at least eliminated one major impediment—gender dysphoria and a false gender self. Think about it: All the time we spend focusing on an autistic child's inability to read *our* social cues, we may have been equally incompetent in reading *their* cues, as in Aline's case, "I am boy."

But supposing Aline is just a rare case? Since one of the signals of autism is obsessive interests, rigidly held and intensely preoccupying until a new obsession comes along, couldn't the autistic child who is insisting on cross-gender presentation just be caught up in gender as one of those obsessions, an intensely held passing fancy, if you will, that will be dropped for something else over time? A reasonable question, and indeed a possibility. I'm thinking of a child I worked with, diagnosed with Asperger's syndrome, who was totally obsessed with Nazi Germany, much to the chagrin of both his parents. But nothing could sway him, and he wanted to tell me about every famous Nazi officer and every World War II German battle, ad nauseam. Until he discovered sex, and then he wanted to read everything there was to read about changing bodies and making babies, and then provide a discourse on it. He even asked if he could see my vagina, because he didn't have one, and after all, I was his therapist, so shouldn't I help him out? And not a word anymore about Nazi Germany. So, couldn't that be the same for gender—intensely here today, then gone tomorrow? Yes, possibly.

And another thing: Autism spectrum is often accompanied with a fascination for anything shiny and/or soft and cuddly. It's a sensory thing. So, maybe that's the reason some boys on the autism spectrum (and there are far, far more boys than girls diagnosed as being on the spectrum) are drawn to "girl"—in our culture, "girl" comes with more sparkles and silky and velvety things;

"boy" not so much. So, it could be not gender, but the enjoyment of visual or tactile sensation that is the real operative here for cross-gender autistic little boys seeking out baubles and beads or soft fabrics. Yes, possibly.

And yet another thing. A fair number of children who are on the autism spectrum do not show a consistent pattern of gender nonconformity throughout childhood. Instead, they are "pop-ups"; that is, their declarations of a cross-gender identification seem to show up out of the blue, often at the entrance into adolescence. Since they don't seem to be consistent, insistent, and persistent from early childhood on, could this late onset signify gender as a solution to one of adolescence's painful social challenges for autistic youth, as with the boy who wanted to become a girl to make friends? Yes, possibly.

So, what are we saying here? That gender forays among children and youth diagnosed on the autism spectrum are simply a symptom of their social communication disorder? Not at all, according to the various explanations people are coming up with for the statistically significant number of children on the autism spectrum who show up in the population of gender-nonconforming children, which include:

- Autism and gender nonconformity are co-occurring conditions. The part of the brain that causes ASD may be the same part of the brain that is responsible for gender nonconformity. Noteworthy here is the finding that both males and females diagnosed with ASD have significantly higher levels of male hormones than individuals in a control neurotypical group. Could it be that the hormones set off one of the conditions in the brain that then influences the other, or could it be that the hormones cause both simultaneously—autism and gender nonconformity—or could it be that one of the conditions creates higher levels of testosterone, which in turn triggers the other condition? Whichever it is, the explanation of testosterone correlated with gender nonconformity and autism resonates with the notion that has been promoted of autism as the extreme male brain, which may be true for both XX and XY autistic children.

- It's just about thinking outside of boxes. Individuals on the autism spectrum are known to have an inherent disposition toward unusual interests. Cross-gender behaviors could simply be one of those idiosyncratic interests correlated with a rejection of gender categorizing altogether.

- The inability to read social cues can extend to gender— children on the autism spectrum do not internalize the social messages about boy behavior and girl behavior and are thus exempt from them. Not registering social cues and being immune to social policing, they actually may have a leg up over neurotypical children in their freedom to go to the beat of their own drum and discover the gender that is "me" rather than the gender everyone wants them to be.

Whichever of these explanations we embrace—and I will mention that the jury is still out as to exactly why we are seeing this high incidence of children on the autism spectrum showing up also as children on the gender spectrum—clinical experiences are telling us that overwhelmingly, when a child shows up with a co-occurrence of gender nonconformity and neuro-atypicality, we are meeting with gender *and* something else rather than gender as a symptom of something else. It might even be that the gender and the neurodiversity are part and parcel of the same thing. Only occasionally might we see the gender as a passing obsession, a clamoring for glitter and satin, or a solution to adolescent ills among our children who show up on both spectrums. And whatever the cause, it is important that we give these children the same respect and listening ear as we do with any other gender-nonconforming children and allow them to live in their authentic gender, if that turns out to be other than cisgender or gender-conforming.

A last note before ending this discussion on autism and gender: We must also entertain the possibility that children suffering from gender stress or distress, particularly if they are growing up in repressive or unaccepting environments and with a certain temperamental style, may be inaccurately diagnosed with an autism spectrum disorder when all they are doing is buckling under the weight of their gender angst. Such a child may show extreme social anxiety; refuse to make eye contact; seem not to be reading social cues very well because they're just not conforming to the gender directives of their community; and appear somewhat rigid or inflexible. What we have here is an extremely gender-anxious child who does not know where to position their true gender self, a gender-nonconforming one, especially if that child is slow to warm up, less adaptable, somewhat more negative in mood, and perhaps just an introvert. In other words, the statistics on the number of children among gender clinics or studies who show up as also on the ASD spectrum may be inflated, with at least some children's extreme gender angst being misperceived as a sign of autism.

WHEN A CHILD COMES WITH GENDER AND . . .

Let's zero in on a child who is showing up with gender issues but with something else as well. Maddie was brought to me by her parents when she was nine years old. Both her mom and dad wanted to know if her "gender stuff" was for real. This is what they reported: When Maddie was three, she asked her mom, "Am I going to turn into a boy when I'm five?" By age four, she refused to wear dresses, but until she was seven, she gravitated toward activities more typically "girl." She hated sports but loved art activities. Most of her friends were girls. Then right after her seventh birthday, she got totally obsessed with sports and wanted to play basketball, and then football and taekwando. She began to dress more and more like a boy, so that a waiter in a restaurant would most likely ask Maddie's parents, "What would *he* like to drink?" That was fine with Maddie. When out in public places, Maddie started using the male bathroom, but never at school.

At about that same age, Maddie's mom was diagnosed with a serious illness that could be terminal. At the time I met Maddie, she was able to talk about her mother's illness, but somewhat dispassionately—just reporting facts. It was directly following her mother's diagnosis that Maddie began asking people to start calling her Matt. Yet she also insisted that they continue to use a female pronoun in referring to her. Within that same year, Maddie attended a cousin's bar mitzvah in another state, a conservative one at that, decked out in a shirt, tie, and sports coat.

Maddie's parents had read about puberty blockers and realized that although Maddie was only nine and not showing any signs of early puberty, it might be the right time to have a consultation with a pediatric endocrinologist. After an initial meeting with the endocrinologist, the doctor referred Maddie's family to me to see what I thought about Maddie's present gender status. She herself felt somewhat stymied by Maddie and, in fact, found her a bit odd.

When Maddie came to see me at age nine, she was playing with both boys and girls, yet, by her parents' report, she had no real friends to speak of. With sadness they shared that Maddie never got invited to birthday parties, even when almost all the other children in her class were included. Maddie didn't quite see it that way. She told me that she had three best friends, all boys; one second best friend, a girl; and a whole list of boys whom she placed in the category of "not friends." She easily shared that she was more into "boy" things—flag football, baseball—but still liked to do "girl" things, although she couldn't say exactly what those were. In each of her visits to me, she always wore the same thing—a white T-shirt with a button-down shirt over it, and pants or shorts, depending on the weather. Her mom said that was her standard dress code every single day.

From Maddie's parents I learned that since she was an infant, Maddie has always been sensitive to loud noises and still could not tolerate them. I did notice during one of her visits that when the sounds of an ambulance sounded in the far distance through my third-floor window, she startled and clamped her hands over her ears in distress. In general, Maddie was hyperalert and reactive to everything around her. She was an early reader, reading fluently by age four, and had always been good with words, although she used them rather formalistically. At age nine Maddie had many fears: of the dark, of bad stories on the news, of tongue depressors and shots at the doctor's office (this fear, I should note, preceded Mom's illness). In Maddie's own words, *"No shots!"*

When I first met Maddie, she informed me that she wanted me to call her Maddie and think of her as a girl, even though she told me she was "in the middle." Later, when I reported this to Maddie's parents, they were quite surprised, as everywhere else Maddie had been insistent that anyone new she met should refer to her as Matt. I should mention that Maddie was initially extremely anxious about coming to see me, "the gender lady," but when she left the appointment she looked up at her parents and announced, "That was really okay. She's nice." (I'm not always that lucky.)

Maddie did not come to me to talk, she came to play. So, that is what we did. She went straight to the toy shelves and pulled out all the hospital and dentist toys. I have a sand tray where children can set up scenes and stories with toy figures, and that is exactly what Maddie did, with no instruction from me. She methodically sorted through the hospital and dentist toys and then pulled down a whole row of military figures from the shelves. Here was the scene she created: Maddie lined up every form of military fig-ure, from ancient Greek to modern armies, and then circled them around a lone figure on a stretcher and a doctor's office in the corner of the sand tray.

I remembered that Maddie's parents both reported that Maddie loved words and could talk forever, yet with me she used very few. But we did get to talking about puberty blockers. Maddie had already been to visit the endocrinologist, where puberty blockers were the main subject of conversation. Very scientifically minded for a child her age, Maddie fully understood what puberty blockers were about—that they were the Pause button on the pituitary gland that stopped you from growing breast buds or getting a period for a while. She told me straight out that she didn't like that puberty blocker idea, because *"No shots!"* overruled any virtues of puberty pausers. As far as she was concerned, she'd be okay just staying in the middle of boy and girl.

In getting to know Maddie, I had no doubt that she was a gender creative child. She was definitely gender fluid, not really gender ambidextrous, maybe a gender Prius, maybe transgender, but it was too early to tell. The transgender child, the apple, typically communicates, "I am a . . ." The gender fluid child, the orange, typically communicates, "I wish I were a . . ." Maddie had not definitively communicated either.

So, here is what I was left with after my initial meetings with Maddie: The history of her gender questioning and nonconformity went back to at least age three. For me, that is very relevant information, an indicator of an affirmed gender that may be opposite to the one she has been living in. Her cross-gender presentation had definitely shown stability over time, yet Maddie was making no firm declarations about her gender identity, instead putting out a mixed message—"Call me Matt but refer to me as 'she.'"

Here were the thoughts that went through my mind: While I was paying attention to Maddie's gender presentation and communications, Maddie also showed me in word and action that she was somewhat idiosyncratic and formal in both her presentation and her interactions with me, very much like some of the other children I've worked with who fall somewhere on the autism spectrum. What should I make of that, and how might her general thinking outside the box influence her gender outside the boxes? Her mom had just been diagnosed with a serious, perhaps fatal illness—did that disruption have anything to do with her switching from Maddie to Matt right after the diagnosis? She clearly was telling me that her mother's illness was on her mind, as she continued with hospital scenes encircled by military figures providing protection, but when asked directly, she seemed quite dispassionate and removed in describing her mother's illness, simply providing me with the scientific facts. I wondered why she presented herself to me as Maddie when to everyone else she insisted on being Matt. She knew she was coming to see the play doctor who knew about gender things; did that have an effect? Was she sending me a message to send to her parents to slow down on all the gender stuff that seemed to have been set in motion?

I knew that one reason the endocrinologist wanted me to take a look at Maddie was to determine whether she would be a good candidate for puberty blockers, since she seemed to be on the cusp of entering into the earliest stages of puberty. Was she?

What I heard while listening carefully to Maddie was that she was a complex child who needed more extensive evaluation and supports to integrate her gender explorations with other aspects of herself. And I suspected that she might have at least a touch of Asperger's. I just wasn't sure. And if she did, I wasn't sure how that looped together with her gender creative presentation and how that in turn looped together with the family stresses brought on by her mother's illness—not that the stresses caused Maddie's gender nonconformity, as it clearly predated Mom's illness, but that they might have confounded the issue and put gender in a suspended state, perhaps by the simple fact that Maddie may have dreaded injections (necessary for receiving puberty blockers) as being too similar to the treatments her mother was forced to endure due to her own illness. What I did do was refer Maddie for a full neuropsychological evaluation, requesting that the psychologist doing the evaluation take gender into account but also assess whether there were any indicators of Asperger's, which might be, for Maddie, one of those "somethings" that either influenced or correlated with her gender nonconformity or functioned as the driving force behind her cross-gender presentation.

Now fast-forward two years. Maddie completed the neuropsychological evaluation and was indeed diagnosed as having Asperger's syndrome. I should mention here that her parents had no idea before they came to see me that Maddie might have Asperger's, whereas I and the neuropsychologist who assessed Maddie suspected it right away. So, now we have another link between autism and gender. In Aline's case, the gender affirmation appeared to function as a partial treatment for autism. In Maddie's case, the gender evaluation facilitated the recognition of her Asperger's condition, so in her situation, gender became the conduit to allowing the family to acknowledge another part of Maddie's self and link it to her gender self. I should add that Maddie's is not the only family in which the progression from a gender to an ASD evaluation has occurred.

Maddie was seen for two years by a therapist in her hometown, to help her adjust to her mother's illness, to explore her gender, and to strengthen her social skills and reduce her social anxieties. In the second of those two years, Maddie revisited the pediatric endocrinologist. By that time Maddie had fully transitioned to Matt, both in name and male pronoun, and was living full-time as boy. Matt returned to me for a follow-up visit. The Matt I greeted was ever so much more confident and relaxed than the Maddie I first met in my office two years previously. His mother was still ill but responding well to her medical treatment. Matt's speech remained somewhat formal, and his thinking aligned somewhat to the beat of his own drum, but he was now able to articulate very clearly that he knew himself to be male. His main concern at the moment was being able to compete on the boys' basketball team—he'd be the shortest boy on the team. With the help of his therapist, Matt has overcome his morbid fear of injections. Shots still made him nervous but no longer over-ruled his desire to stop the onset of an unwanted female puberty. Fully in Tanner stage II of puberty, the optimal timing for beginning puberty blockers, Matt was ready for them to bring on the shots. Matt has Asperger's. He is transgender. With the help of a supportive family and community, he will learn how to weave both together. And Matt's "gender stuff" is as real as it gets.

GENDER AS A "SYMPTOM" OF ADOLESCENT IDENTITY CRISIS

Before we exit our discussion of when it's gender *and* something else *or* something else, I want to make a note about gender cre-ativity and adolescence. In our culture, adolescence is defined as a time of identity exploration and formation; it might even be a time of identity crisis, as outlined in Erik Erikson's "Eight Stages of Man." As social media and the news have increasingly high-lighted the stories of transgender and genderqueer youth, many of us in the mental health field have noticed a swelling number of teens coming to our offices saying something like, "I think I'm like that character in *Glee*. Maybe I'm transgender." Another might say, "I'm so confused. There are so many possibilities. I never knew you could choose your gender." The good news is that perhaps we are finally breaking through the binary gender barriers, offer-ing all youth an opportunity to creatively muse about the ques-tion, "What's my gender?" rather than taking it as a given with no exploration. But at the same time it also hits a population of vulnerable youth who may be completely lost about who they are and are desperately seeking to find themselves. Among all the other things they are trying out, they try on gender for size, in all its shapes and forms.

This is all fine and good, except that youth are also known for their impatience. Teenagers in the heat of identity exploration or crisis might just push, insist, or say they will die if they don't get blockers or hormones tomorrow to "solve" their identity crisis. For some of these youth, gender may just be one more thing they throw up for grabs and then watch it tumble as they try to answer the bigger existential question: "Who am I?" So, be cautious: Beware when gender nonconformity might be a symptom of more generalized adolescent identity confusion; if you suspect that, slow things down and see where gender lands. Once in the full throes of adolescence, when identity crises surface, it's too late for puberty blockers to do the trick of staunching an unwanted physical puberty; it's already happened—so you can relax about that. But it is never too late to introduce other medical interventions, including hormones or gender-affirming surgeries, which can still come later. And there's absolutely no harm in living in the gender that feels most real at the moment sans those interventions, although I would certainly forestall any formal legal changes in either name or gender marker as a youth continues to sort things out. If gender remains persistent, consistent, and insistent, then the drill is the same: Facilitate the youth living in their true gender self.

THE NEW GENDER GAP

In the old days, if we saw a gender-nonconforming child or a child suffering from gender dysphoria, we sniffed for trouble elsewhere—in the psychopathology of the child, in the foibles of the parents, in the traumas that might have befallen the child. In the new days, we have a sea change in our understandings of gender and a celebration of gender variations as creative nuances and textures of life, rather than disorders of being. The challenge for all of us is to create a bridge between the old and the new, not to perpetuate the stigma of gender nonconformity, but to pay attention to each and every psychic meaning of gender in all its expressions and identities.[43] This is no easy feat, bridging the gap between the old and the new, but bridge it we must, so as to affirm children's right to their authentic gender while simultaneously being mindful of other developmental or experiential challenges coming their way that might emerge looking like gender stress, gender dysphoria, or false gender self constructions. To this end, whenever it is a question of "gender and ____" or "gender or ____," bringing in professional supports can be invaluable, if not essential, as long as those professionals start out with the baseline of gender nonconformity as a state of health rather than illness, and as long as we can all hold to the premise that the child who lives in the middle rather than in one of two boxes is not confused and ill but creative and healthy. From there, we can consider all the possibilities of gender, with or without a "something else" in tow.

CHAPTER FIVE

It Takes a Gender Creative Parent to Negotiate the Gender Maze

We allow our child to guide us.
—Michelle Honda-Phillips, daughter of US representative Mike Honda and mother of a transgender eight-year-old child

SINCE THE PUBLICATION OF *Gender Born, Gender Made*, stories of parents describing their journeys with their gender creative children have been cropping up all over the world—in the press, on TV and radio, on the Internet, in articles and books, in school auditoriums, on campaign trails. And each of the stories seems to finish on a note of pride and support. On February 19, 2015, the *San Jose Mercury* reported that US representative Mike Honda of California had announced that Malisa, his eight-year-old grandchild, was transgender. Most moving in the story was his request, following Malisa's social transition from male to female, that the family retake its family photo to be used in his reelection campaign brochure, for, as he explained to Malisa, "We need you to be who you are in the campaign photos." Michelle, Malisa's mother and Mike's daughter, described Malisa as "incredibly touched."[44] Two days later, the story of Zay and her parents, Jason Crawford, a pilot, and Chasilee Crawford, a nurse, from Yellow Springs, Ohio, was published in the Cincinnati newspaper the *Enquirer*. Like Malisa, Zay knew early in her childhood that she was not the boy people thought she was. Jason, her father, described his experience as her dad: "I am really happy that Zay is with us because we are going to try and protect her. There is hurt in everybody's life. There's hurt in the world . . . but that hurt of not being accepted by your family is not going to be something she has to deal with."[45] Four months before that, the *St. Louis Post-Dispatch* published the story of Max, a fourth grader who had transitioned from female to male. Max's mother was fully aware that life might get more difficult for Max as he got older: "There's a loss of some 'normalcy.' Lots of stuff will be harder. What we've done now is create a base of security and love to weather those times. He feels safe and secure with our family. Max has taught us so much, just by being himself."[46]

That same year, the camera was on Angelina Jolie and Brad Pitt, not because they were making a new movie, but because of their eight-year-old child, John Jolie-Pitt, née Shiloh. The photo-op was not Brad or Angelina but John, striding across the red carpet at the premiere of Jolie's movie *Unbroken*. Donning a suit and tie, John looked like a carbon copy of his father. Everyone thought that John had come into the world as a girl, but John let Jolie and Pitt know through both word and action that someone had gotten it wrong and Shiloh was not their daughter but, rather, their son. Both parents listened to Shiloh, who had by all reports been insistent, consistent, and persistent since early childhood that "male" would be getting it right—and helped Shiloh transition to John. In an interview several years earlier, Jolie reported, "She wants to be a boy. So we had to cut her hair. She likes to wear boys' everything. She thinks she's one of the brothers."[47] Not too many years before that, another child of a celebrity, Cher, also made front page news: Cher's daughter, Chastity, now an adult, had come out as her son Chaz. Chaz has become a spokesperson and supporter of transgender issues across the globe, with his mother's blessings: "I admire my son Chaz's courage for sharing his personal journey. Most important to me is that he is very happy. That's what I care about the most. He has my love and support."[48] Politicians, movie stars, ordinary citizens—mothers, fathers, and grandparents are coming out in support of their gender creative children and grandchildren. Yet, truth be told, it is still easier said than done.

Remember the story of *Stuart Little*, born to a human couple? The Little family doctor "was delighted with Stuart and said that it was very unusual for an American family to have a mouse." The situation was, however, not always so delightful for Stuart's parents, such as when Mr. Little banned references to mice in all family conversations and ordered Stuart's mother to tear out the nursery rhyme page with "Three Blind Mice" on it, for "I should feel badly to have my son grow up fearing that a farmer's wife was going to cut off his tail with a carving knife."[49]

Who knew what an allegory this would turn out to be for twenty-first-century parents stretching to creatively raise their gender creative children. At first, the realization of having a child who doesn't conform to social gender expectations or to the sex listed on the child's birth certificate can be quite a surprise. The only difference between the Littles and the parents of a gender creative child is that the Littles knew from the get-go, from Stuart's first breaths, that their child was a mouse. Not so for the parents of a gender creative child. They will have no idea at first—they might discover early on, they might discover much, much later that the child they have is not the child they thought they were bringing into the world—it could be the boy who is a girl, the girl who is a boy, a gender hybrid, a gender-ambidextrous child, a gender fluid child, an agender child, and so forth. And yet, when families come to learn that their child's gender is not the one matching the sex marker inscribed on the birth certificate, or that the child is not complying with the gender norms of their culture, it can be no less shocking than discovering your child is a mouse. Like Mr.

Little, parents may fear for their gender creative child's safety, not at the hand of a farmer's wife, but in the grips of an unaccepting, hostile world. The real question is how they will absorb the shock and take their child in stride over time—again, a task easier said than done.

Basic ground rule for raising children: If we recognize the child we have, rather than the one we wished we had, and if we help our children build resilience to face the challenges before them, we put them in good stead to live a healthy and productive life. Now let's apply that ground rule to children's gender and their parents' role in gender health. Recognizing the child we do have rather than the child we thought we were going to have, coupled with fortifying our child to face life's challenges, become the two key ingredients in the nurture threads of the child's gender web. With the benefit of Caitlin Ryan's work at the Family Acceptance Project, it has become almost a scout motto: If you support your children's gender creativity, your children will do better, both psychologically and physically; if you fail to support their gender creativity, they will not do so well, both psychologically and physically.

Why write more? Because, again, it is easier said than done. Because support is a rubbery concept—what's support to one family is neglect to another. So, what does it take for parents to bring that motto of support to life? How do parents succeed in fortifying their children's gender resilience, in facilitating their children's ability to live in their true gender self with all the accompanying coping skills that will allow them to maintain confidence and good feeling about themselves even in the face of a world who may think otherwise?

FROM THORNY PATHS TO GENDER MAZES

Chapter 2 of *Gender Born, Gender Made* is titled "The Family's Path Is Covered with Roses and Thorns." I wrote that parents find themselves on a road of thorns as they try to carve a pathway for their children who do not abide by the culture's gender proclamations—whether they are boys who are girls, girls who are boys, or young people who defy rules and regulations for how you're supposed to "do" gender. Sometimes parents are called on to police their children's gender, telling them they can't go outside dressed like they are, it's not safe; sometimes they are called on to play God, to be the ones to decide whether the children should socially transition from one gender to another or take hormones with partially irreversible effects. And all the while, parents still travel through a world that blames parents for their children's gender "oddities," albeit far less so than in the past as the public grows more educated and more accepting. But I've learned something profound since finishing *Gender Born, Gender Made*— how quickly the road can morph into a maze, with seemingly endless routes and innumerable dead ends. This is not necessarily bad news. With a half-decade of new knowledge under our belts and an international movement addressing the needs and rights of gender-nonconforming people—a movement nothing less than phenomenal in its emergence and growth—I think we're actually ready to move from traversing thorny paths to finding our way through gender mazes. If you like to solve mazes, you can understand how the experience of negotiating gender mazes can prove no less challenging than carving a path through thorny terrain, but far more pleasurable.

What can gender mazes look like? There are the two mothers who send their gender-nonconforming little boy to a progressive school where it's absolutely fine for him to wear girls' clothes. It's fine for the mothers, too. Yet he flatly refuses and only wears them in the comfort of his own house, even though he lives in one of the most progressive communities in the country. There are the mother and father who have to decide whether they should let their gender-nonconforming (natal female) child-prodigy teen go to a highly coveted summer program for gifted high school students as a boy because the gender-segregated living halls and activities find this teen insisting that the boys' unit is a far better fit than the girls', even though this youth does not identify as transgender but agender.

Let's zoom in on another family caught in the midst of a gender maze. Alice and Morton have a three-year-old girl, Mirabel; at least that's what they think. One day Mirabel announces to her parents, "I'm a boy." What does this mean? As far as they can tell, it means that Mirabel will only wear boys' clothes. A visit to Mirabel's grandparents is coming up. Her grandparents are quite conservative and live in a small town several miles away. Alice knows only too well how her parents will react to Mirabel showing up in boys' clothes—not a pretty picture. The day of the visit arrives. Alice pulls out a dress that has been collecting dust in Mirabel's closet and announces, "Honey, we're going to visit Grandpa Joe and Grandma Jane. So, you'll be wearing a dress today." Mirabel continues happily playing with her dolls, piping up in a cheery voice, "Okay, Mommy, as long as it's a boy dress." The problem of attire for the grandparent visit is solved, but the meaning of Mirabel's pronouncement is not. Is Mirabel telling Alice that she's a boy who wears dresses, a boy-girl, or a girl who is creatively de-gendering all clothes? Alice and Morton have read all kinds of books about boys wearing dresses, but never one about a girl wearing a boy dress. This "boy dress" passageway of the gender maze might take them to a dead end; it might lead them down the path to a transgender outcome for their child; it might require going back to the maze entrance and rethinking what Mirabel has been trying to tell them all this time about Mirabel's gender.

If we go back to the apples, oranges, and fruit salads, the apples—the transgender children—are in some ways the easiest children to traverse the maze with. They are clear about who they are and, if given the chance, they let everyone know. Yes, there is stress, heartache, and grief as a parent comes to terms with the reality that the child they thought they had is not the one they do have—their boy is actually a girl, their girl is actually a boy. But there is also clarity. When it comes to negotiating the maze, the oranges and the fruit salads may prove far more challenging for parents. Who are these children and what are they trying to tell us? How can you be neither gender—or every gender? "Is my child gay? I just want to know." And sometimes it is so hard not to know—especially about something as basic as gender. And the problem with all these questions is that we can't know until the children know, and that could be a long way down the road. But the parents have to negotiate the maze *right now*, because it is their job to shepherd their child through childhood. So, how does a parent find the way out of these complicated gender mazes? Answer: by developing and strengthening a solid gender GPS for traversing the maze while simultaneously cutting new paths so their child can move forward in unique gender creative ways. Let me invite you to think with me about developing a parental GPS for traversing such mazes.

LEARNING TO DE-CENTER

I have discovered that there are many things I learned in my training to become a developmental psychologist that have proved invaluable to me in mapping out the strategies and criteria for becoming a gender creative parent. A central one is the concept of de-centering. To de-center as a parent is to learn how to remove yourself from your own wishes, needs, and desires and instead focus on the wishes, needs, and desires of your child. In the vernacular, it means, in any interpersonal situation, putting yourself in the other person's shoes to understand their experience. It means being able to empathize with what it means to be them, without getting overwhelmed with how their way of being may be so different from your own or for your wishes for them. With our children, it means having the ability to put them first (which is not the same as letting them be the boss of everything). It requires maturity and imagination—imagining what it is like to be their age; imagining what they are feeling; imagining how they are experiencing the world; imagining what they are trying to tell us in word and deed; imagining what they hope for from us.

De-centering is not always so easy to do. Even in the best of circumstances, we as parents will inevitably view our children through our own lenses, projecting our hopes and dreams onto them. We're particularly ripe for these fantasies and projections before a baby is even born, when, in Western culture, all we really have to tell us about who they are is the copy of the fetal sonogram pasted on our Facebook page or stuck on the refrigerator with a magnet, the ebbs and flows of the baby's movements in the uterus—and the sex of the baby, if we have the opportunity to or care to know it. For parents of a baby adopted later than birth, often all we have at first is a photograph. These reveries about the baby who has not yet come to us are all fine and good, because, from our side, it gets the bonding process in gear. Sigmund Freud first alerted us to this natural and healthy phenomenon for new mothers and fathers, and it is what I, in my earlier work, have dubbed "expectable parental narcissism."[50] But once the baby arrives and begins to have a mind of its own, we have to learn how to shift away from our own hopes and dreams and instead nurture our child's. Otherwise, we might end up the truly narcissistic parent, not a good thing.

Leaving gender aside for a moment, what happens when parents have a child who is just so different from them that they can't find a way to de-center and get in their child's shoes and imagine what it is like to be them? Think about it for a moment: We don't value genetic connections just to carry on our blood lines—passing on our genes is believed, sometimes naively, to be an insurance policy that our children will be enough like us that we'll be able to love them. We could say that sameness/likeness seems to function as bonding cement in parent-child relation-ships. We can find this sameness/likeness as cement in nonge-netic family building as well when parents-to-be will make every effort to pick a baby who will match their race, ethnicity, looks, or personality, by making the right match either with a donor, with a birth family, or with a baby or child waiting to be adopted. But it doesn't always work out that way. A child can still end up very, very different from you, even when half of that child's genes are yours. So, what happens when parents end up with a child who is very different from them?

They can feel off-kilter or disoriented and confused, not know-ing how to secure a connection or make sense of this very foreign creature. In *Far from the Tree*, Andrew Solomon explores in depth the parental experience in these situations and devotes an en-tire chapter to parents of transgender or gender-nonconforming children. He introduces us to the idea of *horizontal identity*—that means a child who will have a lot in common with other chil-dren like themselves, but not so much with their own parents. Horizontal identity could apply to the deaf child, to the child prod-igy, to the autistic child, and yes, to the transgender or gender-nonconforming child. Dr. Solomon offers us words of wisdom as to what parents can do in those situations—look deep into your child's eyes, see in your child both yourself and something utter-ly strange, and zealously attach to every aspect of your child. If you can do that, you have arrived at "parenthood's self-regarding, yet unselfish, abandon."[51] That very abandon is the essence of de-centering.

Let's bring parental de-centering into the gender maze. Let's take a family that may come to me for support. You may recog-nize yourself in this family, you may not, so I just invite you to de-center for a moment. Susanna and Sam are a mom and dad who each identify as cisgender. Both have always comfortably identified with the sex assigned at their birth, and both have been pretty gender conforming, living in accordance with their assigned gender and the social guidelines for that gender. They always wanted a little girl, and then their wishes came true—they got one, at least they thought so. For now, Amanda is their only child. She's four. Ever since she was two and a half, she threw anything pink on the floor and cried out, "Hate pink." The only colors she will wear are orange and dark blue. While the other girls run to the doll corner at preschool, Amanda runs outside to play King of the Climbing Structure with the boys. She has begun to tell her preschool teacher, "When I grow up to be a man like my daddy, I'm going to be a rock climber like the guy I saw on TV." Susanna and Sam are flummoxed—what happened to the baby they once dreamed about—the girl in frills? That's how Susanna was when she was growing up. What isn't she doing to help Amanda be the same—to be like her? They're both girls, after all. And Sam feels no affinity for the *Annie Get Your Gun* kind of females; that's why he chose Susanna, in all her femininity, for a partner. He wants to make sure that Amanda knows that she is a girl, and a beautiful one at that, just like he knows he's a guy and Susanna knows she's a woman. And isn't gender bedrock, set as soon as you find out the sex of your baby? How could two cisgender parents have anything but a cisgender child? Sam and Susanna assumed Amanda would be just like them. But she isn't.

Truth be told, at that moment it might be easier to learn your child is deaf than gender creative. Deafness in a child is an immutable difference in hearing that hearing parents have to accept, painful as it might be. They can try to correct the deafness, but it still will not erase the difference between them and their child. Gender creativity, on the other hand, is a difference that is harder to wrap your head around, especially if you believe that you might have caused it, as some experts might tell you. Especially if you are not gender nonconforming. Especially if you believe that with the right efforts you can redirect your child toward more sameness with you and away from this gender difference that may seem so unfathomable to two loving cisgender, gender-conforming parents (remember that sameness functions as bonding cement). But whatever the nature of your child's difference from you, the work will be the same—for Susanna and Sam it will involve de-centering off themselves and trying to get into Amanda's experience and learn about Amanda's gender web and gender creativity, as Amanda lays it out to them. It also means allowing space for the difficult feelings that may accompany the realization of difference, for either Susanna, Sam, or both of them together.

Let's move from deafness to blindness—in this instance, not the child's but the parents'. I'm not talking about actual blindness but, rather, blind spots. Parents may suffer from gender blind spots and have no conscious awareness that they even have them. If de-centering means getting your child in focus as a separate person rather than viewing your child as a mirror of yourself, gender blind spots can only work against that clear vision. Gender blind spots can be caused by lack of knowledge or by resistance to seeing what is there to be seen. Blind spots won't get revealed in an eye exam, only in self-examination and with the help of both the child and a circle of adult support to gently (or perhaps not so gently) point them out.

A gender blind spot shows up most poignantly when a parent insists, "I truly never saw this coming and I can't even see it now." Then the child walks in and another person's first reaction might be, "Wow, you don't see it? That's amazing." I'm thinking of a youth I saw whose parents had on the initial visit described to me their teenage daughter who loved fashion and was stunningly beautiful—how could she possibly be a boy, which she kept insisting she was? The next week I went out to the waiting room looking for that girl, and all I could see was a handsome young man—their daughter. The first thing this youth said to me, with tears streaming down his face, was "Can you believe it? Look at me. What more could I do to get my parents to take their blinders off and see who I am?" The story has a happy ending— the parents, totally committed to the well-being of their child, eventually came to see their child for who he was. This occurred only after they felt safe enough to remove those gender blinders and de-center off their own wishes and hopes for their beautiful, fashion-conscious daughter and get their actual child, a son, in focus. This vision correction was not just an option, but a painful and necessary process to prevent their child from going down the path of self-harm and deep depression, which is where he might have been headed if something wasn't done to acknowledge his affirmed male identity.

It is certainly possible that a parent may be blind to their child's gender because their child has done such a magnificent job of hiding it, constructing a false gender self so airtight that the child's inner desires and sensibilities are masked if not totally opaque, even to their loving parents, maybe even to themselves. This often happens as a result of implicit or explicit negative messages from the social environment that force a child to go underground with their true gender self. Sometimes there are no such messages. Rather, a child's own sensitive temperament, as laid out in the last chapter, will be the driving force behind the masquerade—a child may be so exquisitely self-conscious that they just can't bear to have anyone, even their own parents, peer in on such a vulnerable, core part of themselves. It would be like asking the child to run naked through the streets. So, the parents remain blind to the situation, never given a chance to de-center and discover the child who is so different, unless the child can no longer tolerate hiding the truth and steps out of the masquerade.

I will say from my own observations that it is more common for the parents to be the ones who render themselves blind, with no traces of opaqueness or masking on the part of their child, like in the story of the boy in my waiting room. The parents may fear the worst, given their own gender histories and gender sensibilities. They may want desperately to hold on to the belief that their child is just like them, rather than very different. Often with no conscious awareness, they may operate from the tenet "Hear no evil, see no evil, speak no evil," rendering them unable to recognize the gender creative child clearly standing before them.

To remove gender blinders or gender blind spots so that we can get the children in focus, we need to embark on the process of examining our own gender ghosts and gender angels. I introduced this idea of gender ghosts and gender angels in *Gender Born, Gender Made,* and now I want to bring them back on the scene to see how they can help with or hinder de-centering. In short, gender ghosts are the internalized thoughts, attitudes, feelings, beliefs, and experiences that draw us toward culturally defined binary gender boxes and make us anxious when we or anyone else strays from them. Our gender ghosts may show up in our conscious minds. They may remain deeply embedded in the unconscious chambers of our psyches. Every time a parent walks around with gender blinders or suffers from gender blind spots, we can assume that gender ghosts are in play. Then, we have our gender angels. Those are the internalized thoughts, attitudes, feelings, beliefs, and experiences that allow us to be gender creative and live or accept others living outside of the culturally defined binary gender boxes. Just like gender ghosts, our gender angels may show up consciously, or curl up in our unconscious. Gender angels are what allow us to take our gender blinders off, erase our blind spots, or never have to struggle with them in the first place. And they work marvelously in helping us de-center off ourselves and accept a child who may be gender-different from us.

How do we examine our gender ghosts and gender angels? Starting with gender ghosts: If we want our gender creative children to feel as if they are the fruit of our tree rather than far from it, we begin by challenging our own socialized beliefs about gender. Just like the adoptive Caucasian parents of an African American child who learn about or take part in the black community that their child may identify with, we make a concerted effort to immerse ourselves in a world where expanded gender possibilities are accepted and celebrated. We learn about the risks to our gender-nonconforming child's physical and psychological well-being should we not do this. These efforts will metabolize into the nutrients that feed our gender angels and allow them to come to the light of day. For some of us this process seems to happen rather seamlessly; for others it is a struggle; and for every parent the process will be bolstered by the very presence of our own gender creative child—because I truly believe that love conquers all. It is during this process that mourning may come to the fore—we take the time to mourn the child we thought we had, to make room to embrace the child we do have. It is important to acknowledge this mourning process as a critical component of de-centering. It may seem contradictory to be focusing on ourselves if our task is to focus instead on our child, but not if we understand the mourning process metaphorically as the shoveling that allows us to clear the path so that de-centering on our child's authentic gender is possible.

Then come the gender angels: When the gender angels surface, we call on them to help us de-center off our own desires, hopes, and expectations and offer our children the freedom to weave their own gender web. We get in touch with our good feelings, if we have them, about gender expansiveness and apply them not just to our children's lives but to our own. For many parents, this will involve a major paradigm shift. Others may find they are simply walking in the footprint of a life they have already lived for many years. Whether it's a paradigm shift or a walk in the park, we still have to remain on the watch for our gender ghosts (our internalized genderism, so to speak), who are whisperers, warning us to stay put in those binary boxes and accompanying proscriptions and prescriptions where gender is knowable, predictable, and acceptable. If the going gets rough, it helps to remember that a good predictor of a child's gender health will be the ability of the adults in the child's life to bring both their gender ghosts and angels into the light of day and allow the voices of the gender angels to triumph.

In *My Daughter, He,* Candace Waldron's poignant account of her journey through the gender maze with her child, she quotes from her transgender son's journal, written by Kai at age twenty-three: "I knew I had disappointed her [Mom] by coming out as trans those years ago, but I knew she'd be okay in time." Kai is sharing his own realization of his mother's earlier difficulties in de-centering and focusing on his own gender affirmation rather than her own need or wish for him not to be trans. To disappoint your parents is not the same as making your parents sad. It's about letting them down, not meeting their expectations, getting their hopes dashed. Through his words we have a portal into the ways Kai bore witness to his mother's gender ghosts at work. Indeed, throughout the book Candace is courageously transparent in revealing them herself, as when she wrote about Kai (then Kendra):

> It bothered me how boy-like she was becoming. She was weightlifting and taking protein supplements to build muscle and wanted binding material to hide her breasts. As crazy as it sounds, it felt personal for me that she was so rejecting of her female body. I wondered whether she felt similarly repulsed by mine.

But at the end of the day Kai reveals his belief in the ascendance of his mother's gender angels: "I knew she'd be okay in time." And Candace certainly was okay enough to write a moving book about her gender journey with Kai, a book with the subtitle *Transitioning with Our Transgender Children,*[52] a profound testimonial of gender angels prevailing over gender ghosts.

MICROAGGRESSIONS

I've pulled from my child development training; now I want to draw from my education in sociology. I want to zoom in on the concept of microaggressions. I first learned this concept in the context of US black-white race relations. Microaggressions are not the dramatic violent and sometimes fatal atrocities waged against minority groups, but the everyday oversights, innuendos, slights, disrespectful comments, or actions that a person might endure, based on another's lack of understanding, antipathy, or fear of difference. It was Derald Wing Sue's book *Microaggressions in Everyday Life* that sensitized me to this phenomenon, as he delineated the everyday verbal or nonverbal communications, not necessarily delivered with hostile intent, insinuating to a person of a particular marginalized group that who they are is not acceptable.[53] Microaggressions embody subtle, often unintentional biases. We can think of each one of them as a ping, but when they start to build up, they can morph into a resounding blow. Regrettably, gender-nonconforming children count as one of those marginalized groups, and even more regrettably, the microaggressions can come their way not just from the outside world, but directly from home, even by the most well-intended parents. This may be very different from the experience of children from racial or ethnic minorities whose families share that minority status, because they can at least count on their own family members to watch their backs. Not so for the gender-nonconforming child, who as we can see, can feel far from the parents' tree.

Although this is not about parenting, I want to share my own recent experience as an unwitting perpetrator of a gender microaggression, just to make the point that it happens all the time to gender-nonconforming children, even when we don't mean to and even when we believe we are the most sensitive of gender souls. I was standing on the BART platform waiting to catch a train. Near me was an African American mother with her son, who I would guess was around nine. Large for his age, with a trailing tendril of curls down the back of his head, I noticed he was holding something in his hand, gently stroking it with his other hand, with a contented, dreamy look on his face. His mother had a loving hand on his shoulder. When I looked closer, I saw that he was fingering a small action figure, a girl, which he had dressed up in a home-made cape crafted from a scrap of deep red velvet. He continued to stroke the little figure as we all got on the train. As the train took off, I looked over at him with a smile on my face, catching his eye. Rather than smiling back, he flinched and swiftly threw his arm into his jacket, emerging with an empty hand and no action girl. The figure in the cape never appeared again for the entire ride into San Francisco. I wanted to go over and tell him it was okay and that I would love to see what he had been playing with, but I thought that might make it even worse and perhaps leave him even more defensive and self-conscious in the face of a world that had sent out previous messages, "No action girls for boys." So, I did nothing, except to keep sending smiles in his direction, with the naive notion that he would read my smiles as affirmation and acceptance. Indeed, he was closed up and wanted nothing to do with me. And I wondered how much grief he had already gotten for his doll play, certainly not from his loving mother, but from the kids at school, other people in the family, in his neighborhood, and so forth. Maybe this was going to be a day he was going to get to be free of that, anonymously riding with his mom on the train. So, that, my friends, was a gender microaggression—me, an older white woman, unwittingly but perceptibly infusing dis-comfort and angst into this child's train ride with his mother, his action girl hidden deep in his coat rather than enjoying her ride in his hand.

What would home-based gender microaggressions look like? Let's start with the father who tells his son, "You don't want that Barbie doll; it's for girls." Actually, his son does want that Barbie doll. In telling his son that he really doesn't, the dad might be try-ing to help his son fit in and fare well in their community, where boys playing with Barbies just isn't the norm. But if we delve a little further, maybe it's not the kids on the street, but the dad who feels queasy about his son playing with Barbies. Actually, his son's friends might be just fine with it. They might even want to play, too. In that simple, brief message—"You don't want that Barbie doll"—his son has just been the recipient of a microaggression, like the boy on the train feeling shame for wanting what boys shouldn't want, according to the gender rules. *Ping.* Surely this cannot be in this little boy's best interests if he gets the message that who he is will never be worthy in his father's eyes.

This particular gender microaggression, "You don't want that Barbie," is pretty obvious. Let's move to a subtler one. A little boy announces to his mother, "I like playing with Barbies, and I want to be a girl." His mother, schooled as a child herself on *Free to Be You and Me* and *William Has a Doll*, responds with love and affection, "Honey, you know boys can play with Barbies, too. You don't have to be a girl to play with Barbies." She's proud of herself and counts her response as a supportive parenting moment, breaking the gender barriers of Barbies for girls but not for boys. Except that her son was trying to tell her something very different, which, if she listened carefully, was, "Mommy, I want to be a *girl* who plays with Barbies." At that moment her son could explode and yell, "Mommy, I know, I know that boys can play with Barbies. But that's not what I said. I said I'm a *girl* who wants to play with Barbies." Or he could retreat to his room and never bring it up again, keeping his thoughts and feelings about himself as a girl buried deep inside him where no one will try to correct him. Whatever his response, you have just witnessed a potential microaggression, a subtle unintentional message from his mother that who he is as a girl won't be okay with her. This loving, well-meaning mother only intended to support her child by offering a more expansive world of gender expression, but, unbeknownst to her, she missed her son's need to be acknowledged for the gender he is coming to know himself to be. Instead of feeling cared for by his mother, he may slink away feeling frustrated, putting all his efforts into calming a bruised psyche, all by himself. *Ping.*

Now let's move to the most macro of microaggressions. Do you recall Leelah Alcorn, the transgender teen who left behind a painful but poignant suicide note? After her death, her mother is quoted as saying, "We loved him no matter what. I loved my son. . . . He was a good kid, a good boy."[54] I'm sure she did love Leelah, and I can only imagine the grief she must be going through. The only problem is that Leelah was a good girl, not a good boy. Leelah might even be alive today if someone could simply have recognized Leelah for the girl she was and not let her be taken to therapists who tried to make her the boy she wasn't. Even in Leelah's death the microaggressions persist, and in Leelah's case, added up to the biggest of blows.

To negotiate the gender maze is to monitor all incoming microaggressions coming your child's way, not just out in the world, but right at home. So, when a fifteen-year-old transgender boy of divorced parents tells me that his nineteen-year-old brother moved out of the house to go live with his father because he found his younger sibling disgusting, that's a pretty resounding *ping*. And I wondered, sadly, where his parents were in stopping the brother from delivering such a damning message.

Pediatricians will tell parents not to worry—their child's gender nonconformity is just a phase. In general, whenever "just a phase" is delivered to a parent's ears, we can anticipate the parent's reaction close behind: "Oh, thank God, this too shall pass." Think about tantrums. Think about terrible twos. Think about toileting regressions. Think about grabbing toys from other children at preschool. Think about clinging to Mommy when the babysitter arrives. "Just a phase" = something you hope against hope your child will outgrow. So, the parent comes home from the visit to the pediatrician and reports to the other parent, "We shouldn't worry about Tommy's wearing only dresses. The doctor says it's just a phase. Lots of three-year-olds like to do that." The other parent lets out a sigh of relief. Tommy looks like he's over in the corner preoccupied with his puppets. But he's heard every word exchanged between his parents. He's too young to understand the exact meaning but old enough to pick up the nuance. His parents are waiting for him to stop being who he is. That's a microaggression. *Ping.*

Priscilla plays only with boys. Her parents worry about that. She should have some girlfriends, too. Maybe that will help her be more comfortable at school, because she clearly isn't at the moment. So, the next time she asks for a playdate with Jasper, one of her mothers says, "Honey, let's invite a girl over today." They've already gone to see a therapist about Priscilla's anxiety every morning about going to school. When the therapist heard that Priscilla plays only with boys and likes to wear boxer shorts under her jeans, the therapist connected the dots, or thought they were connectable, and said to the moms, "You need to help Priscilla be more comfortable with being a girl. Buy her some girl underpants she'll like and find some girls for her to play with." And the therapist may be thinking to himself, "There's no man in this house. No wonder Priscilla is trying to be one." So, Priscilla is now being sent a subtle message that her playmates are really not ideal because they're boys, and her underwear is a poor choice, too, and she's missing a father to boot. That's a microaggression. *Ping.*

Katy has been gender nonconforming since she was very little. When she got to middle school, she decided she must be a lesbian. But as the school year progressed, she realized that was wrong. She was a boy. She went to see a therapist, she talked to her parents, and they all agreed that it made sense for her to socially transition to her affirmed male identity. Katy became Kat and asked that everyone use male pronouns. Kat's parents were on board but continued to refer to Kat as their daughter and as "she." Kat would grow agitated, and Kat's parents would say, "Look, you have to give us some time to get used to this. You've always been Katy, daughter, she." Fair enough, but weeks passed, months passed, even a year went by, and still Kat heard, "She, daughter, and Katy." This form of misgendering and misnomering from one's own parents is not just one microaggression, but a series of them, a chronic slight happening over and over again, definitely risking becoming something bigger than a *ping* and more like a cumulative assault on one's self. So, what's in a name? A whole lot.

I painfully bore witness to such misgendering at a visit with a family at the gender clinic where I work. Len, Nadine, and their twelve-year-old child, Emory, showed up for their initial visit. Six months earlier Emory had come out to his parents as transgender, female to male. Emory requested that everyone start using male pronouns. Len is in a lot of pain about this and having difficulty accepting that his daughter is now asserting that he is their son. During the clinic visit, Len uses *she* and *her* to refer to Emory. Every time he does, Emory flinches. Len doesn't notice this at all. Instead, Len begins to cry, explaining how distraught he is, because he was always so close to Emory, but Emory doesn't want to have anything to do with him anymore, and Len doesn't know why. Only meeting this family for the first time, it still seemed to me that each of the *pings* that Emory endured from his dad just in this one visit to the clinic might be the simple answer to Len's question, "Why?" So, this was a moment when I hoped I could blow the trumpet for the gender angels to come out. It seemed clear to me that Len loved Emory very much and didn't want to lose the love of his child. I asked Len whether he had noticed how Emory visibly flinched every time he said *she* or *her*. Len seemed surprised and admitted that he hadn't. I asked Emory whether he could tell his dad how it felt inside when his dad said *she, her*, or *my daughter*. Now it was Emory's turn to cry: "Every time he does that, it feels like my dad has a slingshot and keeps aiming stones at me. And I sink a little lower every time he calls me *she*. And it makes me mad." I explained to Len that for Emory, this was not a little deal, but a big deal, and could get even bigger if the slingshot hits kept coming Emory's way. From that day on Len made every effort to put an end to the *pings*, doing his best to use *he, him*, and *son*. And Emory started talking to his dad again.

The moral of the story is pretty straightforward: If you see a microaggression or are the agent of one, stop it. Anytime you feel an inclination to tweak your child's playmates or tamper with their toy choices, reassure yourself it's just a phase, or edit or correct their gender messages to you, that's a "stop it" moment. Like charity, freedom from microaggressions must start in the home. And it's good to always keep in mind that although any small action might seem like no big deal, gender microaggressions pile up, kind of like the way minor air pollution, if chronic, can add up to serious allergies or asthma. Only instead of breathing problems we'll have anxiety, depression, self-harm—nothing loving parents would want for their child.

PARENTS' BEST INSURANCE POLICY: ACCEPTANCE

Children do best when they get their parents' support. Obvious. The vast majority of parents bring their children into the world or into their family with the intent of supporting them. Assumed. Yet what form that support takes is not obvious nor should it be assumed. What is support in one culture might be considered neglect in another. The same difference may hold true from one household to another on the same block. So, let's talk about the kind of support gender-nonconforming children will need from their family to have a good go of it in life. The secret of navigating the gender maze, with all its potential dead ends and multiple pathways, lies in finding the right ingredients that will constitute true support of gender creative children in spinning their own unique gender web and discovering their true gender self.

Let's stray for a moment from the arena of gender to other aspects of child rearing. Take parents who value education and very much want their children to succeed. To that end they will push their children hard and will tell you this is the best way to support their children's academic success. In certain cultures, placing high academic demands on children is the status quo, and everyone accepts this parental practice, including the children. Yet even within those cultures, some children do not experience this practice as support at all but, rather, as undue pressure, and the result is failure rather than success—the children feel neither seen nor heard and buckle under the load created by their parents' so-called support. How about the parents who want to support their children in being autonomous, confident, and assertive, three traits that may definitely help you succeed in life, at least in Western culture? Such efforts often translate into giving their children an equal voice in family affairs; in other words, every person's vote counts, even when it comes to setting a bedtime or brushing teeth. Part of that package deal: Whenever possible, avoid two words when talking to your children: *stop* and *no*. Such "supports" are rarely in children's best interests, leaving them in a state of perpetual anxiety. They're too young for such participatory democracy and decision-making responsibilities; they will end up desperately seeking some form of leadership from their parents, who are not supposed to renege on their duty as benign authorities who will shepherd the children until they are ready to be self-guiding. In each of these examples, parents' efforts to support their children do not necessarily translate into best practices that will help those children grow healthy and strong.

In like fashion, the support parents may believe they are providing to their children in their gender development may prove to be anything but. The most egregious error in this regard is when parents believe they are the sculptors of their children's gender self, telling rather than listening, enforcing rather than facilitating, imposing their own picture of their children over the children's repeated attempts to paint their own gender self-portrait. But if you ask those parents why they are doing this, with love in their hearts and good intent in their minds they will explain that they are helping their children embrace the gender that was either God's will or nature's way or culture's norms, rather than the children's individual right or choice.

A stands for *apple*, our young transgender children. *A* also stands for *acceptance*, the key ingredient of successful support of the gender creative child, the support that will prove to be parents' best insurance policy in promoting their children's gender health. So, from here on in I would invite us all to dispense with the language of support and stay more strictly with the language of *acceptance*. Here's the riff: All parents negotiating the gender maze have an obligation to scrutinize parenting practices that they consider supportive of their gender creative children. If the contours of that support aren't centrally located around *acceptance* of the children for who those children are, rather than who the parents want them to be, it's time for the parents to take a look at their own gender ghosts and blow the trumpet for their gender angels to show up. Gender-nonconforming children don't just want to be seen; more than anything and most urgently, gender-nonconforming children want to be *accepted* by the people closest to them—their parents or caregivers and family members.

Bart is the single father of Jeremy, a sixteen-year-old high school boy who really wants to wear dresses—at home, at the mall, at weekend social events. Bart calls and asks me for a consultation to sort this all out. In our visit he says to me, "When he's eighteen, he can do anything he wants. But as long as he lives in my house, that's never going to happen." I knew the community Bart and Jeremy lived in, and I wondered with Bart whether he was afraid for Jeremy's safety if Jeremy sashayed out of the house in a dress. That would be a reasonable concern for any parent, one that might force parents to limit their child's gender expressions in the name of safety and well-being. But Bart said, "Nope, I'm not that worried about his safety. He's a big kid and won't let people mess with him. I just think it's *plain wrong*. So, it's not going to happen on my watch."

Is Bart de-centering and getting Jeremy in focus? Not so much. Is he stepping forward in support of his son, rather than just covering for himself? Yes, I absolutely believe that was his intention. I didn't think there would be any point in arguing with Bart about whether it was right or wrong for high school boys to wear dresses. I had another goal in mind: to invite Bart to *accept* his son, with his dresses. So, I said something like this: "I certainly understand your position, and absolutely, until your son is eighteen he should abide by the rules of your household. But I just wanted to share some other information with you, about what the studies show and the statistics say. A lot of kids whose parents tell them they'll have to wait until later, when they're on their own watch, to wear their dress or do whatever they're thinking about their gender—well, they may be at risk for a whole lot of things that aren't so good, psychological turbulence, if you will. Some get anxious and withdraw from the world, some turn to drugs, some to alcohol, some become depressed, some stop doing their schoolwork, some start getting into unsafe or dangerous sex, some start harming themselves, some even become suicidal. I'm not saying this will happen to your son; I mean, I haven't even met him. I just think you should be aware of the risk factors. You know your son best—do you think any of these could happen to him? Or maybe are already happening?" I didn't wish to alarm Bart; I just wanted to invite him to start thinking about whether his dress-code monitoring was supportive of his son. So, now Bart is faced with a dilemma: "I thought I was setting reasonable parental limits for my son by stopping him from wearing dresses" pitted against "Oh, maybe instead it's going to harm him." In my field this is called a situation of cognitive dissonance, where two competing thoughts, beliefs, or feelings contradict each other. To resolve this contradiction, a person has to relinquish one set of beliefs in favor of the other.

In this case, my greatest hope was that love would conquer all, leading Bart, a father who truly loved his son, to replace prohibition with acceptance in the matter of Jeremy's dress-wearing and all that dress-wearing signifies about Jeremy's true gender self.

I saw Bart for only one consultation, but he left saying, "I guess I've got a lot to think about." A few months later Bart called to let me know that he and Jeremy had been talking more openly about how each of them felt about men wearing dresses, and though Bart couldn't in all honesty give Jeremy his blessings, he was able to tell Jeremy that he would accept whatever decision Jeremy made about where and when he wanted to wear dresses and that for the time being they would have to respect their differences on this issue. It was a far cry from total acceptance of his son, but a large step in the right direction.

One last cautionary message: Beware going overboard on acceptance. How could there be too much acceptance of a child's gender? Answer: when it comes from parents' needs rather than their child's. This happens most often when parents want to be acknowledged by the world for embracing their gender-nonconforming children with love and compassion, or when they have their own personal investment or political agenda in promoting their children as the public poster child for the transgender movement, or when they're just too eager to have their children love them for what supportive parents they are. I can usually recognize the surfacing of this hyperactive acceptance when I observe a child squirming rather than beaming as their parents speak of their full-fledged endorsement of their child. As one youth said to me, in considerable distress, after his parents encouraged him to post a video of his coming-out at school, with his parents at his side, on the Internet, "They really don't care about me. They just wanted the video to go viral for the world to see what incredible parents they are. So, me being trans is just their ticket." The lesson to be learned: Go back to the basics. De-center; listen to what your child is saying, not what you want; make sure that your support is about not just who they are but also what they need from you, including respect for their privacy and acknowledgment of their desire to keep exploring their gender rather than being pushed into a gender category. Then you come full circle back to true acceptance, a cornerstone of your child's gender health. And what parents of gender creative children have taught us all: They are doing a superb job of doing just this.

ACCEPTANCE = A FORM OF PROTECTION

I'm hearing a chorus of voices right now: "Well, it's okay for you to promote boys wearing dresses to the mall, because you live in the crazy Bay Area. But we live in a really conservative part of the country, and there's no way we can accept our boys trotting out in skirts. They'll get killed—literally."

All parents, no matter what their culture, are saddled with the identical set of child-rearing tasks, just by the fact that they are responsible for bringing up offspring who start out very little and very dependent. Task Number 1: keeping their children safe. Task Number 2: helping their children grow into thriving adults who can function in the culture they live in. What counts for "safe" and what counts for "thriving" can vary enormously from one culture to another. But the two variables are a constant, and the biggest challenges come when "keeping them safe" is at odds with "thriving." For example, the children who were separated from their parents and sent to the country to avoid the bombing that shattered London during World War II did not necessarily thrive in their temporary foster placements, but at least they were safe. Truth be told, though, the children who remained in London with their parents actually thrived better psychologically, as long as their parents could provide them with comfort and assurance, even when huddled in a bomb shelter.[55]

If you are a parent of a gender-nonconforming child, you may identify with the feelings of London parents during World

War II: How do I keep my child safe from bombings? In this case, the bombings take the form of rejection, malice, even violence that might come children's way because of their gender non-conformity. So, if support = acceptance, but acceptance of who children are saying they are might put their very lives in danger, you're faced with another dilemma: safety versus authenticity: "I want my child to be the most gender creative child possible. I don't want anyone to hurt my child." Let me quote from a parent grappling with this very dilemma—"Look, it's okay for my son to wear his sister's clothes while we're here in Canada, but when we go back to India, where we are from, he'll be attacked in our village if he shows up looking like a girl. I just can't let him do that."[56]

Many years ago Abraham Maslow introduced us to the hierarchy of needs. If you think of it as a pyramid, we build from the bottom up: from physical survival to safety to love and belonging to esteem to self-actualization.[57] Without survival, we'll never get to actualization. That said, it would be reasonable for parents to put reins on their children's full gender creativity if its open expression was perceived as putting the children in danger. I've already pointed out in *Gender Born, Gender Made* that in those situations we want to make sure that the children get the message that if they have to put a cloak on their true gender self to hide it from others, it's not because there is anything wrong with *them*. We need to say, "The problem is the world out there—a lot of people out there haven't learned yet that gender comes in an infinite variety of packages. So, they need to learn. And we're all working on it. But in the meantime, we have to keep your true gender self safe, because sometimes people aren't always so nice to people they don't understand. And while we're working on it, we'll create safe spaces for you where people do understand and you can feel free to be who you are." And so that little boy traveling to India may pack his girls' clothes in his suitcase, to be worn freely in his hotel room, and go in "drag" in his boys' clothes when visiting the village with the relatives who don't know about such things. As long as *he* knows it's because there is something wrong not with him, but with the world, and his parents really mean it that they are working to change it, right now, he can maintain his gender resilience and feel both accepted and protected. I have seen children as young as four years old begin to be able to maintain this differentiation and develop their own creative strategies to meet up with the "unfair" world while maintaining their positive sense of self. As those same children grow older, the parents will best loosen the cords of protection and let the children determine for themselves where they want to express their authentic gender.

This strategy works only if the children feel they will eventually have authorship over throwing these cloaks on and off, which in turn will happen only if they feel totally accepted by the people who love them most. If these factors aren't in place and the unfairness of the outside world is being used only as an excuse to pass the buck from the parents' own discomfort with their children's gender, the children will most definitely smell a rat and lose the protective circle of true acceptance. And even if the parents are not passing the buck but are measuring real signs of potential danger for their children, it will become their obligation to follow through on their promise to become advocates for their children's acceptance in that unfair world, so those dangers can disappear. This is exactly what I have witnessed parents doing, so movingly, with all the courage and risks that takes, and my hat goes off to all of them, because they, along with their children, are our most critical community leaders in the push toward a gender-accepting world.

But the story doesn't stop there. Now I want to flip both acceptance and protection on their head. Sometimes full acceptance, with no censorship or limits, can be the strongest form of protection a family can offer its gender creative child. Its strength comes from building psychological muscles. By telling children, "Go for it. Be the person you are," the children get the message that their parents have confidence that they can stand up to anyone who does not yet understand that they have the right, just like everyone else, to be who they are—everywhere.

Amy is a single mom who explained to me that there was no way she was going to accept her daughter Lucia's insistent demand that she be allowed to change her name to Luke and go to school as "he." It was bad enough that Amy was criticized for raising her daughter without a father. Lucia attended a very conservative school where she would no doubt be shunned as a "freak" if she returned to school after the summer as a boy. Amy had her own grief about potentially losing the little girl whom she treasured so dearly. She assured me that she herself could handle the transition; it was just that she would be "throwing Lucia to the wolves" if she indulged Lucia's wishes. So, here I am again, listening to and totally understanding Amy's worries, but feeling it my professional obligation to weigh in on the other side of the scales: What if Lucia is at risk for anxiety, depression, anger outbursts, self-harm, or something even worse if we hold her back from expressing her true gender, all because of a school that is less than accepting? If Lucia is truly Luke, are we actually harming rather than protecting her by saying she is not allowed to be the boy she knows herself to be? Might not the best protection be to let her be who she is, which is a "he," and build her strengths to live with pride in the world she is growing up in?

Suppose Amy moves in another direction: working through her own issues about being a single mother, so that she could derive pride rather than fear of condemnation from that; putting effort into her own and others' acceptance of the gender Lucia is discovering she is, rather than the gender others are telling her she has to be so as to be safe? Those interventions may very well be the most protective factors Amy could introduce into Lucia's life, lowering the possibilities of anxiety, depression, and/or self-harm, while building gender resilience, so that Lucia, now Luke, would be ready to meet the challenges ahead and promote his right to be the person he is.

Let's revisit Bart and Jeremy. Jeremy wanted to wear dresses outside the house. Bart wanted to stop him. Even though it wasn't clear how much protection from rejection informed Bart's inclination to say no, for the moment assume Bart's prohibition of dresses is intended to be a supportive move, but one that was not necessarily in Jeremy's best interests, given the risk factors I cited. By accepting Jeremy's desire to wear dresses, even if it wasn't necessarily something Bart could approve of, Bart was still offering Jeremy a layer of protection: "I am accepting who you want to be and letting you be that person." As long as Bart doesn't roll his eyes or make derogatory comments when Jeremy leaves the house decked out in his dress for a Saturday night at the mall, Jeremy can feel fortified that his father has his back, or at least accepts what he wears on his back. Ergo, acceptance becomes protection—not through shielding but by building or reinforcing gender resilience and confidence. On the other hand, if Bart were prohibiting dresses to prevent Jeremy from being harassed, that could backfire—instilling fear and contributing to potential shame, anxiety, social withdrawal, or low self-esteem, nothing we would want for our children. So, Bart's permitting the dresses would end up on the side not just of acceptance but of another form of protection: sheltering Jeremy from undesired emotional consequences while simultaneously giving his son the opportunity to enhance his psychological well-being by giving him the freedom and confidence to be the gender that is "me."

THROUGH THE MAZE: ALLY, ADVOCATE, AMBASSADOR

As parents negotiate the maze with a gender creative child, they will encounter a whole lot of people along the paths—their other children, if they have them, their own parents, their extended family, their school, their places of worship, and so forth. This inevitably puts them in the position of ally, advocate, and ambassador.

To be a gender-accepting parent is to watch your child's back, both out in the world and at home. Becoming ally, advocate, and ambassador means being able to take a position of authority. So, it is time for us to amend our dictum, "It is not for us to say, but for the children to tell." What I have learned as a gender specialist: Yes, it is important to listen to the children, but their parents are also our best experts. When parents have questions, concerns, doubts, maybe even flat-out objections to the gender path their child is embarking on, I do not dismiss these as evidence of their gender ghosts at work. These parents may have something very important to tell me, and I want to listen to them, too. For example, recently I reviewed a letter of support from a community therapist endorsing hormone replacement therapy for her teen patient. But I noticed in the letter that reference was made to the mother's having some concerns about the permanence of her teen's cross-gender identity. That, along with other information in the letter that concerned me, led me to recommend that we slow down and do some further assessment and consultation. I asked the parents to call me about my recommendation. When I spoke to the mother, she was immensely relieved and felt her voice was finally being heard. The therapist who had written the letter had not paid heed. This was the first step in this mother's being given authorship and recognized as an ally for her child; and at the end of the day, the additional assessment proved her right. Her daughter was still in the throes of exploration rather than affirmation, and now her mother could advocate for her as such.

Parenting can easily become a delicate affair. We want to do our best. We worry we aren't. To rear a gender creative child in a less-than-gender-accepting world stretches the role of the parent: That parent will need fortifications to go out and be the child's ally, advocate, and ambassador. I learned this one day at our gender clinic when I wondered with the parents of a young child how we could be of help to them. They seemed to have a healthy, happy gender fluid child, and they both impressed me with their empathic and joyful relationship with Gwendolyn, their child, who was way too young to be considered for puberty blockers or hormones. I couldn't think of what we could have to offer this family at that time that it didn't already possess. Yet the parents were quick on the uptake: "We came here because of our parents." "Your parents?" I queried. "Yes, our parents. They're always questioning what we're doing. They think it's so wrong and that we're making a freak out of our kid by encouraging it. So, we figured if we told them that the doctors at UCSF said what we were doing is the right thing and our child is all right, they'll back off." And indeed they did. So, I now recognized a new component of our clinic service: Good Housekeeping Seal of Approval for Gender Creative Parenting Practices. With that endorsement in hand, Gwendolyn's parents gained the strength to advocate for Gwendolyn's gender creative self to both sets of grandparents and then later to her school as well.

Sometimes the role of ally, advocate, and ambassador happens right at home. Arianna is filling out a college application, just as Arianna's brother walks into the room. On the application, an applicant could check Male, Female, or Other. Arianna, who has been exploring her gender and questioning her gender identity, wonders out loud, "Maybe I should check Other." Arianna is pretty distraught about what to do in this moment. Thomas, Arianna's brother, blurts out, "That is so disgusting. What's 'other' even supposed to mean? Sick, that's what it is." Arianna bursts out crying and runs to her room, slamming the door behind her. Arianna's mother hears the commotion and catches the interchange. Before going to Arianna's room to try to comfort her, she admonishes Thomas, "Knock it off. There'll be no disrespecting people in this house." No doubt Thomas needs some help and support in sorting out his own negative or anxious feelings about nonbinary gender and a sister who may be that, but in the meantime Arianna has been empowered by a mother who stood up for her and made it clear that in their house there will be no gender-bashing.

In all areas of life, siblings can be either a child's best ally or worst adversary, roles that can reverse on a moment's notice. But when it comes to gender, the peaks are particularly high and the valleys low. Siblings as allies can be a most important buttress for a gender creative child, particularly at school or out in the neighborhood where parents need not apply and therefore aren't present to protect their child. Alternatively, siblings can be the worst of enemies if they oppress rather than protect, by rejecting or harassing their gender creative sibling. All of that is a roundabout way of saying that parents as allies necessarily includes overseeing the coaching of siblings to be the same.

Sometimes parents, in an effort to protect *all* their children, and with gender ghosts as whisperers, will be heard to say something like: "We can't just think about Jennifer. We have to think about our other two girls, too. Do you know what it's like to have to go to school and have everyone saying, 'What's with your sister and the dude clothes? Weird.' Jennifer's going to have to stop being so selfish and think of her sisters and what this is doing to them and just stop with the crazy dressing." Let's think about this for a moment. The message is that Jennifer should hide her true gender self to keep her sisters comfortable. To become an ally for Jennifer, her mom has to come to recognize the greater harm done to Jennifer if asked to feel guilt and shame and keep her gender fluid self under wraps for the sake of her gender-conforming sisters' comfort. Indeed, both sisters need empathic attention to their own difficulties in accompanying Jennifer along the gender maze, and Jennifer's mother needs help talking about her own angst so that she can be an ally to all her daughters while protecting the rights of Jennifer to be her own gender creative self. And part of her work as ambassador and advocate will be working with the school so that Jennifer's sisters and Jennifer will not have to dodge or be grazed by flying gender bullets. From that work, hopefully new policies and new curriculum will be put in place to help students and faculty alike be respectful and embracing of gender in all its iterations.

Sometimes parents will need to monitor siblings' honest efforts to be allies, which can unwittingly do the opposite by rewriting their gender creative siblings' stories. Alicia was thirteen when she finally came to realize that she could no longer live the lie of being a girl. She had known for some time that she was transgender but hadn't been ready to either admit it to herself or come out to her family. But now she was. And she did. Her parents were understanding, but her mother in particular said she needed time to mourn the loss of the daughter she had. At this point Alicia's older sister, Tracy, who herself was immersed in the genderqueer community at her college, exploded at her mother: "Get over it. You never had a daughter; you always had a son. Alicia's always been a boy, and now Alicia's just letting you know." A good story, but it wasn't Alicia's. Alicia did not feel that she had always been a boy. Her life experience was as both girl and boy, and her journey was an unfolding one—from being a girl who was now going through a metamorphosis, emerging as a boy. To abide by her sister's story would be like telling a butterfly that it had always been a butterfly without having been a caterpillar. Story correction: The butterfly part came later; the caterpillar was as real as real could be. The son came later; before that, the daughter had been as real as real could be. Alicia felt overpowered by Tracy's passionate outcry. Alicia's mother was stewing in her own confusion and mourning but was able to right herself, focus on Alicia, and ask her directly, "Is that true? Have you always felt like a boy?" Alicia mumbled, "No, Mom, not so much," and Mom turned to Tracy, and reminded her that it was Alicia's story to tell and not Tracy's to dictate. So, here we have a sister with every intention of being an ally yet needing a mother to step in as an advocate for Alicia so she could speak her own story and truly be supported. And yes, Mom had more work ahead of her to address her sadness about losing her daughter to make room for the joy of having her son, which indeed she did.

Parents usually don't sign up for being warriors when they decide to have children. But they may find themselves in that very position as they shepherd their gender creative children through the gender maze, with the rest of the family in tow. Sometimes, parents will need to ask other family members to step aside if they are rejecting or unaccepting of their gender creative child; sometimes they will need to let other family members lead the way if those are the ones with the greater facility to accept and embrace. It's a lot of work, but the fruits of the efforts are well worth it—a robust and healthy apple, orange, or fruit salad.

THE GENDER BADGE OF COURAGE—AWARDED TO EVERY GENDER CREATIVE PARENT

I have not minced words about the dead ends or hazardous side paths parents can take as they journey with their children through the gender maze. But I also can't highlight enough the tremendous courage and fortitude exhibited by all the parents who smooth out the bumps, pave new paths, and find just the right end point for children who are not the gender everyone thought they were or who don't do gender the way everyone thought they would. Parents accomplish this by inventing their own GPS device to guide them. In the process, they give a whole new definition to parental gender creativity: It is not simply parents' ability to stretch to new gender horizons, but also their acumen to call on their own wisdom and vulnerability so they can learn from their children while simultaneously teaching them what they themselves are relearning about gender. As any artist will tell you, creativity is not just about having fun; it is also filled with pathos, questioning, and allowing yourself to get lost before you are found. That would be the journey of all gender creative parents as they negotiate the gender maze.

CHAPTER SIX

If Gender Is Expansive, Wherefore a Shrink?

It was the best of times, it was the worst of times, it was the age of wisdom, it was the age of foolishness.
—Charles Dickens, *A Tale of Two Cities*

WHEN IT COMES TO the field of mental health and its relationship to the trans community, Dickens about summed it up. We have been responsible for harm if not atrocities in the name of mental health; we have been responsible for pouring tons of resources into making sure that gender creative people get all the supports they need. You've got to love us, you've got to hate us. And we are not all one.

On December 15, 2015, my email inbox was flooded with messages from friends and colleagues with links to an article: CAMH TO "WIND DOWN" CONTROVERSIAL GENDER IDENTITY CLINIC SERVICES.[58] I learned that Toronto's Centre for Addiction and Mental Health had made an administrative decision to phase out its gender identity services for children and youth. That would be Dr. Ken Zucker's clinic (first discussed in Chapter 1), which engaged in therapeutic practices to help young children accept the gender that matched the sex assigned to them at birth. The hospital had initiated an external review process because of complaints, particularly from local mental health gender specialists and the trans community, that the program, offered to youth ages three to eighteen, performed a type of reparative therapy that was disrespectful of patients' gender identity. The review found the clinic's approach was out of step with currently accepted practice and engaged in techniques that were antithetical to supporting gender creative children and promoting their gender health. Now, not only is our model ascending, we have at least in one instance successfully participated in actions to eliminate potentially harmful child therapy practices.

This has not been a cricket match with a winner and a loser. This is a matter of fighting for what we think is the right and only way to support children's gender creativity, and doing our best to stop harm being done to both the children and their families. And I can breathe a sigh of relief that our model of honoring children's gender narratives and helping them be the gender that they know themselves to be is growing and ascendant. As mentioned in the opening chapter, new gender affirmative clinics are showing up all the time, and we have even established an international consortium of gender affirmative practitioners working to develop and apply the model in our own countries. Yet *ascendant* does not mean *arrived*—we've expended a lot of elbow grease, running just to keep up, and we know there is still much work to be done. But every moment is worth it. In fact, this is the best and most exciting journey I have ever been on. And the people who have joined me along the road are some of the most wonderful I have ever encountered, nothing less than heroic in their firm support for our children of all genders. So, I open this chapter with that sense of exhilaration. And, borrowing from the famous quote of the late President Kennedy, I am putting out a call to myself and my fellow mental health professionals: "Ask not what the families can do for us, but what we can do for the families."

A ROAD MAP FOR MENTAL HEALTH SERVICES

Since *Gender Born, Gender Made* was published, the gender atoms have dynamically shifted and then coalesced into what are now three constellations of mental health practices for gender-nonconforming children and their families. All parents negotiating the mental health system should be aware of the three, so they can make informed choices, know what they are getting back from their investment, and avoid minefields that could harm their children or themselves.

MODEL #1: LEARNING TO LIVE IN YOUR OWN SKIN

I borrow the term "learning to live in your own skin" from Ken Zucker, as he describes his own philosophy and practice for treating children with gender dysphoria, but I also want to say that there are more extreme models than his, usually endorsed by right-wing religious groups, whose goal is to stamp out gender nonconformity altogether. So, let me start with the "learning to live in your own skin" model, the one whose practice was under investigation in 2015 at the Centre for Addiction and Mental Health in Toronto resulting in the closing of his clinic in December of that year. This approach applies only to children below the age of puberty. The model is adapted from the program directed by Dr. Richard Green at UCLA in the 1960s, a program targeting effeminate boys and treating them to become "boys' boys," which equated with becoming straight boys. Overall, the UCLA program proved a colossal failure, as most of the boys went on to be gay in spite of Dr. Green and his associates' best efforts. One, tragically, committed suicide in his adulthood, with family members and friends blaming the suicide on the harm done to him by the purportedly reparative treatment.

In the "living comfortably in your own skin" model, the underlying assumption is that young children are malleable in both their gender identity and expressions; in other words, there is still plasticity to the gender brain. By this way of thinking, if a child exhibits signs of gender dysphoria and if you catch the child early enough, you can help them learn to "live more comfortably in their own skin," or, simply put, to "accept the sex assigned to them at birth." The help comes in the form of: (1) psychotherapy for the child; (2) psychotherapy or counseling for the parents; (3) behavior modification techniques, including removal of "gender-inappropriate" toys and substitution of "gender-appropriate" toys at home, prohibition of cross-dressing, positive reinforcement for "gender-appropriate" activities, extinction of "gender-inappropriate" activities; (4) social engineering of playmate choices, replacing same-sex playmates for opposite-sex playmates; (5) family systems/relational interventions: bringing the same-sex parent closer in, while asking the opposite-sex parent to step back.

The behavior modification interventions are introduced only if that is what the parents want for their child. The goal of the interventions is to ward off/avoid/prevent a transgender outcome. The rationale is that being transgender is a harder way to live your life, so why not offer the child an easier life, with no harm done, given the plasticity of a young child's gender brain?[59] In a 2015 interview with the *National Post*, Dr. Zucker explained the "learning to live in your own skin" approach this way: "You are lowering the odds that as such a [gender-nonconforming] kid gets older, he or she will move into adolescence feeling so uncomfortable about their gender identity that they think that it would be better to live as the other gender and require treatment with hormones and sex-reassignment surgery."[60] In this model, lowering the odds = good outcome, one that ensures better acceptance in the social world and avoidance of medical interventions to alter one's body. However, if you should begin treatment of a child who has already entered puberty and is clear about their transgender identity, it's too late. The train has already left the station. No more gender brain plasticity. In those cases, the recommended treatment is to support the youth in their cross-gender identity and help them receive the services, including social transitions, puberty blockers, and hormones, that will better align their affirmed gender identity with their bodies.

Statistics citing the number of children who benefited from this model, accepting the sex assigned to them at birth and going on to live contented lives as cisgender individuals, are used to support this model. The problem with these statistics is twofold. First comes the apples and oranges issue. Many of the youth treated in gender clinics such as Dr. Zucker's were never destined to be transgender children in the first place. They are more likely our protogay youth. The therapy applied was for treatment of a "condition" that did not exist. These children's gender identity was never in question; they only wanted the freedom of gender expressions. So, it is inaccurate to assess the outcomes for these children as a warding-off of a transgender outcome. They were never headed in that direction in the first place and the success lies in their own persistence in who they were, rather than treatment interventions to make them that way. Second, it appears, regrettably, that such treatment may not ward off but rather drive underground a child's transgender identity. Some of the comments that appeared online in response to the article about the 2015 investigation of the CAMH gender clinic point to such a result:

> It's easy to imagine that his methods—steering parents toward removing pink crayons from the box, extolling a patriarchy no one believes in—could instill in some children a sense of shame and a double life. A 2008 study of 25 girls who had been seen in Zucker's clinic showed positive results; 22 were no longer gender-dysphoric, meaning they were comfortable living as girls. But that doesn't mean they were happy. I spoke to the mother of one Zucker patient in her late 20s, who said her daughter was repulsed by the

thought of a sex change but was still suffering—she'd become an alcoholic, and was cutting herself. "I'd be surprised
if she outlived me," her mother said. This is a success?????

"Repulsed by a sex change" yes, but at what cost?

i was there in 1983-84 they did me no good it has taken me
years to be able to deal with what was done to me.

"What was done to me" is antithetical to what we want to hear
about the patient's experience of our mental health services,
and cutting and alcoholism are never what we want to see as
outcomes.

Dr. Zucker has adamantly insisted that the model he employs is
not reparative therapy, and I agree with him if we define *reparative*
or *conversion therapy* as a comprehensive method for expunging
pathological sexual or gender "disorders," targeting both homosexual and transsexual "conditions." We know of these methods most
often in the context of practitioners, usually associated with the
religious right, who have had no compunctions about using dra-
conian punitive measures, going so far as employing electroshock,
to purge the patient of untoward desires, thoughts, or actions, in
the name of making them either straight or cis, or both. Yet the
"living in your own skin" model, in its employment of behavior
modification techniques and social engineering to alter a child's
gender identity or expressions, does qualify as reparative. This is
exactly why the model is objected to so adamantly by the transgender community and its allies for being at its best ineffective,
at its worst engendering great harm to gender-nonconforming
children and youth. A further complication is that although Dr.
Zucker states very clearly that he will employ these methods only
if it is the parents' wish to do so, parents who decline services after
hearing the treatment options have been known to be labeled as

resistant. And at the end of the day, even if parents want a particular treatment for their child, it does not mean that we mental health professionals go ahead and implement it if it is not in the best interests of the child, an assessment I would say applies to the methods of this model. Two of my colleagues from Toronto, Robert Wallace and Hershel Russell, coming from an attachment theory model (which looks at development from the lens of the relationship and bonds that develop between parent and child), evaluated the "live in your own skin" approach as practiced at the CAMH clinic and published the following conclusion: "We are concerned that this treatment approach may tend to increase shame in both parent and child, thus potentially impacting negatively on successful attachment and increasing the risk of depression."[61] Neither of these outcomes could ever be counted as healthy. My recommendation, therefore: Stay away from "learning to live in your own skin" treatment as defined in this intervention package.

MODEL #2: WATCHFUL WAITING

We have the members of the Amsterdam clinic, spearheaded by Peggy Cohen-Kettenis, to gratefully thank for this model. They alerted the mental health and medical community that young children's gender creativity is not to be squashed but to be observed over time, with the possible follow-up of puberty blockers (this clinic was the first to introduce this procedure as an intervention to put a pause on puberty for youth who are questioning their gender) and then hormones to bring the subjects' body in alignment with their gender identity. Throughout, the children receive mental health services from a therapist trained as a gender specialist. This model has been researched carefully by the highly respected group of practitioners at the Amsterdam Center of Expertise on Gender Dysphoria, VU University Medical Center, and has taught all of us who work as gender specialists so much about gender-nonconforming children and their psychological needs.

But where does "watchful waiting" come in? Because so many of the young children who came through the Amsterdam program did not persist in their gender dysphoria by the time they reached puberty, it was thought that it would be best to let the prepubertal children be gender expansive but not gender changing, the latter meaning socially transitioning from male to female or female to male. The clinic team saw no harm in asking a child to wait, facilitated by living in the social context of a country that was quite flexible and nonbinary in its gender expression norms, particularly for children below the age of seven. This way a child would not be gender-pigeonholed prematurely, and this would also avoid the discomfort if not psychological harm of changing genders again if the child later proved to be comfortable with their natal sex. During the waiting period, the children would be followed carefully by the clinic team, with the support of outside therapists in the community (which is required before a child can receive medical services), to ensure that the children were growing well and getting their emotional needs met, and in preparation for later transitioning and medical interventions if they proved to be good candidates. In this model, the children going through the program also receive a full battery of psychological tests, documenting not only their gender status but also their cognitive, social, and emotional functioning. Some of these instruments are delivered to the children directly, some to their parents or teachers.

I learned a great deal from studying this model, but I also had some questions. First, I wondered about the contradiction between releasing gender nonconformity from the stigma of pathology and yet at the same time running children through a thorough battery of tests just because they show up as gender creative. Do we really need all these measuring rods—for depression, for anxiety, for behavioral problems, for intellectual functioning, and so forth? I wondered what messages we send to the children when we put them under the microscope in this way. At the same time, if we're thinking about medical interventions that affect the course of a youth's life, both physically and psychologically, we do need some indicators that this will be in a child's best interests. Do these measures provide us with that?

It was through perusing the summary of the data amassed on the children going through the Amsterdam clinic that I got my idea about apples and oranges. In going over the data on persisters and desisters, I began to get the feeling that we were talking about two groups of children who were different from the get-go. In delving into my own clinical work with gender-nonconforming children, I noticed that a repeated set of experiences showed up in a certain subset of the younger children—if they said they *were* a girl, for example, rather than they *wished* they were a girl; if the early signs of a cross-gender self were truly very early—such as in the second year of life; if they showed significant distress about their bodies; if all of this already seemed insistent, persistent, and consistent in their young lives. To me it seemed that we could already identify well before puberty that these were our youngest transgender youth.

I had been going on about this for a while when, in June 2013, Thomas Steensma and his colleagues at the Amsterdam clinic published new findings based on a review of the data from their clinic research that corroborated my observations, indeed suggesting that a subgroup of young children could be identified early on as persisters.[62] Yet my Dutch colleagues still held to the watchful waiting approach, arguing that we might otherwise paint children into a cognitive corner where they would get to know themselves as their socially transitioned gender and not know how to get out of that spot if it wasn't right. Moreover, they reasoned, if the children transitioned too young, they might not be able to hold on to a realistic perception of the bodies they were born with, perhaps with no conscious memory of the opposite sex they once were. I should say that to date I have not yet met any young socially transitioned children who weren't all too aware of the bodies they came into the world with—they just might hold some illusions about where those bodies might go in the future. And while I certainly understand the concerns about prematurely fixing a self-label on children that they won't know how to shake off later, (1) I have not had occasion to see that happen; instead, I have watched a small handful of children fluidly moving back into the identity matching their original sex assignment, providing they have social supports to do so; and (2) when I weigh that small potential risk against the higher risks that accompany holding children back from living in the gender they know themselves to be, I'd take a chance on letting them live in their present affirmed gender with no prohibitions. The chances of early transitions being successful will no doubt rise significantly if we work to expand the social environment beyond binary male-female boxes, whether they be cis or trans, to an understanding that our gender may change over the course of our lifetime and may be any-and-all rather than either/or. On the other hand, I will say that watchful waiting is an insurance policy against runaway trains, where families leap forward with social transitions for their young children well before they have time to reflect on what the children are actually telling them.

Ironically, when I was surfing the Internet recently to look for images of "apples," I came across a picture of a young trans girl, whimsically staring into the camera in her pink tutu and long wispy hair, exactly the image I wanted to use for my presentation. Then, lo and behold, when I researched the source of the photograph, I discovered that this very young transgender child was from none other than the Netherlands. Word has it that young children are beginning to show up at the Amsterdam clinic already transitioned, with their parents' support, before any green lights are given by the clinic team. In fact, soon after I wrote this last sentence, I received an email from a mother in the Netherlands that read as follows:

Dear Mrs. Ehrensaft,

You do not know me at all, and your time is precious, but as a mother of 3 wonderful children of which our Bia, born as a boy, with twin brother Sven, 6 years old, I cannot do otherwise than reach out even across the borders of our country . . . all for Bia's well-being.

Last month she told me: "Mumy, until I was 3 years old, I really thought I WAS a girl . . . now I know I am not." And then I explain that how you feel inside is just as real as my oldest daughter knows she is a girl, beyond doubt. In our opinion, Bia is not confused. But the specialist team we consulted tell all parents of children with gender dysphoria: "Do not give too much room, he or she will probably outgrow it . . ." "It is not so hard to dress neutrally . . ." But after a year of struggling, crying of Bia, "Why can't I dress the way I want to, Mom?" We felt we had to give more space . . .

What do you think of our way of responding?

Thank you so much for your time

A mother with tears in her heart . . .

I think her way of responding is just right, and I wish she could wipe the tears from her heart and just feel the love for Bia running through. All these signs lead in one direction: It appears that the waves of historical change may be overriding the norms of the watchful waiting model. For some twenty-first-century families of gender creative children who are hooked into ever growing local, national, and international networks that support children of all ages living in their authentic gender, like the mother with tears in her heart, action seems to have transcended waiting.

MODEL #3: LISTEN AND ACT

I've already laid out the gender affirmative model in its general dimensions, but now let's consider this third model, "listen and act," from the perspective of mental health care. The "listen and act" model promotes allowing children to live in their authentic gender, whatever their age. This includes the possibility of facilitating social transitions early in life, as young as the preschool years, providing a child's gender identity is clearly in focus at that time. And yet it does not presume that a young child will necessarily hold that gender for the rest of their lives, although most will. The "listen and act" approach does not assume that the professionals will know best. Instead there is a collaborative support or treatment team, if you will, a team that includes the child, the family, and any professionals involved in the child's life. At the same time, each of the professionals on the team has a responsibility to apply their expertise to ensure that the child gets the best care they can.

Now, let's turn to the mental health member of that team. Traditionally, the mental health professional serving the trans community, whether it be little ones or adults, bore the reputation of "gatekeeper." They were the people who wrote the letter to say whether a person was eligible for medical services (actually, they still are those people). They were the people who looked for "comorbid" conditions that might put a halt on forward movement toward gender affirmation. So, how is that different in the gender affirmative model? Simple: We have expertise, but we don't consider ourselves the primary experts. The main expert is the child. Alongside the child is the family. The parents are going to know this child far better than we do, even when they have blind spots.

In the gender affirmative model, the mental health people are essentially the translators—taking in information from the child and family to reflect back what we see as the child's gender web. We don't assume therapy is mandatory for every child who goes against the gender grain. But we do recognize the value of therapeutic supports in helping a child undo knots as they spin their web and in helping parents align with each other and mirror back to their child the child they know themselves to be. Therapeutic goals include building gender resilience, soothing the strains of gender stresses or healing the wounds of gender distress, solidifying and expanding the circle of gender acceptance surrounding the child, and helping the child consolidate their true gender self. Sometimes parent consultation is all that is needed, in which case we spend time only with the parents and never meet the child. Sometimes we do family or sibling therapy. Sometimes we create groups—for the children, for the parents, or both. Sometimes we see a child alone, either briefly or in very long-term therapy, depending on the child's needs.

We've been bothered by the binary nature of the psychological measures that exist to assess a child's gender, and we have searched to develop alternative assessment packets, which we are successfully accomplishing.[63] We know that the children's gender well-being will not be ensured by the work we do in our offices unless it is accompanied by the work we do in the community to offer new paradigms for thinking about gender, promote gender expansiveness, and protest against harm when we see it being done. And we struggle to figure out the puzzle about diagnosis: If gender pathology lies in the culture rather than in the children, we ask ourselves why we have a psychiatric gender diagnosis for children at all. At the moment, there is actually no consensus among us on the answer to this question.

If not primary experts, who are we mental health professionals other than translators? From the start, we abide by the principle "If you want to know a child's gender, ask the child; it's not for us to tell, but for the child to say." At one level, that makes it easy for us, because it calls on the basic listening skills we learned a long time ago in Becoming a Mental Health Professional 101. The challenge comes in the translation—making sense of what we are listening to. How do we know what children are saying? They don't always do it in full or coherent sentences. Much of the communication will come not in words, but in actions, as when a gender-distressed child, natal male, buries a boy figure in the sand tray and firmly plants the girl figure on his grave (that's an easy one to figure out, but we're usually not so lucky). We learn to stay suspended in a state of not knowing, training ourselves to be patient as the story unfolds while simultaneously being at the ready to shift gears quickly if a sudden urgency emerges in a child's gender signals. If we have been trained psychoanalytically, as I have, we put every effort into culling the good and extracting the bad from our training. From my own training I have discovered, in my efforts to promote gender health, that I possess the gift of wonderful social capital, thanks to my psychoanalytic training—a cache that includes listening skills, interpretation, attention to the unconscious, suspension of judgment, knowledge of the interrelationship between outer and inner worlds, and the use of play as a means of discovery.

Our biggest surprise as child therapists is our new role in the medical world—learning to make sense of the appropriateness or a youth's readiness for puberty blockers, hormones, top surgery, bottom surgery, hysterectomies, and so forth. We have had to educate ourselves in physiology, stages of puberty, bone development, and so forth. In the age of attention to body-psyche linkages and availability of new medical interventions, we find ourselves right in the belly of that beast—how do we help gender creative children make adjustments or create harmony between the bodies they were born with and the gender they know themselves to be? Would there be any harm in doing so? Are we too caught up in the microcosm of body adjustments, rather than working at the macro level to confront the gender-binary social mores that make such adjustments feel so essential to some of our youth? We have had to get over our qualms, and there have been many, about weighing in on medical decisions that may have permanent effects on a child's future life, all the while with gender ghosts whispering in our ear, "Don't mess with Mother

Nature." Many of us, save the psychiatrists, may have chosen the field of mental health over the field of medicine with the intent of avoiding just such involvement in children's medical issues. And here we are, right in the vortex of those very issues; there's no escaping it if we are to be gender experts. We're the ones who are asked to write the letters of *support* or do the psychological assessments to determine whether a specific youth is a good candidate for any number of gender-affirming medical interventions. This is no small burden, and a task we must take very seriously if we are to do well by the youth.

Coming full circle, the proponents of the "listen and act" model are in total agreement with Model #1's goal of helping children feel comfortable living in their own skin. But our definition of "living in your own skin" is diametrically opposed to the one outlined by Dr. Zucker. We consider a child's gender skin to be determined not by either chromosomes or genitalia but, rather, by the brain, mind, and experience. It is what is called in my psychoanalytic circles "the ego rind," the psychological outer covering that envelops the self. So, yes, we very much want to help children live comfortably in their own skin, if that means living comfortably with their true gender self.

I know I do not hide my biases well. In my estimation, the gender affirmative "listen and act" model is the one that makes the most sense to me in promoting children's gender health. I can suspend judgment about the worth of the "watchful waiting" model, as I always tip my hat to thoughtful, cautious, well-researched approaches, even if I have my differences with the idea of holding children back when they know they are ready. What I can say with no qualifications is that the original "live comfortably in your own skin" model that attempts to get young "apples" to accept the gender that matches the sex assigned to them at birth makes no sense to me. Children going through the multifaceted interventions in this model are at risk for repeated microaggressions, if not outright trauma, if they feel coerced into relinquishing their gender desires, inclinations, and identifications and burying their true gender self so as to become a gender-acceptable human being by other people's standards, rather than their own self-knowledge. It is no accident that there is a move afoot to outlaw this therapeutic practice with children and youth. To do otherwise would be to abandon our oath—to do no harm.

PUTTING OUT FIRES

For those of us who are gender affirmative practitioners, even though we are committed to our model of care and look forward to the time when we have completed the longitudinal research that will validate this approach, we also know we cannot wait for those results to appear. There are fires burning all around us, fires we must put out now—the fires of transphobia and genderism that bear down on the children's gender health. For myself, I have been accused of being in consort with the devil or the actual devil incarnate, straying from good Christian values, and even worse. My crime: advocating the gender affirmative model. So be it.

I hear about patients who have experienced a course of therapy aimed at altering their gender creative journey, leaving them feeling so much shame about the treatment and about themselves that they retreat into silence rather than speak up. I have heard about a recent situation of a young transgender child living two thirds around the world from me who was removed from her mother's care by the local social service agency, on the advice of child psychiatrists, because her mother had been bringing her up as a girl. Sometime later, after attempting to cut off her penis because of the distress of being denied who she was, she ended up in an inpatient psychiatric ward where she was put in the seclusion room if she did not behave like a boy, part of the unit's behavioral program to try and discourage any "atypical" gender behavior. A member of our international gender affirmative community, a psychiatrist, had been doing his best to intervene in this tragic situation, but with only limited success. I myself have had to pick up the pieces in my own work with a young adult who had the same thing happen several years ago, right in my own country, removed from his mother's care by the courts and forced to return to living as a boy in his father's care after the estranged father accused the mother of child abuse for her acceptance and support of their child's transgender female self. This youth was abusing drugs, expelled from his school, and in trouble with the law, exhibiting almost every one of the risk factors faced by youth who are thwarted in their gender journey. My colleague's efforts across the globe and mine right at home are emblematic of the "firefighter" work that becomes part of our daily life as gender affirmative mental health clinicians. We not only struggle to put out fires; we also take on the cleanup work of undoing the harm that has already been done and replacing it with an accepting, supportive therapeutic environment.

We mental health professionals need to expend an inordinate amount of energy on pushing back whenever we see harm being done. The perpetrator might be an ill-informed mental health professional; it could be an individual, such as Laura Ingraham (see page 10), whose lack of knowledge, surfeit of prejudice, and access to a bully pulpit tap into the media to infuse fear and hatred in people's hearts—toward the children, toward the parents, and toward the gender-affirming professionals who serve them.

OPENING THE GATES

Recently a beloved patient of mine sat in my office very distressed. I have worked with this patient, Remy, for many years. Remy was now in young adulthood and wanted to pursue surgeries to better align Remy's body and gender identity. The facility where Remy sought services has a good reputation as a gender-sensitive program. In accepting a patient for gender affirmative surgeries, the staff requests that the attending mental health provider fill out a mental health summary form and then have a phone interview with one of the mental health specialists on the facility's team. Then the patient meets with the team for an interview. I was very supportive of this young person receiving the surgeries and spoke to that effect. But in the interview at the program, my patient revealed some recent recreational activities that alarmed two members of the medical team. Remy was told to wait for six months and then be reevaluated. Distressed, Remy pleaded with the team to please contact me again before making that decision. The team agreed. I spoke with the mental health liaison for a second time, and the final outcome was that "the verdict was overturned." My patient was relieved and grateful, but also quite angry. To paraphrase, "They say they're not gatekeepers. But they *are*. And I was just trying to be honest. I should have just kept my mouth shut and told them nothing. And they didn't listen when I tried to explain. So let's just call it for what it is—*gatekeeping*."

This wasn't the first time I had pondered the question about gatekeeping myself, but my patient's tirade propelled me to think about it a lot more. We mental health professionals who practice from the gender affirmative model pride ourselves on being something other than gatekeepers. We think of ourselves as participating in a collaborative process with the youth and families we work with. But are we just fooling ourselves? Especially when it comes to gender affirming medical interventions for minors? Even though the parents have the last word in deciding whether to consent or not consent to treatment for their child, if a mental health professional recommends against any of those procedures, parents will never even get a chance to have that final word.

At the UCSF gender clinic, we, like the program my frustrated patient went to, ask for reports from attending mental health professionals. We have rejected the notion of letters of readiness, disparaged by so many in the trans community as the hoop they were forced to jump through for the price of admission into the hallowed halls of sex-reassignment surgeries. In its stead, we have asked for letters of *support*, in which the mental health professional writes a narrative answering questions along several dimensions, including present gender status and stresses, gender history, nature of the relationship with the mental health professional, family support system, general social and emotional functioning, and cultural issues that might be relevant. And we certainly request that the mental health professionals make a recommendation, if they feel they can, as to whether it would be in the youth's best interest to receive puberty blockers or hormones (which are the two main medical interventions we offer at the clinic). We invite input from the parents and child and give the parents access to the letters submitted. Some other clinics engage in more extensive and formal mental health evaluations to get a reading of a youth, assess the appropriateness of various interventions, and collect aggregate data on the children who attend their clinic. But whether we use letters of support or test batteries, I have to ask myself, "Are we just deceiving ourselves, convincing ourselves we're not the bad guys? At the end of the day, are we mental health professionals, no matter what our persuasion or what techniques we endorse, the toll takers who decide who can pass through and who can't?"

So, here are my answers to these questions, definitely a work in progress. If we were to say that whatever we write in either a letter or a more formal evaluation is the last word, then we are nothing more than toll takers or gatekeepers. But if we are willing to see our evaluations and letters as plastic rather than rigid, process rather than product, available for discussion and reflection in a collaborative process with the parents and the child, perhaps we can strike the balance between inserting our expertise and professional opinions and simultaneously leaving room for the perceptions, sensibilities, and self-knowledge of both the child and the family.

Ironically, the most difficult situation is when two parents are in conflict and one parent is actually imploring us to be a gatekeeper who says no, while the other parent is imploring us to provide a green light for going forward. For example, a mother and a father, divorced and fighting in court, were in total disagreement about the appropriate way to raise their young gender creative child, Addie, who, by my estimation, completely qualified as one of our apples. The mother, Sheridan, was advocating for full acceptance of her child's transition from female to male, because, as she saw it, that was who their child truly was. The father, Richard, accused Sheridan of unduly influencing Addie by permitting and even encouraging Addie to act like a boy (indeed, he was attending school as a boy that year). Richard endorsed a "neutral zone," not pushing or encouraging one way or another, because who knew which direction their child would end up going in? Richard didn't make up this strategy—it was recommended by the first therapist the family saw when they began seeking help for their gender-nonconforming child, which both parents agreed they had.

By my estimation the train had already left the station, and the direction was clear. When asked if he could have three wishes, what they would be, here was Addie's first: "That I could be a boy all the time." As Addie sat listening to Richard and Sheridan talk, or should I say argue, Addie kept busy drawing pictures on a sketch pad—multiple stick figures of boys. But as soon as Addie's father started talking about the neutral zone, expressing hope that Addie would understand that Addie was female because Addie was born a girl, Addie suddenly switched the subject matter of his artwork and began frantically drawing something quite different and bold—an ominous black gun, smoke pouring out of the barrel, aimed directly at his father, who was sitting next to him. After listening to Sheridan, who, I must say, looked as if she was going to leap across the room and throttle Richard, Richard turned to me and said, attempting to remain calm, but not very successfully: "So, Dr. Ehrensaft, it seems like we need to think of something that would be somewhere in the middle of where we [he and Sheridan] are."

In that moment I felt pressure from Richard to exercise my authority as a gatekeeper, asserting that Sheridan must stop letting Addie present as a boy, substituting instead a gender compromise, so to speak. I am indeed a trained mediator, taught to help divorced or divorcing parents iron out their differences and come to common agreements they can both live with. But this was not a mediation moment. My response, paraphrased, was: "Well, no, Richard. You sought me out as a gender specialist. My responsibility is not to find a middle ground but to learn about your child and determine what would be in your child's best interests to keep your child happy and healthy, which is what both you and your ex-wife have shared as being a common goal. If I did anything else, it would be like saying to two parents who disagreed about the worth of antibiotics for treating an infection that I had just diagnosed, 'Well, how about meeting in the middle and giving the antibiotics only every other day?' I would never do that, because that could harm your child. You've asked me to provide a professional opinion, and I will. You and Sheridan are definitely part of the team, and as Addie's parents, you will be the ones making the final decisions. But at the end of the day, my job is to offer my professional assessment of who your child is and what will be best practices for your child. I can do no less."

Richard had implored me to be a gatekeeper. I said no. In other situations, parents or a youth have insisted that I simply sign on the dotted line, giving them what they want. I say no. If I'm going to be part of the team, I have to have an opportunity and the necessary time it takes to bring my brain and mind (and my heart as well) to the table. I'm thinking of another situation experienced by a colleague, in which a parent hurled at the clinician, "My child says if you don't give her a vagina by the time she's nine, she's going to kill herself. So, what are you going to do?" That was an easy no. Are we gatekeepers there? No, I think we're benevolent overseers, listening to the children, allying with parents when we can, and foremost infusing our own expertise to guide these children, who are not yet old enough, mature enough, or legally able to make independent medical or legal decisions toward their gender health.

BUILDING DAMS AND SLOWING CURRENTS

Being gender creative comes with excitement. It comes with confusion. It comes with challenges. The story of the nine-year-old's insisting on a vagina—*now*—reminds me that a child's gender creativity can also come to a therapist with a sense of urgency or insistence. A book I wrote several years ago, *Spoiling Childhood*, targeted two words that seemed to have dropped out of some modern-day parents' vocabulary: *stop* and *no*. Now link that to the rubric of the gender affirmative model: Listen to the children. To give our children a chance to assert their true gender, we want them to be both seen and heard. Now link that to the fear many parents carry that if they don't listen and if they don't act immediately, their children may be at grave risk—for all those ills that come from being thwarted in affirming their gender, the worst being suicide. Parents might be culpable of inducing trauma if they miss the boat and don't get the children the medical interventions they need in a timely manner—puberty blockers to stem the flow of an unwanted puberty, hormones to bring a body in sync with an identity. Now link all that to the psychology of children and youth, for whom waiting is anathema; patience, an acquired taste; and the longest the future should be is the day after tomorrow. Add all that up and what do we get? Possibly a feeling of urgency ringing out no less shrilly than a hurricane siren. So, we mental health professionals are not only firefighters. We also build levees and dams to protect against the flood of gender angst.

Distressed parents who demand a vagina for their child by age nine to avoid her threatened suicide will need some help taking a deep breath and slowing down. Another divorced parent I was working with, Samuel, had come around to acknowledging his fourteen-year-old's legitimate pleas to be recognized as the boy he was. Samuel contacted me after one of their heart-to-heart talks. During this conversation Samuel lovingly gave his child, Ren, the green light to fully transition from female to male, which by almost all means the youth already seemed to have done anyway—except for name and pronoun change. Dad was now on board for both name and pronoun change, although he wondered with his child why he couldn't keep his present name, as it was a gender-neutral one. Ren, angry at both of his parents not just because they hadn't been listening to him but because of their acrimonious divorce, threw a curve ball—he wanted to change not only his first but also his last name, the latter to a name that would be neither his father's nor his mother's.

At that point I was meeting with Dad regularly to sort out his own feelings about his daughter who was showing him that she was his son. In his high-powered professional life, Samuel was a force to be reckoned with. Not so when it came to parenting—in every respect, he was quite wobbly on his feet. After providing me with all the information that transpired during the name-change conversation, he added, "I'm inclined to ask Ren to accept us continuing to use his last name for a while longer, but I'd love your view of it." This was a new one for me, but every day I always anticipate a new one. I gave myself a little time to think before I responded to the dad in an email: "Last name should be off limits regarding a change. Has nothing to do with gender. Issue of gender should be separated from issue of wanting to shed one's entire identity." Samuel thanked me and said, "I thought so, but I just wanted to check."

One of our assigned tasks as mental health professionals is to slow things down. We try to dredge out other issues that get tangled up with gender issues so we can concentrate on the latter without getting distracted by the former, or understand how the two are getting woven together, or explore whether the gender issues are actually symptoms of another underlying trouble having nothing to do with gender. In this youth's case, for good reason he would have an adolescent fantasy of purging himself of any identifiable ties with either of his parents. But do we want to endorse putting those fantasies into action as teens work out their separation issues with their parents? If we did, the registrars at the high schools would go out of their minds trying to track all the daily last-name changes. And would changing his last name facilitate his gender authenticity? Not so much, especially as he was about to enter a school where no one would be there from his past. But we do want to make sure that youth feel affirmed and recognized in the gender that fits them most comfortably, and if that involves changing their given name, that's where we don't put up a dam but open up the locks. In this case, even if the given name was gender neutral, for this youth it might be associated with his female self, which no longer felt like a good fit. In the English language, gender is marked not by a surname but by a given name, and here is where the mental health professional can play a hand in injecting a bit of common sense into an otherwise fraught situation.

We've all learned that living with ambiguity about gender in a world that has heretofore perceived gender as bedrock (at least in Western culture) is perhaps one of the hardest challenges both for parents and for mental health professionals, and sometimes for children and youth themselves. We speak of the gender journey but have to remind ourselves that it is a walk, not a race. A mother came to me for a parenting consultation about her five-year-old gender-exploring child. She challenged me: "If my child is going to be or is transgendered, isn't it better to know early?" She had heard about the concept of "consistent, persistent, and insistent," and also the ex post facto test, that kids calm down once allowed to transition. Unfortunately, partial information can lead to lopsided equations: The word on the street about the ex post facto benefits of early transition gets morphed into the myth that early transition is *always* better, so let's just *find out* and get things moving. One problem—there's an overriding variable: What's best for the children is to let the children unfold at their own pace, driven by their own quest rather than our need to know. So, the dam building involves helping whoever on the team can't tolerate not knowing—to slow the current of their fears and anxieties, remembering always what it feels like to move from gender as bedrock to gender as moving boulders—that it's destabilizing, if not terrifying. Such dam building is effective only if accompanied by a soothing reminder: "What we all need to do is let children unfold at their own pace, and then make space for them to live their gender as they have discovered it to be."

But now let's go back to firefighting. Sometimes the fire alarms are set off not by the actions of the transphobic world, but by an explosion erupting within a child or youth. So the real finesse for the gender affirmative mental health specialist is to recognize when to switch gears—to drop the dam-building equipment and run for the fire truck and hoses. What I'm trying to say is that mental health gender intervention sometimes requires swift and dramatic responses, particularly when a child is rapidly moving toward heavily troubled waters of distress, depression, and self-destruction. Let me give an example. I have been consulting with Tory and her parents about Tory's gender needs. Tory is just leaving grade school and has been on puberty blockers for two years. She has been living in her female identity for three years.

Tory is desperate to go on hormones so she can enter high school with an onset of puberty that will fortify her female presentation and put her in sync with her peers. If she has to go on experiencing herself or being seen as a prepubertal child of nebulous gender, she doesn't know whether she can keep going. She already has a history of self-destructive behaviors, including one suicide gesture. What is delaying getting hormones? Not her young age, but her phobic fear of needles. She has tried every form of therapy to reduce her needle phobia. Nothing has worked. Medication could—short-acting antianxiety medication to get her through the medical procedures. At first one of her parents doesn't want to do this, preferring to wait it out until she can overcome the phobia and handle the shots. After all, aren't we not supposed to rush forward? So, here is where I switch from my dam-building hard hat to my fire hat. Spending time with Tory, my reading is that overcoming her needle phobia may not happen for a very long time, if ever, maybe when hell freezes over. I hear an SOS—I think we need to act fast, and this is what I have told the parents. Unlike the nine-year-old screaming for a vagina, Tory has been crying in my office, both in anger and distress, convinced that she's doomed to be a gender freak because now she'll never be able to get hormones, ever. In general, I am not a promoter of psychotropic drugs for youth, unless absolutely essential. In Tory's case, I assessed the administration of antianxiety medications as absolutely essential, with a high risk of suicidality if we keep slowing down this youth who knows who she is, knows how she will finally feel comfortable in her own skin, and may drown behind the dam if they don't open the locks and let her move to where she needs to go. So, the lesson to be learned is: Slow down until you need to hurry.

FAST OR SLOW, DO GENDER DIAGNOSES HELP?

In 2013 the *Diagnostic and Statistical Manual of Mental Disorders* issued the newest edition of the manual. Gender identity disorder was removed as a diagnosis, replaced by gender dysphoria, in which there must be a marked difference between the individual's expressed/experienced gender and the gender others would assign to the person; in children, the desire to be of the other gender must be present and verbalized; and there must be evidence that the incongruence causes clinically significant distress or impairment. In other words, the diagnosis of gender dysphoria signifies that a child has gender concerns and is stressed out by them. The new gender diagnosis is definitely a step up from the gender identity disorder classification, the latter with its implications of pathology and enforcement of culturally dictated binary norms of gender acceptability. Yet the new diagnosis has not quieted the turbulence of an ongoing debate among mental health professionals—should there be a diagnosis at all? When it comes to the diagnosis for prepubertal children, a recent survey of WPATH members at the end of 2014 indicated that the membership was split right down the middle—half were in favor of a childhood diagnosis, half wanted it eliminated.

Those who are in favor of the diagnosis argue that it is necessary because (1) it captures a particular form of psychiatric stress that certain children experience related to their gender, particularly those who feel anguish about being delivered the wrong chromosomes and genitalia; (2) it provides access to services—without the diagnosis, children would not receive needed psychosocial interventions or be able to get insurance coverage for them; (3) it alerts parents to a condition that they had best attend to in their children; and (4) it allows us to aggregate clinical data about the children who come to us, creating a pool of children diagnosed with gender dysphoria, necessary for both research and public health purposes.

Those who are against the diagnosis argue that it should be thrown out because: (1) it continues to cast gender nonconformity as a psychiatric condition rather than a healthy variation in development, and for that reason alone should be eliminated just as homosexuality was struck down as a psychiatric diagnosis in the 1970s; (2) children suffering from the *effects* of gender nonconformity in an unaccepting world can receive relevant diagnoses, such as adjustment disorder or generalized anxiety, just as children of divorce receive just such diagnoses in light of their divorce experience, rather than a psychiatric diagnosis of childhood divorce syndrome or some such thing; (3) when homosexuality was taken off the books, gays did not stop receiving mental health supports; in fact, such services have increased since that time; (4) yes, the diagnosis may alert parents to the need for their children to get help, but couching it as a psychiatric problem may lead to just the wrong kind of help—trying to "fix" children through reparative forms of therapy; (5) insurance companies and state-run subsidies for mental health should not be dictating what is a mental disorder and what is not; rather, we should be dictating it to them, along with the demand that they provide medical gender affirmation services when needed without a mental health diagnosis but rather with a clear need for gender integration; (6) there are plenty of ways to collect data about gender-nonconforming children who are receiving mental health services without giving them a psychiatric diagnosis; and (7) the pathology lies in the culture, not the child.

My own bias: Down with the diagnosis. Why? Because gender nonconformity is not a disorder of childhood but, rather, a healthy variation of gender possibilities that may show up over the course of a child's life with good effect if social supports are in place. Difficulties, if faced at all by gender-nonconforming children, are psychosocial, rather than psychiatric, and typically come in one of two forms: (1) a discrepancy between the norms and expectations of gender within the children's social environment or culture and how these children identify and hope to express their gender; and (2) a discrepancy between the perceived sex assigned to the children on the birth certificate and the gender those children identify as being. Neither of these in itself qualifies as a disorder. Instead, we could say that gender dysphoria is a social condition, not a psychiatric one. As long as penis = male and vagina = female, we will induce gender dysphoria, particularly body dysphoria, in our gender creative children. When we can move the social order to think in terms of a penis-bodied or vagina-bodied person, the boy with the vagina and the girl with the penis will be less of a socially startling phenomenon. It is the anxiety, depression, and distress surrounding this externally induced problem that are expectable psychological responses to the social imposition of gender rigidity, both regarding bodies and roles, that should be of our concern.

Comparing the gender dysphoria diagnosis to the now-defunct *DSM* classification of homosexuality as a disorder, I have yet to encounter gay people who long for the return of homosexuality as a designated psychiatric disorder; instead, they report that they felt affirmed and liberated by its removal from the *DSM*. They still find ways to get the supportive mental health services they might want or need, as early as their childhood years, and researchers are still able to locate them for the purpose of conducting psychological studies. Regarding the present requirements of insurance companies and funding agencies to provide their organizations with diagnoses in order to get gender-related services—if we have to live with that for now to ensure our patients get the services they need, so be it, but we shouldn't leave it there. We should work to change it.

Of most concern to me are effects of a mental health gender diagnosis on the child. The obvious one is the stigmatization of the child. As with gay individuals, I have yet to meet a child or youth who embraces a diagnosis of gender dysphoria as a healthy attribution of self—maybe a ticket to care, but not a proud self-label.

Receiving this diagnosis is especially risky in the context of social environments that are hostile to or condemning of both children and adults who do not conform to the culture's gender norms. For example, one public school refused admission to a transgender child because that child had a diagnosis of gender identity disorder (pre–*DSM V*), which qualified as an emotional disturbance for which the staff claimed their school could not provide adequate services. Beyond stigmatizing children in the outside world, bad effects of mental health labeling can also show up in the inside world. For a child, the gender dysphoria diagnosis runs the risk of leading the child to think that "there must be something wrong with me," when there is no scientific evidence that there is, perhaps even causing the child to repress, suppress, or go into secrecy about gender desires and feelings, lest they be seen as "sick." And then there is the danger that the parents will take the diagnosis and run with it—in the wrong direction, indeed believing that their child is sick and needs to be cured or brought back in line with culturally acceptable gender behaviors and presentations. After all, their child has just received a psychiatric diagnosis. The same danger goes for mental health professionals of a certain type, who might take the diagnosis of gender dysphoria as a green light to proceed with therapeutic interventions that attempt to realign a child's gender identity or expressions with gender conformity so as to rid the child of the "disorder." So, the diagnosis runs the risk of imposing unneeded or harmful health services when, with the provision of family and social supports, a child may have needed none.

I would liken the risks of the childhood gender dysphoria diagnosis to the situation for left-handed people. Historically and in certain cultures today, left-handedness is perceived as deviant, disordered, or even sinister. A child observed to prefer the left hand in such cultures is "counseled" away from using that hand and steered toward the right hand, with the goal of eradicating the left-handedness and avoiding social stigma or even punishment. The treatments have proved to be successful at the surface—the child uses the right hand; however, the underlying "condition" of left-handedness remains intact; it is simply suppressed, with subsequent risks for stuttering, learning problems, anxiety, or other psychological difficulties. In cultures in which left-handedness is accepted as a normal variation of handedness, albeit appearing in only a small minority of the population (approximately 10 percent worldwide), the children are left alone to embrace their left-handedness, show no such psychological stresses, and are even reputed to be overrepresented in the highest echelons of the arts and sciences. Isn't that just like the varying experience of gender-nonconforming children, depending on whether they find their place in an unaccepting social environment that perceives them as ill versus an accepting social environment that perceives them as healthy?

One last thing about gender diagnoses. Increasingly, I have come to see gender as cure rather than disease. It came to me the day after I saw our little patient at the clinic who was both autistic and gender nonconforming and who then returned to the clinic, nine months after being put on puberty blockers and allowed to do a social transition, seemingly remarkably cured of his autistic symptoms. Then I began to think about all the ex post facto tests— if we got it right about a child's authentic gender and allowed the child to live in that gender, previous psychological symptoms dissipated, if not disappeared altogether. So, how about thinking of gender, or more precisely, gender affirmation, as the cure, rather than the problem? I leave you with that to ponder, and simply alert you to be mindful about the effects, both good and bad, of a gender diagnosis.

PSYCHIATRIC HELP 5 CENTS—THE DOCTOR IS IN

Why would a family of a gender creative child seek us out for help? Put another way, what good are we mental health professionals to families? I have said before that for the most part I like to meet with parents and do what I call "behind the scenes" work, in this case working with parents and other caregivers or family members to think about their children's gender web and create a space and put in place supports so their children can freely traverse all the paths along their gender journey. Sometimes children need a room of their own to sort out their conundrums. Sometimes their siblings do, too. Sometimes the children need a forum with their whole family present. There's space for that, too.

I am happy to say that "blame the parents" is dying out. "Support parents in supporting the child" is on the upswing. A new form of gender policing is in—instead of policing the children, we are beginning to police the mental health professionals who are doing harm to our gender-nonconforming children and youth. I'm all for that, but my best hope is that we can reeducate rather than subjugate the offending parties, so they can begin to do some good.

Parents and caregivers: If we give you a chance to bring all your feelings about your children's gender to us, the good, the bad, and the ugly, keep us. If we give your children a chance to say who they are, rather than dictate who they must be, keep us. If we pay attention to your whole family, keep us. If we use our expertise wisely, never withholding, never imposing, keep us. If we recognize you as an expert and work as a team in mapping out a gender support plan, keep us. If we are willing to leave our offices and advocate for gender rights, keep us. If we fail to deliver on any of those things, let us go.

Chapter Seven

Do We Want a Doctor in the House?

*I will remember that there is art to medicine as well
as science . . . , and that warmth, sympathy, and
understanding may outweigh the surgeon's knife
or the chemist's drug. . . . I will not be ashamed to
say "I know not." . . . I will respect the privacy of my
patients. . . . Above all, I must not play at God. . . .
I will remember that I remain a member of society,
with special obligations to all my fellow human
beings. . . . If I do not violate this oath, may I enjoy
life and art, respected while I live and remembered
with affection thereafter.*

—Excerpts from a modern version of the Hippocratic
oath written by Louis Lasagna, dean of the School of
Medicine at Tufts University (1964)

IF YOU ARE a parent of a gender-nonconforming child, you will
benefit from the care of a medical doctor who holds paramount
the oath taken by all health professionals—above all, "Do no
harm." Until recently, we saw no need to go to the doctor to learn
how to deal with our children's gender. The lessons were simply
passed on from generation to generation, to be either accepted
or rejected by the next. There were basically three gender issues
that called for a doctor in the house: If there was some question
about our children's genitalia—they were ambiguous or confusing; if our children didn't seem to be going through puberty like all
the other youth of the same gender—either too early or too late;

if our children weren't doing gender "right" or were saying such things as "I'm not a boy, I'm a girl" or "I'm not a girl, I'm a boy" when everyone knew that was obviously not true. The point person was typically the family doctor or pediatrician who sounded the alarms, possibly preceded by the ob-gyn specialist who may have detected a problem of ambiguous genitalia at the baby's birth. From there, other specialists may have been brought in to fix the problem, including a surgeon, a pediatric endocrinologist, and a psychiatrist: one to fix the genitalia so they were either male or female, one to study genetic and hormone anomalies to see if they could be fixed, one to help children accept the gender that they were expected to be.

I grew up during that era and ended up having the most familiarity with the doctors in the last category—psychiatric gender fixers. When I was going through my graduate school training as a developmental psychologist beginning in the late 1960s, with gender development as my main field of study, Dr. Robert Stoller was considered one of the top experts in the field. I continued to keep up in the field after leaving graduate school, and here is what I learned as late as 1985 from Dr. Stoller:

> I have presented a hypothesis that I believe is being confirmed plus a guess that is beyond confirmation . . . a mother who tries to create a limitless and unending blissful merging between herself and her yearned-for beautiful son will put him at great risk for becoming feminine if his father does not interrupt the process. The guess is that this malignant process is . . . the result of a developmental arrest that prevented the otherwise expected unfolding of masculinity.[64]

The implication was that this little boy needed to be treated for his gender malignancy and the parents needed guidance to undo their toxic influences on their child. That is not the kind of doctor I would want to send anyone to today, although sadly, such doctors are still in practice in the twenty-first century.

The world I grew up in is changing dramatically. Today, in the United States, we recognize that intersex children have a right to the bodies they were born with, that children can assert a gender that does not conform with the sex marker on their birth certificate with no question about their sanity, and that parents create not malignancy but positive growth in their nurturing interactions with their gender-nonconforming children. So, why would we need a doctor in the house? Well, to track our children's gender development over time (that would be the family doctor or pediatrician who might follow our children from birth to maturity), to track our children's puberty development (that would be the family doctor, pediatrician, or the pediatric endocrinologist), to administer puberty blockers and hormones where appropriate (that would be the pediatric endocrinologist or pediatric gender specialist), to provide surgical interventions where appropriate (that would be the surgeon trained to do gender affirmative surgeries).

PEDIATRIC POINT PERSON

Like mental health professionals, your pediatrician or primary care provider can offer either the best of times or the worst of times when it comes to the care of a gender-nonconforming child. For the medical doctor, training about gender will typically fall within old-school models, if there is any training at all. And not uncommonly, whether well- or ill-trained, the child's primary care provider may be the first person who hears from parents of a very young child, "There's something about my child's gender that I've been noticing." And for the parents of the gender-nonconforming child, their child's pediatrician may be their only point person in the helping professions. The communication "There's something about my child's gender that I've been noticing" can be spoken in a tone of pure curiosity; it can also come with a cry of utter panic. It may be a spontaneous offering from the parents or, more rarely, follow a query from the doctor's general protocol that includes questions about gender development. Alternatively, without such a standard protocol, the doctor may notice something that seems "different" about the child and be the one to bring it up to the parent. However it enters the room, the manner in which the doctor responds can have profound effects on the unfolding of the child and family's gender journey, either opening up smooth pavement or heading the family toward the bumpiest of roads.

I have had the good fortune of working with the most wonderful of pediatricians who will make every effort to ensure that their gender-nonconforming and transgender young patients get the care and attention they need to grow up healthy. I would encourage the parents of any gender-nonconforming child to search high and low for just such a doctor, which sometimes means having to leave the pediatrician who has up until then served all the children in the family. But in some communities there are no such gender affirmative doctors, and in other situations, a family does not have much choice in its doctor or may not even consistently have the same doctor from one visit to another. In those cases, as if parents did not already have enough work, yet another task for gender creative parents is the guidance of their child's medical provider in the direction of gender-sensitive care.

When that is the case, there are three simple sentences to watch out for: "It's just a phase," "Let me give you a referral to a psychiatrist," and "I don't know anything about this." Let's start with "It's just a phase." Embedded in this communication is the subtext "Don't worry," because in child development and pediatrics, phases are typically childhood phenomena that we count on children's outgrowing—such as terrible twos or adolescent rebellion. And buried in that subtext is yet another subliminal message—that gender nonconformity is not something we celebrate, but something we hope shall pass. Indeed, sometimes gender nonconformity is a phase along the child's gender journey as they spin their gender web, a way of being that may look very different in its future iterations. But most commonly a child's gender nonconformity is not a status that they outgrow. Saying "It's just a phase" gives false hope to parents who are not yet at the place where they can accept and celebrate their child's gender creativity but, rather, hope it will just go away. So, in one fell swoop, "It's just a phase" is one of those microaggressions against the smallest members of a minority group and simultaneously a child development inaccuracy. Therefore, beware of pediatricians who bear such gifts, and invite them to dispense with this assessment, replacing it with an open curiosity about what the child is showing people about their gender, both now and in the past.

As for "Let me refer you to a child psychiatrist," I do not think much needs to be said about the doctor who immediately jumps to the conclusion that a gender identity disorder has just walked through the door, one that needs to be fixed ASAP. In those situations, if at all possible, changing doctors would be the best course of action. Yet that doctor may be a good fit in every other way and may be following another of your child's medical needs as an expert in that area. In that case, or in the case of the doctor who is assigned and for whom a parent has limited choice, inviting the pediatrician to read literature that offers a different perspective on gender nonconformity, such as publications written for medical professionals by our interdisciplinary team at the UCSF Benioff Children's Hospital Child and Adolescent Center clinic,[65] can actually lead to enlightenment and change. Recall the Hippocratic oath. All we ask in those situations is that medical providers abide by the oath by reeducating themselves or perhaps for the first time exposing themselves to education and training about gender. This is where we, professionals who do trainings, come in— sometimes I think of us as ghost busters and itinerant teachers all in one: moving across the country from institution to institution to rid the buildings of gender ghosts and replace them with gender angels, by providing coherent and cogent trainings on the gender affirmative model and its application to pediatric practice.

We also write about gender from a pediatric perspective. Here is a sample of a written invitation to pediatricians to implement a gender affirmative pediatric practice:

> The first step is to examine our own feelings, attitudes, and beliefs about gender and consider how these affect our work with youth. Equally important is educating ourselves on the diversity of gender in our patients and the corresponding interventions available for supporting them. Adopting supportive, affirming practices, such as intake forms that allow for the patient's preferred name and pronouns (and using them accordingly), is another critically important step for helping young persons feel comfortable.[66]

Some of these tasks are easy, others are easier said than done, but all are achievable in the context of a supportive and informed teaching environment and a commitment by pediatric professionals to ensure a gender affirmative experience for their young patients and their families.

Now we come to the last of the three sentences, "I don't know anything about this." I would say, "See above," but I also want to add that it is far better to admit ignorance than to operate with conviction informed by misconceptions and biased attitudes. As long as a provider is willing to move from not knowing to knowing, there is hope for gender-sensitive care. And as long as there are interdisciplinary teams of trainers providing the education, there is a good chance that there will be a growing cadre of such sensitive providers. But if the statement "I don't know anything about this" is really a euphemism for "I think it would be better for you to go elsewhere," I'd take the provider up on that offer and find a new doctor for your child. I have found that the role of primary providers has been invaluable in the ongoing supportive care of the gender-nonconforming children and youth I have worked with. I know I could not do the work without them, so it's best that they be the right ones.

The last thing I want to say about gender affirmative care and pediatricians (and I should say all medical doctors) is that most medical doctors have been trained in a model in which practice is informed by data and results, in the form of research studies, be they clinical or in a lab. Providers are often hesitant to proceed until the studies have come in validating a particular form of intervention and its outcomes. I, too, have been raised in a profession that turns to such studies to inform our practices, and I honor that tradition. But I am also a clinical psychologist who honors a different way of knowing—and that is the knowing that comes from spending day after day with children and youth who are going against the gender grain. We are scrambling to get the studies of our gender affirmative interventions under way so that we can document whether our model indeed works, but in the meantime, we already know just by watching. And we also know that the studies about gender-nonconforming children that exist to date have many flaws and need to be reanalyzed with a critical eye. So, I would invite pediatricians to pay attention not just to the reports in the medical journals, but also to the lived experience of the children and families and the clinicians working with those children, to get a full picture of the lives of gender-nonconforming and transgender children.

At some point, there may come a time when the pediatrician will want to make a referral, and that would be to the pediatric endocrinologist or trained gender specialist who is in the business of providing medical interventions to gender-nonconforming and transgender youth, in the form of puberty blockers and hormones. So, let's wander over to their offices now.

MEDICAL 101

One of the challenges we mental health providers have encountered is our new involvement in medical practices and decision making. Gender is no longer just a psychological phenomenon.

For gender-nonconforming youth arriving at puberty, it is a state of being that may be enhanced by medical interventions. And we mental health providers are now asked to weigh in on these medical interventions, through assessments of a child's gender status and observations of their readiness to receive either puberty blockers or hormones, and then later, gender affirmative surgeries. Since the publication of *Gender Born, Gender Made*, I have studied hard to hone my medical knowledge, as basic as it might be. As the attending psychologist at the Child and Adolescent Gender Center clinic at UCSF Benioff Children's Hospital Department of Pediatrics, I have had the opportunity to have a close-up look at the youth and their parents as they contemplate the youth taking puberty blockers and/or hormones. Let me start with what I've learned about puberty blockers.

PUBERTY BLOCKERS: THE PAUSE BUTTON THAT GIVES US PAUSE

I am now adept at explaining to parents and youth that puberty blockers, also known as GnRH inhibitors (full name: gonadotropin-releasing hormone inhibitors), coming in the form of either agonists or antagonists, are a substance that, if released in the brain, will decrease the gonadal secretions that set off the beginning of puberty and all the sex-related body changes that go with that. A child can receive puberty blockers in the form of either injections throughout the year or a yearly implant just under the skin, a procedure that can happen in the doctor's office with a local anesthesia. The best time to maximize the effects of puberty blockers is in Tanner stage II of puberty, when children show the first signs of pubertal development. They are not administered before a child enters puberty. The procedure is fully reversible. If the child chooses to discontinue the blockers, the puberty that had begun to take its course will proceed forward within a short time period (within six months). To get puberty blockers, as one of my patients explained to me, "You have to go to the blocker doctor." That would be the pediatric endocrinologist, particularly one who is trained in gender care. If there is no such person in a family's community, it may be necessary to travel a distance to work with a specialist or else to locate a pediatrician or family doctor in the community who is willing and able to administer the blockers. The functions of puberty blockers are twofold: (1) to staunch the flow of an unwanted puberty that at its most extreme could prove traumatic to the child (it should be noted that suicidal feelings and thoughts often spike at the onset of puberty for youth who are troubled, if not horrified, by the onset of pubertal body changes that don't fit who they know themselves to be); and (2) to buy the youth some more time to explore their gender if their true gender self is still not in focus.

In the United States, the two main problems with puberty blockers is that they can be exorbitantly expensive and, as of this writing, are not yet FDA-approved for puberty suppression related to gender. And some children hate shots—to the extreme. I don't know how many times a patient of mine has asked, hopefully, "Did they discover a pill yet?" Leaving needle phobias aside, what we know is that puberty blockers have been used successfully for precocious puberty for nearly forty years with no ill effects. The only caveat there is that we do not know whether stopping a precocious puberty that came too early is exactly parallel to stopping puberty in children who were going forward at a normal rate in their pubertal development. We will have to wait for future studies to answer that question, but what we do have as reassuring evidence is that since the 1990s puberty blockers have been administered to hundreds of youth in the Netherlands, youth who have been studied over time into adulthood. No untoward effects have been identified. There has been some concern that the puberty blockers interfere with healthy bone development, particularly bone mineral density. However, studies to date indicate that bone density does not change or simply remains at its prepubertal rate of change during the course of puberty blockers, and once adult hormones are introduced in the form of either cross-sex hormones/hormone replacement therapy or the child's natal hormones, the bone mineral density picks up again to normal levels. There has been some concern expressed, by both professionals and parents, that puberty blockers might interfere with forward brain development in early adolescent youth, either temporarily or permanently. To date, we have no evidence to indicate that this is the case, so we can only state that every effort is being made to engage in research to determine whether any effects exist. What we do know is that a twenty-two-year follow-up of a youth treated at the Amsterdam clinic with puberty blockers followed by hormones showed perfectly fine brain functioning.[67]

For both puberty blockers and hormones, the gender affirmative mode of practice is moving away from ages to stages as the guideline for when to introduce either blockers or later hormones. With puberty blockers, that's a simple procedure: When the child arrives at Tanner stage II of puberty, that is the time to start, whether the child is ten years old or fifteen. The real problem for the children who start on the early side is the length of years they might be staying on puberty blockers before the time when it would be appropriate to start hormones, if that seems like the treatment of choice. To date, we do not have any documentation of harm being done to the body by staying on puberty blockers for an extended time, but, erring on the cautious side, it remains a concern.

CROSS-SEX HORMONES/HORMONE REPLACEMENT THERAPY: YOU CAN'T GO BACK, AT LEAST NOT ALL THE WAY

Cross-sex hormones/hormone replacement therapy allow youth to bring their bodies more in line with their affirmed gender. We often think of them in binary terms—through the hormonal effects on the body, we can take a natal female and, with testosterone, affirm the boy; we can take the natal male and, with estrogen, affirm the girl. More recently, genderqueer youth have seen the myriad other possibilities—for example, a touch of testosterone, but not too much. Through their demands and requests, these youth push for us to open our horizons to understand medical interventions not just to achieve gender reversal, but also to afford the opportunity for gender in the middle or in unique iterations.

We do know that there are long-term medical risks to estrogen and testosterone treatments, albeit small, but we also know that cross-sex hormones/hormone replacement therapy have saved the lives of many youth and adults, transforming suicidal ideation into glorious dreams of a gender affirmative future.

For an affirmed male, taking testosterone will result in "masculinization" of his body, including a more buff body (increased lean muscle mass), fewer layers of fat, and facial and body hair, all of which are reversible effects if the youth should decide to discontinue the hormones. If an affirmed male goes straight from puberty blockers to testosterone and started taking puberty blockers before the closure of growth plates, there is a chance he will grow to a normal male height (this is a big, if not a tremendous plus for many young transgender men, who might otherwise always be the shortest guy—another sometimes unwanted visible tag of being a trans rather than a cismale). If a transgender boy has already developed breast tissue, the testosterone may cause some atrophy of the tissue but not make it disappear completely. Some of the effects of testosterone, however, are irreversible, and this is what gives many parents pause when it comes to signing off on this intervention for a child who is still a minor. These include the deepening of the voice and the enlargement of the clitoris. The biggest price tag for many transgender youth who go on testosterone is acne, sometimes fairly acute. But this is only temporary and goes away, just as acne shows up and then dissipates or disappears in cisgender youth as they move through adolescence. The biggest primary health concern is later development of polycystic ovarian syndrome, and this, among other things, is why many transgender young men are eager to remove their ovaries (and usually their uterus) as part of their care.

What about transgender girls and hormones? They will be taking estrogen. If they had been taking puberty blockers, they can continue to do so, to keep their testosterone levels low, making room for the estrogen to have its full effect. If they never took puberty blockers or cannot afford them, they can also take another drug to suppress testosterone, most commonly spironolactone, used in combination with the estrogen. Once on estrogen, a transgender girl will notice decreased facial and body hair, if she ever had it, a redistribution of her fat creating a more "feminine" presentation, a decrease in spontaneous erections, and softer skin, all of which are reversible to some extent. Estrogen can also make breasts grow and might have the effect of closing the growth plate and reducing the possibility of a "too tall" woman (the complementary angst to the short boy syndrome in transgender males). These two changes are irreversible. Unfortunately, estrogen cannot whisk away some male features if they were already there. Body hair and facial hair will not disappear completely, and a low voice will stay low, leading many transgender young women, either on hormones or not, to seek out electrolysis or laser hair removal along with voice therapy or vocal cord surgery.

All of these interventions should be monitored carefully and consistently by a trained medical professional. Blockers, hormone suppressants, estrogen, and testosterone are all prescription drugs and should be respected as such. Many youth seek out hormones on the street or on the Internet, because of either necessity or desire and no other access. We do not want to deny them the hormones they so sorely need, but we do want to make sure they can get the same quality of medical care that is the right of every youth, which means, of course, that we have a lot of work ahead of us to make sure this happens.

One thing needs to be highlighted if a youth has chosen a course of puberty blockers beginning at Tanner stage II, followed directly by cross-sex hormones/hormone replacement therapy: the implications for fertility. At this moment in history, those youth will not produce mature eggs or sperm of their own, meaning they will forgo the possibility of conceiving a genetically related child. These are important considerations that need to be shared with both parents and the youth, which is tricky business. In our culture, youth of that age have typically not reached the stage of family building, making it challenging for them to project into the future as to whether conceiving or bearing their own children or having children at all will be critical to them or not, and parents in these situations are catapulted into the position of signing off on their child's medically induced infertility. On the other hand, if a youth has already gone through the puberty of their natal sex before starting a course of hormone therapy, they can choose, before starting their course of hormones, to preserve the gametes they already have, with egg extraction and freezing for the XX youth, and ejaculation and sperm collection and freezing for the XY youth. Gamete preservation will afford them the opportunity to use those gametes in the future if they desire genetically related children, albeit through assisted reproductive technology techniques. Egg extraction is a more complicated and invasive procedure than sperm collection, placing an added medical burden on transgender male youth. On the other hand, many transgender females have reported to me how awkward it is to go to a fertility clinic or medical office and ejaculate into a bottle on their way to becoming girls, especially if their sexuality has been put on hold as they consolidate their gender, putting on them an added *psychological* burden.

SURGERIES: NO GOING BACK

Surgeries are the most permanent of gender affirming medical interventions, which is why so many people are nervous about performing them on youth before they've reached the age of majority. In fact, a prominent hospital in the San Francisco Bay Area recently put a stop to just such surgeries, questioning the ethics of these procedures for minors, but also concerned about the perceived liabilities for their institution, leaving a whole group of youth and their doctors temporarily medically homeless as they searched for other hospitals to take them in, which fortunately did happen.

Since completing *Gender Born, Gender Made*, I have seen an increasing number of youth who are requesting and being granted surgeries over the course of their adolescence, before the age of eighteen. As children are socially transitioning at younger and younger ages, by the time they reach adolescence they have already been waiting for years to benefit from the medical interventions that will align their bodies with their affirmed gender self. Although the WPATH standards of care set sixteen years as the minimum age for such interventions, common practice has led to the amendment of those guidelines in accordance with the stage, rather than age, measure of readiness. The most common form of surgery is chest surgery for transgender males or for some genderqueer youth, followed by hysterectomy (partial or radical), and genital surgeries. Later might also come tracheal shaves, vocal cord surgeries, and facial adjustments. Some youth also request electrolysis or laser removal of gender-discordant body hair. These are definitively irreversible interventions, and, except for electrolysis or laser removal of body hair, performing these procedures on minors can really make people nervous, because there's no turning back, and the majority of the surgeries target the most fundamental body icons of the gender binary—genitals, breasts, and internal reproductive organs. However, this angst may be soothed by the realization of the increased sense of well-being and mind-body harmony in a youth who is given the opportunity to affirm their gender through their body.

If a child has started puberty blockers by Tanner stage II of puberty and then proceeded directly to hormones, some of these gender affirming surgeries can be avoided. A transgender male in those circumstances will never grow breasts. A transgender female will never grow an Adam's apple or have facial and chest and back hair. Genitals, on the other hand, are another story. A clitoris may enlarge and count as a micropenis in a transgender male on testosterone, but it won't be a fully functioning penis. A functioning penis or vagina will come only with surgical intervention. More and more youth are requesting such surgeries, while others are happy with staying with the apparatus they have, challenging the notion that penis = boy and vagina = girl.[68]

On June 17, 2015, an article appeared on the front page of *The New York Times*, NEW GIRL IN SCHOOL: TRANSGENDER SURGERY AT 18. The subhead: "A Debate over How Young Is Too Young."[69] The story features Katherine Boone, an eighteen-year-old transgender high school student who completed vaginoplasty surgery in April of her senior year. The surgery was not without medical complications, but Katherine, who likes to be called Kat, also had a gender history not without complications, including self-harm and suicidal thoughts, due to gender distress. At age eighteen, Kat reported that even with the postsurgery complications, she had no regrets and looked forward to entering college fully affirmed in her female identity, with a vagina in place. Yet the article also expresses the doubts of both professionals and the general public—teenagers are in flux, so how could one know this is a stable identity? If so many young children are desisters, how could we know whether a youth who is requesting surgery will end up being one of those desisters? Dr. Paul McHugh, professor of psychiatry at Johns Hopkins Medical School and former psychiatrist in chief of the hospital there, looks askance at the use of surgeries to treat a "psychological" condition, both for adults and especially with children. To quote him directly, referring to the coming out of Caitlyn Jenner, formerly Bruce Jenner, the Olympic champion:

> Bruce Jenner—who cares? He's a wonderfully successful person. He's got all kinds of social networks. He's got plenty of money. No one's objecting to him if he wants to live as a

woman. This is America, be my guest. But we are talking about children with a future ahead of them.[70]

Actually, we are talking about children who may not have a future ahead of them, given the rate of suicidality among transgender people who do not receive supports and acceptance, including the ability to access medical interventions now available to bring their bodies in sync with their psyches. And we are talking about a situation that is not just psychological, but biological as well.[71] Dr. McHugh played a part in closing down the transgender surgery program at John Hopkins in the 1980s. I'm imagining he sees this as an accomplishment in his career. One wonders what has happened to all those transgender individuals who found the doors to potential gender affirmative surgeries closed to them.

There is no doubt that surgeries, which are irreversible and involve moderate to extensive medical interventions and aftercare, are to be done only with careful forethought and collaboration to determine whether any one of the surgeries would be in a youth's best interests. We have already established that one indeed can differentiate the persisters from the desisters, and that a clearly identified transgender identity that is present from puberty and beyond is typically a stable one, into adulthood. The reactive sentiment that youth are just too young to make such irreversible life-changing decisions, in terms of both their gender status and their maturity, leads us into the psychological manifestations of the new medical interventions, to which I would like to turn now.

PSYCHOLOGY 202

Let's start with puberty blockers, and the story of a youth who has been on them. Tex, now age fourteen, started puberty blockers when he was ten. At that time, Tex was still Tess, a girl who was going on puberty blockers to buy more time to explore her gender while heading full-on into puberty. By age eleven, Tess had finished her exploring—she was clear that she was male and requested a full social transition, changing her name to Tex and her pronouns to *he*, *him*, and *his*. Tex presented as a handsome young boy at the new middle school he entered that fall. But by the end of middle school, all his male friends had voices that were cracking, faces that were showing the early signs of acne, and peach fuzz tickling their top lips. By freshman year of high school, some of his friends were full-out shaving. The endocrinologist treating Tex had a policy that no one under the age of sixteen could receive cross-sex hormones, and even that seemed a bit too young to the doctor. This left Tex in a suspended prepubertal state, out of sync with his same-age peers, and anxious that this suspension would flag him as the transgender boy he was, which he had chosen to keep private.

All right, Tex was simply put in a position no different than any other youth who starts puberty at a late age, known in medical terms as delayed puberty, defined as anyone who has not shown signs of puberty by age thirteen. Let me pause for a moment to give a personal account. I was what my mother called "a late bloomer." I did not show even the first signs of puberty until age fourteen. By the time I reached high school I was an "A" kind of girl—A's in my grades and AAA in my bra size, and even that was filled with some padding. I did not get my period until I was approaching fifteen. While all the other girls were filling out bodily and getting excused from gym class because of menstrual cramps, I still looked like a ten-year-old string bean. And I never had a good excuse to get out of gym. I wondered whether someone, maybe God, had forgotten to give me a uterus and ovaries. I wondered whether maybe I really wasn't female—after all, I was good in math and sports, and wasn't that supposed to be the domain of boys and men? Ergo—maybe I was actually male. At a time when Marilyn Monroe was the icon of beauty and Audrey Hepburn had not yet made her debut in *Breakfast at Tiffany's* as the elegant, skinny girl, this was no easy journey for me. As with many of the strains of adolescence, this, too, did pass. My period came, I stopped being the shortest girl in class, I got some shape, I dropped my doubts about my sex and gender, and life went on.

Nobody and no medical intervention had put a stop to my puberty; its natural onset was just a long time in coming. And finally it did, but not without leaving traces of that discomfort and painful knowledge that I was out of sync with all my peers. I can still feel it today. As hard as it was for me to be a flat-chested skinny girl who looked ten when everyone else my age looked sixteen, I can only imagine, and indeed have witnessed, how much harder it is for a teen who is artificially suspended in a state of prolonged prepuberty precisely because they are indeed not the gender inscribed on their birth certificate. They wait because the doctors or their parents either prohibit or express hesitancy about their taking the next step, which would be hormones to align their bodies with their affirmed gender identity. They are asked to be patient and to keep waiting for the puberty that will not only affirm their true gender but also protect them from being the one kid who stands out in the crowd. Propelled by my late puberty, the ensuing angst about my gender left some psychological stains, but that only pales in comparison to worrying that your gender is being withheld from you. Conclusion: It behooves us not to leave a transgender teen in a suspended prepubertal state, watching all their peers pass them by into their adolescent bodies with all the secondary sex characteristics (breasts or beards, and so forth) accompanying that, if we can avoid it. Waiting until age sixteen makes no sense if a youth shows up firm about their gender, typically already having lived in it for several years, and simply ready to take the next step in consolidating their stable adolescent gender identity. And yet setting an arbitrary minimum age for estrogen or testosterone treatment, which is the prerogative of any practitioner in the United States, is standard practice among many medical professionals and clinics. Why would we want to withhold hormones if a teen is clear about their gender identity and anxious to get to do what all their peers are doing or already have done—to go through the pubertal physical manifestations that establish to themselves and to all around them the gender they know themselves to be, whether that be cis or trans? If hormones could help transgender teens do that, it seems cruel to withhold them due to an age requirement rather than a more flexible stage readiness, which might be as young as age twelve or thirteen. Setting an arbitrary minimum age for hormones, without considering it case by case, is one of those situations where doing nothing is actually doing something: in this instance, putting youth at risk for undue psychological stress and social tension.

To make that point, I'm thinking of another transgender youth I was working with, Omar. Omar had been on puberty blockers since he was eleven years old, the age at which he fully transitioned from female to male. Now he was attending a high school not known for its gender sensitivity. One day Omar came into my office and began sobbing as soon as I closed the door: "I can't stand walking around my high school looking like an eleven-year-old boy. I'm a freak." Not only was it exquisitely painful, as it had been for me looking like a ten-year-old girl in high school and for Tex feeling forced into a suspended Peter Pan state, but it flagged Omar as different. He might as well wear a target on his back—a horrifying thought, given that he was not disclosing at his new not-so-friendly high school that he was a natal female. His prolonged prepubertal state stood a good chance of outing him, made much worse because Omar was a very shy, introverted guy. There was a solution for him—he could start testosterone and catch up with his peers. But only if the doctors would give him the medicine. His parents had a limited income and didn't have a lot of choice in the doctors available to them, due to their stringent insurance plan. The first doctor they found met with Omar and told him, "Sorry. You have to wait until you're eighteen. That's the way it works. You're too young now." Given what the doctor said, Omar thought that was the rule he had to live with. Through his sobs, Omar was able to tell me that he didn't think he could make it that long, living in a frozen state looking like an eleven-year-old boy. He might not even want to live any more.

I first listened to Omar with great concern (keeping to myself my frustration with the endocrinologist he had seen) and told him not to worry: I would help him and his parents find another doctor who would be able to see him, one who wouldn't make him wait until he was eighteen. I assured him that waiting until eighteen was just this particular doctor's practice, one that made no sense to me. I was appalled that the doctor Omar had first seen hadn't done his math to calculate that asking him to wait until age eighteen meant that Omar would be suspended in a prepubertal state for seven years after reaching the natural age of puberty, with a prolonged use of puberty blockers that conceivably could affect his health, and certainly his psyche. He would graduate from high school looking like a child prodigy, which was not one of Omar's aspirations. Or, in desperation, he might not even make it to graduation, were he to follow through on ending his life to put an end to the misery.

With a transfer to a gender affirmative endocrinologist, Omar finally got his hormones at age fifteen, so we could say that all's well that ends well. In Omar's case, this was not without some scarring along the way. Omar had been catapulted unnecessarily into a state of gender distress after the first doctor informed him that he would have no choice but to wait until he left high school to enter puberty. Withholding testosterone, the next step in his gender journey, had he taken that advice, would have been nothing short of harmful practice. Perhaps if all pediatric endocrinologists went through either a prolonged prepuberty or a delayed puberty themselves, as Tex, Omar, and I did, because of either natural or medically induced causes, they would be more sympathetic to the problem and more willing to substitute stages for ages in their standards of care for transgender youth.

The use of puberty blockers and then hormones to allow youth to further explore and/or consolidate their affirmed gender identity has been nothing less than manna falling from the sky when we consider the possibilities for enhancing gender health among our adolescent gender creative children. At the same time, these interventions are not always magic bullets (a drug or treatment that cures a disease quickly and easily without producing bad effects). Following the Boy Scouts' motto "Be prepared," I think it is helpful to know in advance some of the shadow sides that may follow in the wake of the interventions, especially after a teen starts a course of hormones. It begins with a story of hope—"If I've just started puberty blockers, I might just have put a stop to an unwanted puberty that doesn't match my gender identity and could range from somewhere between horrific and traumatic if it were to occur. If it's hormones we're talking about, either I've successfully dodged an unwanted puberty or I didn't, but now I'm going to be getting hormones that will provide me some body features that will validate and solidify my gender identity. If I'm an affirmed female, I'll grow breasts, my skin will soften, my hips will spread, my muscles won't bulge, I won't have to worry about unwelcomed and embarrassing erections. If I'm an affirmed male, my voice will deepen, body hair will grow (I just hope I don't go bald later), my hips will be slim, my muscles will get bigger. If I already grew breasts, they might shrink in size. If I already started menstruating, I won't have to worry about that anymore. And so forth." And yet . . .

Nicco is thirteen. His assigned sex at birth: female. By age seven he knew he didn't feel like other girls; by age twelve he figured out that was because he was a boy. Nicco continued to present himself as a girl at school, but this was becoming increasingly stressful to him, as it just didn't feel right. So, in his eighth grade year, he decided to transition from female to male. His parents were okay with this but wanted him to wait until he went through puberty before considering any medical interventions, as they wanted him to keep the option open of having genetically related children through egg preservation once he started menstruating. At first, Nicco was in agreement with this, carrying the intergenerational weight of a history of genocide in his family's country of origin, in which many family members had perished, and thus recognizing how important regenerating their family lines was for both of his parents, and for himself as well. But then something exploded inside him. As he watched his breast buds begin to grow, he panicked, to the point that he felt like killing himself, which he revealed to his parents. They definitely took notice, as they certainly did not want to lose yet another beloved family member. In consultation with their therapist (that would be me), Nicco and his parents recognized that asking Nicco to wait until he had gone through puberty was causing Nicco great distress and was not at all what he wanted. So, Nicco's parents took him to see a pediatric endocrinologist, who started him on a course of puberty blockers, just in time, because he was just at the end of Tanner stage II of puberty. Initially, Nicco was ecstatic and came out to his peers in a moving community event at his school. His friends all hugged and held him, and he was flying high on the newly felt euphoria that was enveloping him. The clouds had lifted and the sun was shining brightly.

But the euphoria soon wore off and storm clouds appeared on the horizon. Relieved of the angst of ever having to menstruate, Nicco discovered that on the school camping trip, he still couldn't go out in the woods and pee against a tree like all his male friends. Instead, he had to go hide in the bushes and squat. His friends, although accepting, were not as welcoming as he would have liked them to be. He had a crush on a girl, but she showed not the least bit of interest in him, and he wondered whether it was because he wasn't a "real" boy. He grew increasingly agitated. Coming from a religious family, he railed at having been skipped over when God was giving all the other boys penises and XY chromosomes. In despair, he blurted out that he would never be able to be the boy he wanted to be. He started cutting to express his level of despair and deflation. Obviously, his parents were very worried about him and wondered whether the puberty blockers and the coming out might not have been a terrible mistake, because he had never openly expressed such distress before.

It was not the puberty blockers that were a mistake, but the lack of preparation regarding what to expect once he was on them. Given Nicco's personality, taking more time to forecast the events to come, incorporating what would change with what wouldn't, might have helped him be better prepared for life on puberty blockers. Stopping to pay attention to his fantasies and aspirations for life as a boy, and specifically life as a boy on puberty blockers, would have facilitated that work. On the other hand, sometimes we can't foresee what is ahead of us, and in Nicco's case, the work came after the crash, when through therapy he could articulate his gender deflation and its causes, have an opportunity to mourn and vent against what couldn't be, then open up the part of him that was now ready for him to explore, realistically, what could be.

The same euphoria followed by dysphoria can show up even more poignantly in youth who have started hormones, particularly if they have been preceded by puberty blockers. I am specifically talking about body dysphoria—angst about the body one has in contrast to the gender one knows oneself to be. Hormones are supposed to remedy that, at least partially, allowing the youth to develop the secondary sex characteristics of the gender they identify as. But hormone treatment cannot turn a vagina into a penis or a penis into a vagina. The best it can do for a transgender male is to create a micropenis in the form of an elongated clitoris. Estrogen treatment cannot grow a uterus, fallopian tubes, and ovaries in a transgender girl and cannot eliminate them in a transgender boy. The hormones might help with desired height, if timed appropriately, but they might not. So, it makes sense that the dysphoria attached to puberty blockers and hormones would be a body dysphoria. The medical interventions offer promise to the body, but when they fall short of their mark, it is the body that remains the problem.

I'm thinking about Rachel, a transgender girl who fully transitioned from male to female when she entered sixth grade. As soon as she hit Tanner stage II of puberty, her endocrinologist started her on puberty blockers. Right before she entered high school, she requested estrogen so she could begin growing breasts and be on a par with her high school friends. Her endocrinologist agreed, and she was ecstatic. She became much more outgoing, joined clubs at school, and was doing well in all her academic classes. It was a pleasure to watch her blossom. But then one year later, she was showing signs of wilting. Yes, she had breasts now, yes, she had a tall, slender build that gave her a graceful, doelike appearance. But she was still a girl with a penis, and how weird was that? she asked. She, like Nicco, came from a religious family, but now she didn't want to go to church anymore and she was having real doubts about God, because if God really loved her, God would never have done this to her, and so she was really angry at God. And, for the first time, she was depressed. Even though Rachel had spent many, many hours exploring her feelings about being female and her desire to have the opportunity to take puberty blockers and then hormones to fortify her female self, she still had the feeling that she had been sold a false bill of goods.

As with Nicco, the medical interventions—this time, hormones—failed as a magic bullet. Rachel's symptoms of body dysphoria resurfaced, perhaps more strongly than ever before. When I think about the stage of adolescence, I think about the resurfacing of the magical thinking of early childhood—the soaring belief that anything is possible. But on the other side of those exhilarating fantasies is the crash—the risk of disappointment and feelings of betrayal in the face of the sobering reality that there is no such magic and not all is possible . . . and perhaps some agitated accusations: "But you promised."

I was present at our clinic to witness Rachel's expressions of angst and frustration upon realizing that she could never be the whole girl she wanted to be, even with estrogen treatment. I watched one of the medical members of the team, in an effort to soothe her distress, offering words of encouragement, pointing out how much better her life was than before and itemizing all the good things estrogen had provided her with. Another member of the team chimed in, assuring her in calming tones that she wouldn't always feel this way, to the tune of "It gets better." I felt a need to stop them, and to give Rachel the opportunity to stay with the upset feelings she was having. Anything else was like cheerleading at a funeral. I left that meeting with a heavy heart but with the realization that just as we always talk about giving parents the room to mourn the child they thought they had, to clear the way to embrace the child they discovered they did have, we need to give the youth the same opportunity: not to mourn the gender they've left behind, but to mourn the loss of the affirmed gender they will never have the way they wish they could—as a cisgender person. They need space to confront the reality that all the hormones in the world, and surgeries as well, will not make that possible and there's nothing we can do to change that. All we can do is facilitate their being the truest transgender person they can be.

Will Nicco and Rachel's future look better when they have the opportunity to choose gender-affirming surgical interventions that could allow Nicco to have a penis and Rachel to have a vagina, if they so desire? Perhaps yes, as the final stage in gender affirming medical intervention, but actually, I would say that Nicco and Rachel's future will look better far before that, whether they go on to have surgeries or not. They both just need the time and space to metabolize the letdown feelings they are having now, without anyone trying to cheer them on to victory. They also do not benefit at such a time from "Uh-oh, did we get it wrong about you being transgender?" messages from the world around them.

Not just the youth themselves, but we, too, need to be prepared for these potential psychological tumbles and turbulence that these youth may confront. I will say that I've noticed deflations, like Nicco and Rachel's, showing up more in youth who come to their gender identity later in comparison to children who socially transitioned at an early age and thus have consistently lived their lives in their affirmed gender from early childhood through puberty and beyond. The early transitioners have had years to assimilate their bodied self with their gender mind, afforded many years of adjustment to being a girl with a penis or a boy with a vagina. That very experience equips them with shock absorbers for the medical ride ahead, if they should choose to go in that direction. It is the latecomers, those who become aware of their transgender identity only later in childhood, often with puberty as the wake-up call, who are more at risk for the downward slope from euphoria to dysphoria following the introduction of medical interventions in adolescence. They have not had the advantage of years to prepare. But suffice it to say that no child is exempt from the risks of such deflation; some are just more protected from it, and we should be at the ready to receive painful feelings with enveloping arms, without being alarmed by it, wherever and whenever we see it.

Another psychological side to highlight is the experience for youth who did not take puberty blockers, went through the puberty of their assigned sex, and then later began a course of hormones. This means that these youth will go through not just one puberty, but two. Actually, this is true for a transgender person of any age, but we're sticking to youth for the moment. I don't know about you, but for myself, once was quite sufficient. Tackling puberty for a second round can be a challenge and quite draining psychologically. With the influx of new hormones, you can feel off-kilter, your emotions may feel as if they're lacking a surge protector, your sexual energy may shift, your skin might start to break out, parts of your body are morphing into something quite unfamiliar. I'm recalling an eye-witness report from the college-age siblings of a younger high school–age transgender sib who had recently started on estrogen. Returning from a year at college, it was the older siblings, all three of them, who lost the surge protector on *their* emotions as they expressed their feelings. They were furious—their sister was not only absorbing all the attention in the family, she was hell on wheels, a PMS nightmare with no respite of a menstrual flow to alleviate the symptoms. The three sibs had only one thing to say, in unison: "You try living with that shrew for a day." How about trying to *be* that shrew for a day? For an older teen, it is not easy to be catapulted back into an earlier developmental stage, in this case puberty, one that many await with eagerness before they enter but are totally relieved to exit. Psychologically, this is what we are asking all youth who have already gone through puberty to do before starting a course of estrogen or testosterone to align their bodies with their psyches. Let's have sympathy for that.

An ongoing point of dissent regarding medical interventions for youth under the age of eighteen is that psychologically they do not have the wherewithal to make such heavy decisions that, excepting puberty blockers, are partially to completely irreversible. Further, they are not typically steadfast in how they define themselves—that's what adolescence is all about. That is, what they feel today may vary drastically from how they will perceive themselves later, once they mature and enter adulthood, or even before that. Which means that they could grow to regret these medical decisions later in life, with potential accompanying serious psychological distress, questioning what they had wrought and why their parents did not stop them when they could. What I would say about that is that we would never want to move forward cavalierly with such interventions in adolescence; they require careful forethought. But the data to date indicate that regrets are quite low; in fact, a study of youth going through the Boston

Gender Management Service (GeMS) program and another of youth going through the gender program in Amsterdam revealed that with their clinical population, regrets were actually nonexistent.[72] What we know on the other side is that transgender youth who remain in a state of gender dysphoria with no access to medical interventions have their own set of regrets, and those regrets are many: that they are prevented from living a life that feels most real and integrated to them, or that they have been barred access to surgical interventions for what seem like no good reasons. Such regrets may interfere with their ability to live a fulfilling life, or have any life at all. I don't think we want that for our children.

We need to advocate for the ability of youth to make informed medical decisions about their gender affirmations and to give them a voice in their own gender care, acknowledging the goodness of these decisions for their gender health. I have come to realize that in doing so, we are simultaneously doing something much broader—challenging our cultural understandings of adolescent development. We need to accept that sixteen-year-olds have the maturity to do long-term planning for themselves, the foresight to project into the future and envision where they will be across time, and the stableness of self required to make informed medical decisions with permanent effects. In other words, we must give teens in our culture more credit than they often receive for sanguinity and level-headedness, and reconfigure their adolescent stage from an emotional platform of Sturm und Drang to a place of wisdom and self-reflection.

PARENTS' GENDER CREATIVITY AT ITS WEIGHTIEST

Sixteen may be the new thirty, but sixteen-year-olds in the United States, unless emancipated minors, have not reached the age of legal majority. Although we require that they give assent to their medical care, only their parents or guardians have the legal authority to consent to any medical intervention, be it puberty blockers, hormones, or surgeries. This means that for parents or guardians, the gender journey is not just about what you call your children and how you signify their gender marker, the latitude you give them to express their gender as they see fit, the steps you take to make sure they get the support they need at school, in your extended families, and so forth. You also carry on your shoulders the inordinate weight of making medical decisions for your children—some reversible, some only partially reversible, some irreversible—because your children are not old enough to medically sign off for themselves. As some parents have put it, "We've left the world of playing policeman to our children's gender and are now in the position of having to play God." And while they're put in the position of playing God, a lot of people are looking over their shoulders with a critical eye, even going so far as to accuse them of child abuse for consenting to these medical procedures.

If you are a parent of a youth who has reached the age of legal majority in the country in which you reside and is seeking a medical intervention to affirm their gender, you may be on the opposite side of the fence: now left in the situation of holding your breath and hoping against hope that your child, barely an adult, can make wise medical decisions, decisions over which you now have no legal control. You may feel helpless to stop them if you feel that they are headed down the wrong path and might make a decision about an irreversible medical intervention that can't be undone and that they'll deeply regret later. If you should find yourself in this situation, you can call on your bond with your child to open up a discussion, to express your concerns and listen to theirs. If you are paying for their medical care, you can elect to not cover the cost. But what you cannot do, legally, is stop a youth of legal majority from moving forward with a medical gender intervention.

In your child's early years, you may also bear the weight of watching your child be burdened with information and decisions that they shouldn't have to be dealing with at such a young age.

Why should a twelve-year-old have to grapple with assenting to a procedure that might render them infertile? Why should they have to make informed decisions about their own future fertility, or lack of it, at an age when their friends only have to think about the latest Facebook postings? Aren't we robbing them of their age of innocence by forcing them to create an avatar of themselves at age thirty? Why should a child have to make the decision to undergo a second puberty if gender affirmation using either testosterone or estrogen comes only after that child went through the puberty of their natal sex? Wasn't one puberty quite enough?

In your darkest moments, you as a parent might feel guilty for not having given your child the chromosomes and biological accoutrements that would have made all these medical interventions irrelevant. I'm recalling when my young adult daughter, who was dancing professionally at the time, discovered that she had a torn meniscus flap in both her knees that required surgery to repair. Her doctor informed us that the condition was not caused by Rebecca's dancing but was a congenital condition, present at birth and only later aggravated by her intense dance regimen. All these years it was a surgery just waiting to happen. I sat with Rebecca in the doctor's office listening to the news, and what did I think?— *It's all my fault. I made her that way. I should have done better in making her. And now she has to suffer through surgery and take a leave from her dance career.* This was not a passing thought; it took me a while to shake the feeling. You can imagine how much more profound that same "blame thyself" feeling can be when it's not just a knee but your child's whole gender self at stake.

You might not take it to that extreme, but it is not uncommon to feel the pangs of a gender ghost pulling at your heartstrings— maybe there really was something you did that made your child unhappy with the sex assignment on their birth certificate. Maybe if you had gotten your child early enough to a therapist like the one in Toronto who could have helped them live comfortably in their own skin (that would be a cisgender skin), these medical burdens could have been lifted. And now you have to worry about the potential side effects of the hormones your child will be taking, already fretting about whether your trans son should have his uterus, ovaries, and fallopian tubes taken out or, if it's your trans daughter, about whether she should have her gonads removed, to prevent in either case the risks of cancer.

And what about the burden of making medical decisions on your child's behalf that your child might regret later? A scenario pops up on your mind's eye of your child coming back some day and throwing it in your face, accusing you of being a negligent parent for letting them go forward, when just a kid, with a medical intervention that has no backsies. What if your child hates you forever, or you've spoiled their life?

With all these images potentially dancing in your head, you are faced, as a layperson, with the daunting task of sorting out the controversies in the field about whether and when a youth should receive medical interventions to enhance their gender health. We know that parents hold the right to veto a medical intervention requested by their child, a request often accompanied by a recommendation from a medical or mental health professional. Some parents are opposed to any medical interventions or don't want these decisions done on their watch, and so they take the stance, "When they're eighteen, they can do anything they want." That is certainly a parent's prerogative. The problem with that approach is, their child may be one sorry mess by the time they're of legal age to make their own medical choices. It therefore behooves parents who are leaning in the "You can do anything you want once you're a legal adult" direction to remember the adage "Doing nothing can equate with doing something," in this case something that will not be in their child's best interests and could cause their child unnecessary pain and suffering, either now or in the future.

Circling back to the fertility issues, this angst about parents' decision making on their children's behalf comes up most poignantly around reproductive choices to be made. At this moment in history, we are on the brink but have not yet mastered the art of turning nongamete tissue into reproductive material. Therefore, if you don't have viable mature eggs, you cannot reproduce. Likewise, if you don't have viable mature sperm, you can't reproduce. So, parents learn from the doctor what we have already discussed: that a child who goes on puberty blockers prior to the onset of menses or the production of mature sperm ejaculate and then goes straight to hormones has foreclosed the possibility of having genetically related children in the future. This prospect may lead some parents to shy away from consenting to a medical intervention that forecloses those fertility options. They might refuse puberty blockers until their child is menstruating or producing sperm, so that even if they go on hormones later, they have the options of going off their hormones and having their reproductive system kick in again. Or if their child has already gone through natal puberty but now wants hormones, before consenting to hormones the parents may insist on creating a security deposit box of gametes for the future by collecting and then freezing eggs or sperm. It should be mentioned that this option, especially egg extraction and preservation, is quite costly, available only to those with the financial means. Furthermore, right now the shelf life of frozen eggs is only about ten years. Of course, these procedures cannot proceed without the youth's assent as well, but the youth may feel pressured into assenting to fertility preservation procedures so as to get the parents to sign off on the hormones.

Here is where the shadow of a grandparent shows up before its time. Many parents are focused on their children's future fertility not so that their children can become parents, but so that they will have grandchildren. This is the moment where the parents might need some help: "Let's think about who you're really doing this for, you or your child." I'm reminded of another family I worked with, similar to Nicco's. Their thirteen-year-old daughter, Karyn, began to question her gender identity. She wondered whether she might be trans. They were exploring together as a family whether it would make sense for Karyn to go on puberty blockers. Her parents were very clear that this would be fine, but only after Karyn started menstruating. Karyn's parents had no other living relatives, so keeping the family going was very important to them. Karyn, with what seemed like an inordinate level of maturity for a thirteen-year-old, appeared to agree, saying, "Yes, I will wait until I menstruate so that I may have an opportunity to have my own kids someday, which has always been important to me." Yet somehow the words did not ring true to me. As time went on and Karyn and I began to meet individually, it didn't take long for her to break down and sob, "I don't want to have periods. And I sure don't want boobs. And I don't care if I adopt children. I can't do this." Karyn was acceding to her parents because she was a compassionate child and empathized with her parents' desires. But Karyn couldn't be the receptacle for her parents' longing for grandchildren; the weight was too much for her. And she knew, beyond a doubt, that if she grew breasts she would want surgery later, and if she got periods she would be horrified, experiencing the flow of menstrual blood as a betrayal of her burgeoning male self. Fortunately, Karyn's parents were as compassionate as she was, and after recognizing that she was in agony, they made sure Karyn got the puberty blockers she urgently requested, to help her go forward more securely and authentically in her gender journey.

I hope Karyn's story will be a helpful message to parents. Time and again I watch youth weigh keeping their fertility options open against postponing obtaining their true gender identity, and time and again I watch the decision to affirm their gender and forgo fertility win out. Can a thirteen-year-old truly know that? Yes, I think so, in the same way that a thirteen-year-old is capable of making a choice that will save their life even if it means losing a limb or living with only one kidney. We could say, "Well, yes, but that's a matter of life and death." So is this for many gender creative youth—to affirm their gender or face crushing despair.

OH, THE DOCTOR AND THE THERAPIST SHOULD BE FRIENDS

I would like to bring this chapter to a close by endorsing a model that is being discovered all across the continent, certainly at our gender clinic at UCSF. The best medical decisions for gender-nonconforming and transgender youth are made when the circle opens up to include the doctor, the therapist, the educator, and even the lawyer . . . and of course, the youth along with their parents or caregivers. We all put our heads together so we can see every side of the elephant.

In the midst of writing *Gender Born, Gender Made*, I helped give birth to the Child and Adolescent Gender Center. It was not fully born by the time the book was published, but now it is. And the birthrate has been phenomenal in the past half-decade for other programs like ours. Many of us have reached our hands across the continent and beyond to share what we've learned and establish ourselves as an international gender affirmative consortium of medical professionals, mental health professionals, attorneys, educators, academics, researchers, community advocates. Each month I hear about another program that has popped up to offer services and supports to gender creative children and their families. And those who are the children and parents have been our greatest teachers in alerting us to what we are doing right, what we are doing wrong, and what needs to be tweaked. So, I want to share what we are all learning together. It sounds so trite to say it takes a village, but that is the simple truth when it comes to promoting gender health. We are learning that the best way to help gender creative children's garden grow and make sure they get the medical and mental health care they need is to populate that garden with professionals and parents working together as a collaborative team to fertilize the children's gender creativity and affirm their true gender self. We couldn't do it without a doctor in the house.

CHAPTER EIGHT

Into the Streets/Onto the Screens

I have always pinned my faith to that spirit which is slowly coming into its own in America.

—Emma Goldman

IN THE BURGEONING OF community psychology in the late 1960s, we who were training to become psychologists were urged to think of psychological services as a storefront operation. The personal was both social and political, and many of us were trained that if we just stayed in our offices or up in our ivory towers, no real change would ever happen. Little did I know then what fine preparation this was to be for working with our gender creative children and their families as we clear the path for their gender journey. And to create those pathways, I am definitely pinning my faith on the spirit coming to its own in America, and beyond.

When it comes to what makes a child's gender, I adhere to the model of the feedback loop: The child influences the parents who in turn influence the child. Now let's create a series of concentric loops around the parent-child loop. The world around the gender creative child and family influences the child's gender, while the gender creative child and family and their allies influence the surrounding world's sensibilities about gender—the world of extended family, the world of the neighborhood, the world of school, the world of the local community, the world of religious institutions, the world of media—entertainment, news, print, and social; the world of academic studies and research science; the world of medical practice; the world of local and national social mores, action, and advocacy; the world of government law, legislation, and policies; the global world. John Donne was already hinting of these loops four centuries ago when he wrote "No man is an island / Entire of itself,"[73] poetically signifying the ways we are connected to all around us. But I think he missed the two-way street of that connection: Each of us is strongly influenced by the world around us, just as we influence that world.

It is that two-way street that represents the quintessential equation of action for gender creative children and their families. Andrew Solomon in *Far from the Tree* couldn't have put it better, "A tolerant society softens parents and facilitates self-esteem but that tolerance has evolved because individuals with good self-esteem have exposed the flawed nature of prejudice."[74] In that spirit, substituting the word *acceptance* for *tolerance*, all of those who are part of such families live within a set of concentric circles that have an influence on their child's gender opportunities; whoever lives in those families will inevitably enter those circles and alter them, by either stretching them or breaking them open where necessary, whether by conscious intent or simply by being present in the world.

This chapter is all about the inside/out of gender. We'll zoom in on two specific subsets of social forces—(1) schools, and (2) social, entertainment, and news media—each in its own way strongly influencing the directions of our twenty-first-century children's gender journey. Then we'll reverse directions and highlight the incredible force field of the child and family that, in unison with the activism and advocacy of themselves and/or their allies, have come to be the movers and shakers catapulting us into a new world of gender, in schools, on screens, and beyond.

Just five days before I embarked on writing this chapter, the US Supreme Court declared marriage a constitutional right of every American. If you had asked me five years ago while I was in the final stages of writing *Gender Born, Gender Made*, whether marriage equality for all people in the United States could be possible in the very near future, I would have said, "Only when pigs can fly." But flew they did, at incredible speed. In a remarkable combustion of community advocacy and shifts in attitude, gay and lesbian individuals have been secured rights to a central arena of life in which they can finally be recognized as full human beings who fall in love, marry, and have children, if they desire, just like anyone else. And although I have said repeatedly that sexual identity and gender identity/expressions are two separate tracks, they do sometimes cross. Right now the victory for marriage equality in the United States gives us tremendous hope that the next terrain of gender victories is close at hand and already in evidence. It now seems imminently possible that the gender force field in place will pay off from the inside out and then back to the inside: There will be a universal end to conversion therapies for gender-nonconforming youth; our children will be granted full protection at school and in their communities—to be acknowledged with appropriate names and pronouns, ensured their rights to engage in activities and use the facilities that match their affirmed gender rather than the sex originally listed on their birth certificate, and so forth. It has already begun. Let's test it out by looking at schools, screens, and streets.

SCHOOLS

All that I have to say about schools I have primarily learned from Gender Spectrum and particularly from Joel Baum, senior director of Gender Spectrum, director of education of the Child and Adolescent Gender Center, and my close colleague and friend. Gender Spectrum has set a mission: to help create gender sensitive and inclusive environments for all children and teens. One of its major targeted environments: schools. What the speakers do when they get there—I call them the gender ghost busters, but, borrowing the words from their Web site:

> In a simple, straightforward manner, we provide consultation, training and events designed to help families, educators, professionals, and organizations understand and address the concepts of gender identity and expression. Our accessible, practical approach is based on research and experience, enabling our clients to gain a deeper understanding of gender all along the spectrum.
>
> We present an overview of how society currently defines gender and how these restrictive definitions can be detrimental to those who do not fit neatly into these categories. We then help you identify and remove the obstacles so all are free to be their authentic selves.[75]

In the United States, children as young as two years of age begin to spend a good proportion of their waking hours in school or day care. They learn their colors; their letters and numbers; to read; math and science; new languages; about the world around them; to think; the rules of society and how to get along with others; and to trust their teachers (or not). It is within those last two modules that things can either go belly up or blossom beautifully when it comes to "gender learning." As soon as a teacher asks all the girls to line up on the left side of the room and all the boys on the right, every child in the class has been taught an important gender lesson: there are only two choices, boy or girl, and you have to fit into one or the other, and it's the teacher's choice, not yours. Too bad for children who think they may be both or haven't yet broken the news that they're not the gender everyone thinks they are, but the other or another one altogether. Too bad for children who get along better with the people in the other line because their gender expressions are a better fit with those little folks. The lesson to the young children: Gender is a very narrow path with only two tracks within it. Anyone who doesn't fit is an oddball or a rule-breaker.

Now switch to an alternative method of lining up: Everyone with birthdays from January to June line up over here; everyone with birthdays July to December, over there. Presto: No more gender-boxing; no more stopping in your tracks if you don't know where to line up; no more lessons about just two tracks. You might be embarrassed that you don't know what month you were born in and have to ask the teacher, but that's a far less daunting task than having to hide behind a gender mask to suit the teacher's line-up rules. The former—an awkward moment; the latter—a marker of many more gender microaggressions to come. And this alternative nongendered line-up routine comes with the perk of a learning moment—you can learn the months of the year, you can memorize your birth date if you haven't already. What you won't learn is that gender is only boy or girl, and the teacher, not you, decides who you are. And that is a good thing.

I won't belabor the point about schools and bathrooms. Similar to the hysteria that erupted in the late twentieth century about the dangers of gay men teaching young children and either molesting or converting them, the apoplectic mania about bathroom use for transgender and gender fluid youth is amazing in its reactive emotionality: It will open up the doors for boys to break into girls' bathrooms posing as girls and molest them; expose children to private parts different from their own; freak out our cisgender, gender-conforming children; and so forth. All these gender creative children want to do is relieve themselves throughout the day in a milieu that feels most comfortable to them, like any other child. California has mandated that all public schools in the state allow the children to do just that. But other states do not have such statutes, and private schools that do not receive public funds are not bound by those directives in states where such statutes exist. So, we have children who end up with urinary tract infections because they avoid school bathrooms altogether, or who sneak into the bathroom matching their affirmed gender when they're sure no one is looking, as if they were either committing a crime or entering a potential war zone. I'm thinking of an eleven-year-old I met with who was in the throes of sorting out gender. Assigned female at birth, at the end of the first session this youth whispered to me, furtively looking around to make sure nobody was listening, "Sometimes I go into the boys' bathroom and it feels so good. But promise, promise you won't tell anyone." Our toileting functions are definitely private affairs in Western culture, but they shouldn't have to be dark secrets.

Yet children do not spend most of their school day in the bathroom, unless they're hiding out altogether from the stresses in the hallways, classroom, or playgrounds. Moving to the classroom and to the schoolyard, we also know the potentially disastrous psychological effects when gender creative children and youth are teased, harassed, or even physically attacked because of the gender they are. Studies repeatedly indicate that gender-nonconforming children and youth may encounter such abuse on a regular basis in the course of their school day. This puts them at risk for anxiety; depression; drug and alcohol abuse; self-harm; and suicidal thoughts, attempts, or successes.[76] And we know that children do not learn as effectively when they are not accepted for who they are or feel they have to hide who they are.

In the last five years, there have been tremendous efforts, led by parents, community activists, outside professionals, and school personnel themselves to free their schools from transphobic fear or thoughtless actions and replace them with gender-expansive practices. Advancements have included asking all children what pronouns they like used for themselves at school and what names they like to go by, and making sure this information is communicated to all school personnel, if the children so desire, as well as eliminating gender divisions in activities and programs and providing reading materials that represent children of all genders rather than just two. In August 2015, *Schools in Transition: A Guide for Supporting Transgender Students in K–12 Schools* was released online.[77] It is a joint project of the ACLU, Gender Spectrum, the Human Rights Campaign, the National Center for Lesbian Rights, and the National Education Association. In my view, this was an act of activism and an act of love by the heavy hitters in our field. We could call them a concentric circle around the families; I'd prefer to call them a halo. In the foreword to the guide, Janice Adams, superintendent of the Benicia Unified School District in California, sums up the guide very succinctly:

> This guide to supporting transgender students builds on the experiences of educators like myself and the advocates who have supported us along the way. Moreover, it ensures that the knowledge we have gained as we worked to support these students can serve as a model for other educators, parents, counselors and students. In doing so, we hope to provide a foundation so that schools and classrooms become more accepting of gender diversity and where all students can feel supported and safe.[78]

The opening chapter puts out a call to all educators: "Instead of 'putting out fires' by treating the needs of each transgender student as an issue to resolve, schools should engage in 'fire prevention' by fostering a school environment that celebrates gender diversity."[79]

Increasingly, schools are doing just that. Scout is a six-year-old attending public school in a large urban area. Scout is in the midst of gender exploring. Scout is gender-ambidextrous—on some days exercising a girl self, on other days, a boy self. Scout just completed kindergarten. The kindergarten had its own bathroom attached to the classroom, available to all children—girl, boy, or other. It also had its own outside play area, separate from the older grades. Scout, a somewhat shy and withdrawn child by temperament, did fairly well in kindergarten, although sometimes thrown off by classmates' questions—"So, are you a boy or a girl?" But first grade was coming up, which required children to leave their classroom in search of either the boys' or the girls' bathroom in the hallways, throwing the first grade children into the melee of all the older students in the school. Arlene, Scout's mother, was extremely anxious about first grade: not just the bathrooms, but the exposure to older children who might bully and harass Scout for Scout's gender creative presentation. And then along came Scout's new first grade teacher: a young gay man. The first thing this teacher did before the start of the school year was to push the school to create a school-wide gender-neutral bathroom for any who would want to use it. He made sure there were books in the classroom demonstrating gender in all its diversity, next to the books about the rainbow spectrum of families. Then he called in Scout's parents, having heard from the kindergarten teacher about Scout's gender ambidexterity, and asked them how he could help make sure Scout had a positive first grade year, given Scout's gender creativity. Arlene burst out crying in the meeting and expressed her fears about Scout, a gentle child, being teased or even beaten up because of Scout's gender presentation, concerned that since Scout was also not a very verbal child, she would never find out if he was being harassed. The teacher assured her that he would (1) provide a learning curriculum for gender acceptance for his classroom and push other teachers to do the same in theirs; (2) set up a team of adult allies for Scout, especially having one of those team members available during schoolyard time, so Scout would know who to go to and so the team could also monitor for any gender-rejecting/harassing behaviors; and (3) contact Scout's parents immediately if there was an incident at school, so they could all work as a team to both support Scout and ensure Scout's gender resilience. Au contraire to the irrational homophobic fears of gay teachers' being allowed to teach young children, it was this teacher's own early history of teasing and harassment, not for his sexual identity but for his early gender-nonconforming expressions, that both informed and bolstered his dedication to making his classroom, and the school beyond his classroom, a gender-safe and gender-expansive environment for all students, with a special eye on Scout.

Scout lucked out with this amazing teacher, but I would like to say that more and more schools, individual teachers, and educational organizations around the country have been contacting gender specialists and gender organizations to ask, "How can we do it better?" Understandably, not all schools are on board, and it is a work in progress, but progressing it is, and the more this concentric circle around gender creative children and their families fortifies their school-based gender-expansive practices, the more the psychological risks to gender-nonconforming children will go down, along with the worries of their parents. Caitlin Ryan and her colleagues poignantly demonstrated the positive mental health effects when LGBT youth are supported by their families. I would argue that schools, where children spend most of their day and build the bulk of their peer relationships, are the second in line to provide this same good effect.

SCREENS

A book about gender in the second decade of the twenty-first century would not be complete without addressing the relationship between gender creativity and screens, and print media as well. Since I wrote *Gender Born, Gender Made*, there has been nothing short of a media explosion on the topic of transgender and gender creative children and youth, not to mention adults (witness Caitlyn Jenner on the cover of *Vanity Fair* in July 2015). Also in 2015, within just a few months of each other, three significant documentaries were released featuring gender creative children and youth: *Three to Infinity: Beyond Two Genders*, by Lonny Shavelson; *Growing Up*

Trans by Miri Navasky and Karen O'Connor, broadcast on PBS's *Frontline*; and *Louis Theroux: Transgender Kids*, broadcast by the BBC. Each of these films had a unifying three-pronged message: Children and youth come in a variety of genders; the journey, for both parents and child, can be a challenging but rewarding one; there are professionals out there supporting the children to be who they are.

Documentaries are not the only show in town. The character Billy Elliott danced across both stage and screen, sending the message to youth across the globe that working-class English boys can be ballet dancers and they and their male friends can wear dresses in happy celebration, rather than dark closets. Before that, the character Ludovic in the film *Ma Vie en Rose* brought to life the poignant story of a child in Belgium struggling to affirm his gender creativity against great odds. Kids all over the world have been watching *I Am Jazz*, a young girl's happy and confident account of her gender journey from male to female, as well as reading the acclaimed children's book of the same name, coauthored by Jessica Herthel. Transgender actor Tom Phelan plays a transgender boy on *The Fosters*, which airs on the ABC Family network. Alex Newell has become a regular actor on the TV series *Glee*, playing a transgender teen girl, Unique Adams, at McKinley High. Moving into adulthood, Laverne Cox plays the vibrant character of Sophia Burset, a transgender woman valiantly struggling with life in prison, while Jeffrey Tambor plays the compelling role of a father discovering he is a woman and transitioning from Morton to Maura in the acclaimed TV miniseries *Transparent*, which received a Golden Globe Award in 2015.

A major tool of oppression in any society is to render people invisible. The oppression lifts when people are seen and acknowledged, but also when they can find themselves reflected back in the community and society in which they they live—when there is a positive social mirror for them, not one marred by distortions, but an accurately reflecting one. When they can find nobody like them, they are indeed an island, if not stranded on one. We are seeing the proliferation of such social mirrors as more and more gender creative children find themselves in movies, television shows, on billboards, on YouTube, in tweets, on Tumblr, on Web sites, in front-page newspaper articles. Far from a freak show (although this might be how the far right would prefer to have it), what we are finding are positive images of children and their families as they carve out a gender path for themselves. These new social mirrors both reflect and effect attitude changes among the populace viewing these images of children, their families, and their allies, but the mirrors also do something critically important for the children themselves. The images allow them to find them-selves and to celebrate their visibility. Moving beyond the direct mirroring from family and friends, these positive media represen-tations provide one more mirror in which to discover themselves and be able to say to other people—"Look everyone, this is who I am, too, just like the kids in the movie."

Some years ago a youth that I was seeing in therapy, prior to seeking me out as his therapist, had just by chance turned on the radio to the NPR radio program "Two Families Grapple with Sons' Gender Preferences," in which I had been interviewed alongside Dr. Ken Zucker. On the show, I had given a description of trans-gender children in positive terms. In shock, my patient, listening to me talk, turned to his mother and blurted out, "Mom, that's me! I want to find that woman and go see her." A determined young person, he did seek me out and was able to come see me, since we both lived in the larger Bay Area, although he came from a very small town nearby, while I was a big city girl. One of the transgen-der teens showcased in the 2015 *Frontline* film *Growing Up Trans*, reported an identical experience to my patient's. He said he never knew who he was until he read about someone on the Internet, and then he shouted out, "That's me!"

These are not rare incidents, and not just the youth but their parents or caretakers may also have the same "Aha" moment, as a result of exposure to media accounts. Let me illustrate with an excerpt from a story written by a foster parent about her gender journey with her then eight-year-old foster child:

> When he was between six and a half and seven years old, we were at Disneyland in our hotel room, when our daughter-in-law (staying in another room) opened the door and said, "You need to come and watch this." It was a talk show on TV where they were talking to a family with a transgender child. We couldn't believe what we were hearing! It was as if they were telling our child's story, even to the obsession with princesses, mermaids, and fairies!

One year later, this family, with the support of educational and mental health professionals, had facilitated their foster child's social transition from male to female, and she is now a beaming transgender girl. Would that have happened without the mirror provided by that TV talk show? No doubt eventually, but because of the opportunity to view the show this family more quickly discovered a clear reflection of the child they had, which translated into that child's finally being seen for who she was, rather than remaining invisible. So, the mirror can benefit the child both directly or indirectly, as illustrated in each of these stories.

Now let's turn to the Internet and social media. Before the advent of Web sites, YouTube, and smartphones, youth who were questioning or exploring their gender might easily experience themselves as the only one in the world with this "problem." "Trans" was the issue of which we did not speak and also the image that we could find nowhere. Now, with a click of a button, you can connect to people just like you all over the globe—trans people, agender people, genderqueer people, gender fluid people, and so forth. No longer are you stranded on a desert island with just yourself. And this time, with access to interactive chatrooms, instant messaging, Skype, FaceTime, and so forth, the mirrors are two-way rather than one-way—they are you viewing someone else as someone else is viewing you. And then you can actually step inside the mirror and make contact with the image you are seeing. Unlike passively viewing a documentary, you can talk, see each other on-screen or perhaps later in person, and share experiences with another gender creative person like yourself. And you can connect to a whole lot of people at the same time. This is a boon to all gender creative youth, but especially to those from isolated areas in which gender diversity is hardly celebrated but instead rejected or maligned. It is also a boost to shy and intro-verted youth who would be hard-pressed to reach out in person in their own community, yet feel safe having virtual interactions via Internet and smartphones. This distance-connecting may also be the most comfortable means for gender creative youth who are somewhere on the autism spectrum, reducing the elements of social anxiety through virtual rather than in-person interactions. Friendships and support groups are built through just such medi-ums. When you are of minority status and/or when you live in an area of the world where you cannot find anyone else like yourself, meeting up with other gender creative youth through the Internet and social media not only can be a perk, it can be a lifesaver. And for some who would otherwise feel desolate in their gender jour-neys, by hearing other people's stories and connecting with those people, it makes a tremendous difference to know that indeed "it gets better."

The only caveat here is that when "virtual" friends substi-tute for real-life friendships, it can make for a very "as-if" life and also leaves youth at risk for connecting with made-up char-acters rather than true gender creative friends. For example, So-nia tells me about her wealth of transgender friends, including her best friend. As we explore further, I discover that she has never been in the same room with any of them. They are, to a person, online friendships. On the positive side, Sonia has been able to test the waters of friendships as a newly transitioned transgender girl, without having to worry about people entrapping her in her previous ill-fitting male persona. But her virtual connections are also getting in the way of reaching out to real people in her community, supportive or like-her people she could hang out with, go to movies with, or meet for dinner. In retreating from a world that did not treat her well, Sonia, by clinging to her online friends, has at the same time insulated herself further in a virtual world, albeit a safe world, but one in which she is suspending herself rather than overcoming the inhibitions and fears about being herself in the "real" world. Real genders need real worlds to live in. There is a risk to them if they exist only in virtual reality. In situations like Sonia's, best to rely on the Internet as an adjunct or stepping stone whenever possible, not as the central venue of relating. And just like parents of any other teen, parents of gender creative youth reaching for connection through the Internet will need to be on board to monitor contacts and coach their children on Internet safety to make sure that they are not falling under the influence of individuals posing on the Internet with less-than-friendly intentions in making contact with the youth seeking them out.

Moving back to the positive attributes of online connections, everything I have just said about gender creative youth applies to their parents as well. The journey can be equally as isolating for parents, and discovering families throughout the country and beyond through Internet support groups may be as life-saving for them as Internet connections are for their gender creative children. I would like to take a moment to pay tribute to Edgardo Menvielle and Catherine Tuerk for setting up the first of such parent support networks in the United States through the Children's Gender and Sexuality Advocacy and Education Program based in Washington, DC, a network that continues to this day. In the words of Menvielle and his colleague Darryl Hill, through such support networks:

> Gender unconventional children and parents increase their
> self-esteem and protect it from future attacks. Supportive
> communities offer alternative relationships in which to feel
> included, valued, and respected.[80]

If the Internet can provide just that for both the gender creative children and their families across the country and beyond, we should be all for it.

But just as it is the best of times and the worst of times when it comes to mental health and gender creative children, so it is for screens. There is no doubt that a media explosion has occurred in the coverage of transgender/gender-nonconforming children, their families, and the professionals who serve them. Regarding exposure, mirroring, and education, this has been a very good thing. Yet there are some drawbacks in the media explosion of which we all need to take heed. Some of the media presentations, particularly the TV talk shows, have turned a child's personal story into a dog-and-pony show for the voyeuristic interest of the audience. Right-wing pundits have jumped on the bandwagon to create a platform for their own histrionic and hostile defamations of gender creative children and their families. And then gender affirmative experts have to spend an undue amount of time confronting these misconceptions and setting the record straight about the care of gender creative children—no, six-year-old children are not receiving genital surgeries; no, puberty blockers are not a form of child abuse; and so forth. Recall that gender is no longer bedrock but, rather, moving boulders. This can kick up some pretty thick dust. And those who are threatened or outraged by the dismantling of the binary gender system have the opportunity to use screens to broadcast hurtful messages. Stay tuned to Fox News and you will see it happen. Exposure to such vitriol can never be in any child's best interests. Hopefully, these negative and harmful tropes will be eclipsed by the increasing number of gender affirmative messages available, on-screen and in print, but know that these hellfire-and-brimstone narratives still remain toxic pollutants for gender creative children and their families, not to mention for the society at large.

Many youth will come to see me and dictate scientific facts about their gender, about medical interventions, and so forth. Increasingly, they are coming in as their own experts. I have said that we learn from the children, but they are also learning from the Internet. They not only find themselves reflected in the Web sites they seek out; they educate themselves—about gender categories, puberty blockers, hormones and surgeries, legal name and gender marker changes, social networks available to them, medical providers, support groups, binders, voice-training apps, stand-to-pee devices, packing, coming out . . . about anything they want to know along their gender journey.

Self-education is a tool of empowerment, a tool that can only serve gender creative youth well—unless they are getting inaccurate information. And herein lies the underside of an Internet knowledge base for gender creative youth, particularly one that then gets passed on by word of mouth. We all know the old game of Telephone—you whisper something to one person who whispers it to the next person, and by the time it gets to the last person, it bears little resemblance to the original message. Such is the fate of some of the information that comes across the Internet into the mind of eager learners—including gender creative youth. Fifteen-year-old Celine came for a visit with me and explained that even though she had already gone through male puberty and had to shave every morning, as soon as she started taking estrogen, which she hoped would be any day now, her whiskers would disappear and her voice would become feminine and her Adam's apple would just fade away. A friend of hers on Facebook assured her of that and said that's exactly what happened for her. Celine was temporarily crushed when she found out this was myth, not truth, and that to eliminate her facial hair she could pursue laser treatment or electrolysis, and to feminize her voice she could pursue voice training, and she may have to think of a tracheal shaving further down the line, but estrogen would not do the trick. Celine recouped fairly quickly, but only after getting angry and accusing me of being outdated and ill-informed, and only after shedding many tears upon the realization that estrogen was not a silver bullet and was going to be able to do only so much for her. Youth itself is a bundle of fact and fancy, as it should be, and so it is for the Internet education of gender creative youth. The residue of misinformation can easily be removed through dialogue with a trusted person who possesses the accurate information, but keep in mind that not all youth have access to such an individual and so are left to the vagaries of the Internet to build their repertoire of gender knowledge. To that end, it behooves all who are experts in the field to publish material for youth that is accessible, readable, and accurate, such as *Trans Bodies, Trans Selves*,[81] for knowledge is powerful only if it is accurately informed.

Then there is the problem of "scripting," made available through the eloquent personal stories showing up daily on the Internet. Remember the dictum "It is not for us to say, but for the children to tell." Our job is to listen. So I do. Occasionally I will hear a narrative from a teen that sounds like an audition for a play—that is, a memorized script. Here's how it might typically unfold: A youth comes in and reports to me their newfound discovery that they are transgender. As I listen, I notice flatness in the account, almost like that of a younger child reciting aloud from a reader in class. And then I begin to think that I've heard the words before, as if maybe I read from the same reader. It is not from a reader but from the Internet that I recognize the words. This youth is borrowing someone else's narrative. I can't tell yet whether it's really who this youth is, or whether they are borrowing someone else's clothes. It doesn't mean that the story isn't the youth's own, just that the words aren't. What I have to figure out is whether the borrowed words are expressing a true gender self that matches those words, or if this is a posing of sorts, perhaps trying on someone else's identity for size.

Why are youth pulling scripts off the Internet to describe their gender self or gender identity? For many reasons, including: They borrow the words of others because they fit perfectly and are articulated so much better than they could say themselves; they are still searching or perhaps floundering and, to right themselves, appropriate someone else's story as their own; they have an agenda in coming for a visit and use a set script to accomplish their goal (e.g., getting a letter of support for cross-sex hormones); it is safer to tell someone else's story than their own. Regardless of the motivation, the Internet-recited script, so available to our youth, presents a conundrum for parents and providers alike. How do we sort out the authentic words of a gender creative child from words adapted from a narrative so readily found online—a narrative that may turn out to be a real story, but perhaps not *that* child's story?

We've already established the challenge of finding the children in translation. Youth's access to both the Internet and social/ popular media only complicates the tasks of interpretation. The child may have borrowed an Internet script because it's a perfect fit; the child may be suffering from TMI—flooded by too much Internet data—and simply grabbing on to one piece of it as a life raft; through adapting an Internet script, the child may be hiding behind a false gender self while struggling to let the authentic one come out. All of this becomes grist for the mill in the gender journey—brought on by the Internet, one more element to consider when bringing children's authentic gender into focus and helping them discard what is either inaccurate or inauthentic.

Sometimes it's not a script but a label that is borrowed. In Chapter 2 we talked about all the possible categories of gender available to children today. Popular and social media play their part in broadcasting gender in all its rainbow of colors. This can potentially influence children toward one self-label or another. So, how do we know when a label is borrowed rather than hatched from within? The answer: with time and exploration. Sooner, or perhaps later, the "real me" will emerge. And are children being bombarded with too many possibilities? Perhaps, but better too many than not enough. In no way does borrowing scripts or adapting self-labels cancel out the virtues of the Internet as a nurturing concentric circle surrounding the family with feedback loop possibilities, for we must remember that not only does the Internet influence the children, but the children (and their families) are also responsible for the postings, YouTube videos, and blogs that are appearing daily and influencing others. In essence, the gender creative children and their families are speaking to themselves from themselves.

One last cautionary reminder about social media—it is a way of connecting, but it is also a means for "outing." Youth who thought they confided something in confidence may find their newly discovered gender self broadcast across the globe on Facebook before they were ever ready to go public. Parents who have no idea about their child's gender explorations may suffer gender shock if they unexpectedly and by happenstance receive the message through social media. When we say, "If we listen, the children will tell us who they are," we also have to provide a space where it is safe to speak and the listeners have the supports they need to hear. Social media has the capacity to provide that safe space, but it also runs the risk of robbing children and their families of safety and privacy, instead leaving them at sea knocked about by the jetsam and flotsam created by gender outing or gender shock.

Yet, on balance, the ability of gender creative children and their families to learn, to connect, to seek support, and to tell their stories through social media, and see their own stories told in positive terms through popular media is one of the most gender-expansive phenomena that has occurred in the first part of the twenty-first century. Could we say that it reflects the spirit that is (not so) slowly coming into its own in America (and beyond)? Indeed.

INTO THE STREETS

When Abe finally gets up the nerve to dance down the street in his favorite red velvet dress, that's taking to the streets. When Julie's parents politely but firmly correct the local shopkeeper who keeps misgendering Julie, because, even though told that Julian has transitioned to Julie and prefers the pronoun *she*, he keeps using "he" because he thinks this "trans stuff" is nonsense, that's taking to the streets. When Melinda appears at least once a week in the principal's office to bring up an incident or a policy that has been less than supportive to Franklin, her transgender little boy, and ask that it be remedied, that's taking to the streets. When a father calls to make an appointment for his child at our gender clinic, seeking out professional support for his child's gender creativity, that's taking to the streets. In other words, every time a gender creative child and their family moves through the community, confident in who they are, social change in happening.

Another way to think about the families is as snowballs. A family works to support the gender creative child they have. Each time another family does that, it is like a snowflake being added to a snowball. The snowball gets bigger and bigger. Soon it rolls down the street and grows into a snowman, or snowwoman, or snowperson. You don't even have to leave your house to get the ball rolling. But when you do leave the house to advocate for your child at school, attend a Gender Spectrum or Gender Odyssey or Transhealth or Gender Infinity or True Colors conference, or solicit your local legislator to support a gender affirmative initiative, the snowball grows even bigger and the forces for change toward a gender-expansive world grow even stronger.

Yet it is not up to families alone to make that change, and it will take more than skipping down the sidewalk, walking to the corner store, showing up in the principal's office, or making an appointment at a gender clinic. Others need to contribute to the gender affirmative snowball as well. It appears this message is getting across. In August 2015 the American Psychological Association released its first set of guidelines for transgender care. Going through them, it warmed my heart to read:

> In educational settings, psychologists may advocate for TGNC [transgender and gender-nonconforming] youth. . . . Psychologists may consult with administrators, teachers, and school counselors to provide resources and trainings on anti-trans prejudice and developing safer school environments for TGNC students. . . . [P]sychologists may consider and develop peer-based interventions to facilitate greater understanding and respectful treatment of TGNC youth by cisgender peers. . . . Psychologists may work with TGNC youth and their families to identify relevant resources, such as school policies that protect gender identity and gender expression . . . , referrals to TGNC affirmative organizations, and on-line resources, which may be especially helpful for TGNC youth in rural settings.[82]

The American Psychological Association has never been known for street protests, rabble-rousing, or formal demonstrations, so when a fairly conventional professional organization sends a missive to its members to infuse themselves in the community in the name of promoting gender health in youth, we have a social movement that's both deepening its roots and spreading its wings.

We would expect as much and far more from such an organization as the Transgender Law Center, based in Oakland, California, and indeed, it has far exceeded anyone's expectations in what it has delivered, taking to the streets and to the halls of justice in advocating for the rights and protection of gender creative children. In the center's own words:

> Things are changing, and momentum is on our side. Countless students and their families have courageously come out in town halls, school board meetings, on social media, and in mainstream news stories to build visibility and support for transgender youth. And across the country we are seeing schools, communities, towns, and states update and change their policies and laws to make sure all students have a chance to thrive.[83]

The Transgender Law Center has invited the youth to lead the way, and the youth have turned to the center as their guiding light and to its staff as the folks they can count on to watch their backs. And the Transgender Law Center is definitely coming through. The same is true for other gender advocacy programs throughout the country, with new ones continually popping up—our own legal director at the Child and Adolescent Gender Center, Asaf Orr, helping to lead the way.

All of these actions have the effect of stirring up our feisty and our creative juices. For example, at a recent monthly meeting of Mind the Gap, our mental health group at the Child and Adolescent Gender Center, one of our members cited the story of a transgender teen who was given an endless amount of grief simply for requesting access to a gender-neutral bathroom at their school. The principal was resistant. First he said it wasn't possible, then he explained that it would take at least a year, then he said the only way it could happen sooner would be to allow this student to use the staff bathroom, and that would be unfair to the other students and give this student preferential treatment. Then the principal compromised and said, "Okay, you can use the staff bathroom, but you'll have to come to me and request that a key be made for you for that bathroom [which was kept locked] and then you'll have to wait until the key is made before you can get access to the bathroom." This solution was something close to mortifying for this student—he was quite shy and didn't want the whole office staring at him if he had to come in with this request. But this was still a better situation than having to go into the misgendering student bathroom. So, our group came up with a transgressive solution: Organize the student body to rally around their transgender classmate by having each and every one of them appear in the office requesting that a key be made for them to be able to use the staff bathroom—for their own comfort. After all, the principal made it very clear that he did not want to give preferential treatment to any one student, so the other students would be asking for the same treatment to which they were entitled. Even if only ten or fifteen students showed up, that would be enough to send a message. And if two hundred showed up, well, I guess the principal would have gotten his just due for being so insensitive to a transgender teen's needs. And maybe it would be a learning opportunity for him—wouldn't it be a lot easier to have an unlocked gender neutral bathroom for everyone, rather than have to make two hundred copies of a key and have all the students storming the single-stall staff bathroom?

As our creative juices flow, we also have to keep in mind that the streets are filled with many kinds of gender-nonconforming and transgender children and youth. They will be of different races, ethnicities, and religions. Some will come from nice homes; some will have no home at all. Some will live with a parent or parents; some will have guardians other than their parents. Some will be rich; some will be poor. So, we have to pay special attention to the specific needs of the children and youth walking or marching alongside us. CeCe McDonald, a twenty-six-year-old African American trans woman, reflects on her life as black and trans and its relation to social action:

> As I figure out who I am as a person, it is hard not to consider my black and trans identities. There is so much misogyny,

racism, sexism . . . I navigate this world knowing that I'm in this world, in this body, and that is challenging. I can get harassed, I can get stopped by police, I can get harassed for being black, I can get heckled for being trans . . . I have to know that's not my fault. I'm doing nothing wrong—this is about other people's ignorance.

It will be a struggle . . . But there's nothing worthwhile that's not worth fighting for. For myself, my community, for change in our society. I'm going to have to fight for it. And, that's my mindset.[84]

CeCe's community is all of our community, her society is our society. Her fight is our fight. As CeCe points out, there are a lot of sharp nails tossed right in the middle of the street, so when we take to the streets, we're going to need the soles of our shoes to be tough enough to march right over those nails. As far as I can tell, the best way to fortify those soles is by linking arms and working together to make this a place where gender health—the freedom to live one's authentic gender protected from harassment or violence and surrounded by love and acceptance—is available to a child of any age, race, religion, ethnicity, or class, along with their elders.

Before I leave the streets, I want to say that not all marching is done with our feet. As the old saying goes, the pen is mightier than the sword. We who are writers have an obligation to advocate for gender health in written words—in the books and articles we write; the blog entries we post; the stories we document about gender creative children's lives; the research we conduct about gender creative children, their needs, and the methods for meeting their needs. We who are not writers but have a story to tell, like so many parents of transgender and gender creative children, can also make use of the written word to get out the message—the children are all right, even though the journey may be challenging. I would refer you to *Raising My Rainbow: Adventures in Raising a Fabulous, Gender Creative Son* by Lori Duron, a book Lori generated from the blog posts she had been writing under the same title. Her book stands as a superb example of one mother's eloquently written story making a tremendous difference in the social fabric of gender beyond her own household.

We also have to fight back with our pens (or more precisely, our computers). We fully expected to meet the wrath of right-wing conservatives and religious fanatics, but when it is our fellow professionals—research scientists, academics, clinicians—who we discover in print vilifying the gender affirmative approach and the concept of a world beyond the gender binary with an infusion of inaccuracies and misinformation, many of us feel compelled to take action and fight back by writing back, setting the records straight. For example, in 2015 Eric Vilain and J. Michael Bailey published an op-ed piece in the *Los Angeles Times* titled "What Should You Do If Your Son Says He's a Girl?" and then they answer in the text, "As scientists who study gender and sexuality, we can tell you confidently: At this point no one knows what is better for your son."[85] Really? I couldn't get to my computer fast enough to write a response, which was published in the *Los Angeles Times* the next day. Instead of paraphrasing, let me present to you my letter to the editor in full:

> "What should you do if your son says he's a girl" (May 21, 2015) only highlighted for me the work to be done in counteracting the arguments made in the guise of scientific evidence that is in itself faulty and in its implications alarmingly damaging to the number of children who need to be heard about what their gender is. If either of the authors has ever spent an hour with a young child sobbing in their office, "Why did they get it wrong? I'm not the boy you think I am" and if either of them has ever witnessed the remarkable transformation from distress and anxiety to happiness and well-being when these children are listened to and allowed to transition to the gender they know themselves to be, they might think twice about putting the decision in the parents' hands rather than in the child's affirmations. There

are different ways of knowing, not just from numbers in boxes in research studies but from clinical experience documented day after day in our offices. And as for the research statistics about the number of children who by adolescence "desist" from their early diagnosis of gender dysphoria, I would ask the authors, "Don't you know the difference between an apple and an orange?" As reviewed by the team of researchers who originally collected the data on desisters and persisters in the Netherlands,[86] from early on the persisters are not the same group of children as the desisters and should never be lumped together. The apples, the persisters, are our youngest cohort of transgender folks, showing up early in childhood, saying "I am a girl" rather than "I wish I was a girl" and being insistent, persistent, and consistent in their declarations. We can find them if we look for them, and the worst thing we could do for them is deny who they are and try to force them to be someone else. If we don't do that, and continue to promote approaches that attempt to twist a child's gender to parents' or professionals' demands, we will end up with more Leelah Alcorns ending their lives in despair. This is never what we would want for our children.

This is just a sample of how many of us are spending our days as allies and advocates of gender creative children and their families.

SCHOOLS, SCREENS, STREETS

As I came to the close of writing this chapter, I picked up my *New York Times* to discover that the present (conservative) mayor of Venice, Italy, Luigi Brugnaro, is attempting to ban forty-nine children's books from the city's preschool libraries. Included in the list: a story of the male dog who aspired to be a ballerina; the tale of a little boy who wanted to be a princess; and a book about a princess who wanted to be a soccer player.[87] No gender diversity in his city, at least among the youngest set, not if Mayor

Brugnaro can help it. So, yes, I know that we have miles and miles ahead of us before we are done with our work of instilling in the minds of people the notion that when applied to gender, rainbows are good; boxes, not so much. But I do believe that in the course of negotiating the moving boulders that gender has become, we are making tremendous inroads—at school, on-screen, and in the streets—advances that can only make it a safer and more expansive journey for our gender creative children.

In *Gender Born, Gender Made* I underscored that gender creative children would never be totally free to exercise their creativity until we also laid the path of a gender-accepting world for them. I can say with great excitement and good feeling that in the past five years, one pathway after another has been paved for the children and their families, all by the love, sweat, and labor of parents, providers, educators, attorneys, community activists, and most important, the children themselves bonding together to both educate and demand change. There are trainers ready to go into any school and help them set up a gender-expansive environment—for all the children. There are attorneys who are entering the halls of justice to fight for the rights of transgender and gender-nonconforming children. Parent support groups, both local and virtual, have proliferated—and generated larger social movements advocating for gender diversity. PFLAG, originally established to support the friends and family members of gay and lesbian individuals, has now opened its arms to the transgender community. I might even go so far as to say that we have finally created a civil rights movement—to promote gender acceptance for all children and youth and to stop the oppression that continues to stifle them in their growth and development. And we can never forget that it is the children who are leading the way—they are out in the world making change and raising consciousness just by growing up and shaping gender in their own creative ways that we never could have imagined.

CHAPTER NINE

What's Left to Learn?

*I have come to view gender less as a riddle that
should be solved and more as a collage, which we
each assemble in our fashion.*
—Deborah Rudacille, *The Riddle of Gender*

I'VE COME TO the very same conclusion as Deborah Rudacille, and
my greatest hope is that this book can provide not a puzzle to be
solved but a map to guide you along the pathways of an infinite
variety of gender journeys. Before I sign off, I thought I would do
something unorthodox (for isn't that what this is all about?) and
admit to you that I know things now that I didn't know when I
began Chapter 1 of this book, which of course opens the door to
exploring what I still don't know at all. I am going to label these
new nuggets of information, knowledge, and reflection my epiphanies, and run them by you one by one. Theoretically, I could take
all these epiphanies and edit them into the earlier chapters to give
you the impression that I've known these things all along. But
that wouldn't be the truth. Instead, I wanted to be transparent and
show you how much I've learned just in the process of writing this
book, so you can experience my own evolutionary gender journey
from Chapter 1 to this concluding chapter.

EPIPHANY #1: TIME AS A FOURTH DIMENSION

With the help of a close friend who attended one of my talks at a local hospital,[88] I came to realize that I had forgotten the fourth dimension of the gender web—time. Each child's unique gender web is an interweaving of nature, nurture, and culture (three of the dimensions) over time (the fourth dimension). By factoring in time, we clear up the misconception that authentic or true means permanent, never-changing. On the contrary, what is true today may not be as true tomorrow. Some people reading these words might grow squeamish about young children being given the green light to declare their gender before they're even old enough to actually cross the street on their own. You might feel compelled to say, "If children are going to change over time, how can you let them jump forward into a new gender so prematurely?" We are not talking about leapfrog when we speak of the dimension of time and the potential of a child's gender web to change over the course of their childhood or beyond. Think molasses, not raging flood waters. Think evolutionary rather than revolutionary time. Yes, we are struggling to comprehend the intricacies of brain functioning and gender messages from that brain. We observe a strong constitutional component to gender identity, but that does not equate with absolute permanence of that identity. Thus we factor in time as the fourth dimension of the gender web. In doing so, we tip our hats to the growing realization that gender is mapped out in an ever-expanding playground, a space that reflects the circle between our inner selves and our outer lives as they dance together around the mulberry bush—over time. To quote Jody Norton, the author of "The Boy Who Grew Up to Be a Woman":

> That paradox—that one can stay, moving—stands for me as a metaphor for transgender. May we all stay where we love to be, moving as much as we need to.[89]

EPIPHANY #2: STABLE GENDER IDENTITY BY AGE SIX: YOU CAN'T HAVE IT BOTH WAYS

How can a child know their gender? That is the question raised again and again in response to what is seen as our careless practice of allowing young children to transition from one gender to another "prematurely," words seemingly expressed as a query but typically lodged as a formal complaint.

Can a young child know their gender? Traditional developmental theories say they can, will, and should, by age six, for normal development to unfold. But that dictum, by conservative standards, applies only to cisgender children. If they are transgender children, they can't and they shouldn't, and they are not normal if they insist they do. I don't think you can have it both ways—you can know your gender by age six if you're cisgender, but you can't if you're transgender. Common sense would tell us that there is a contradiction in theory if cisgender children are expected to know without a doubt their stable gender identity by age six, but transgender children are considered pathological, confused, or in need of intervention and redirection if they are equally clear.

Epiphany: How about if we put it this way instead? Developmentally, at age six or before, all children are quite capable of knowing their gender. That does not mean this self-identity will remain stable throughout their entire lifetime, but it does mean that on average, children by that age will exhibit a core consistency and cohesion of self, whether cis-, trans-, or everygender. And it does not mean that the gender they know themselves to be, by age six, will match the sex listed on their birth certificate.

EPIPHANY #3: GIRL BRAINS AND BOY BRAINS?

Many people hear us talk about the strong constitutional component of transgender identity and listen to tropes about being born in the wrong body and come to the conclusion that we who promote the gender affirmative model are essentialists who believe gender is innate and inborn. Nothing could be further from the truth. We recognize the intricate interplay of nature, nurture, and culture that goes into the making of each child's gender web. It's just that some threads have a stronger pull for certain children. By our and parents' observations, we locate a small cadre of children who are experiencing a disjuncture between the sex assigned to them at birth and the gender they know themselves to be. We recognize that they just show up very early in life, rather than being shaped by their environment. Put differently, gender lies in our brains and minds, rather than in the formation of our genitalia and our chromosomal makeup. The latter obviously play an important part but are not deterministic. Here comes my epiphany: Gender lying in the brain does not mean there is a female brain and a male brain. Instead, it alerts us to the phenomenon that a small minority of people receive messages from their brain telling them that the gender they are is not in congruence with the *F* or *M* marked in their birth records or the body part showing up between their legs. It is those brain signals that are not malleable and should never be tampered with by adults hellbent on getting the children to accept the sex assigned to them at birth as the gender they must be. I suppose another way of saying it is that we are talking about *brain waves*, not *brain functions*, when we talk about gender emanating from between our ears rather than from between our legs. And that brain is not a binary one—male or female—but, rather, a gender-expansive one.

EPIPHANY #4: GENDER AS CURE

Gender as a cure was a lightbulb going on for me when I observed with wonder the autistic features receding in our little clinic patient once he received hormone blockers and once he was allowed to socially transition to the boy he kept trying to communicate he was. Having worked with autistic children for many years, I had never in all those years witnessed such a radical transformation. That got me to thinking about gender as a cure rather than a disease.

I thought about the worries people have about regrets—youth, still in the throes of development, will make decisions about medical interventions (hormones, top surgery, bottom surgery) that they may be really sorry for later. After they mature, they might look back with dismay, lamenting, "What was I thinking?" followed by an accusation hurled at their parents: "Why did you let me do this? I was just a kid." We cannot rule out the possibility of this ever happening, but if we weigh the tiny odds of such a lament occurring against the assuredly higher risks for psychological upheaval and psychiatric symptoms if we withhold from youth the opportunity to align their bodies with their psyches in gender consolidation, that seems like a no-brainer of an equation to solve. And if we consider further that such youth may assuredly discover greater happiness and better life satisfaction if afforded the opportunity to receive gender affirmative treatments, then we can say that we have provided gender as a cure for angst. In which case, if gender is a cure, how could it also be a disease? If the answer is "No, it can't be both," then we are led to the logical conclusion: dispense with psychiatric diagnoses of gender pathology, because gender is the cure, not the disease.

One more piece of gender as cure is gender as a protection against trauma, such as my earlier example of girls in Afghanistan who found safety and freedom in assuming a male identity. In their case, gender became a cure for women's oppression, socially induced but internally embraced.

My epiphany of gender as cure reinforces the notion that all three dimensions of the gender web—nature, nurture, and culture—hold the threads of gender authenticity. Therefore there is no reason why a youth couldn't weave together an authentic genderqueer or transgender self to cure the disease that stems, for example, from a foster child's traumatic history of repeated molestation in their birth family only to be repeated in their foster family, or in the example of the Afghani FtM youth, to cure the disease of repeated oppression, repression, and violence against females. So, I leave you to muse on the concept of gender as cure as a replacement for gender as disease.

EPIPHANY #5: "I HATE THE WORD *TRANS*"

In recent months I've been repeatedly meeting up with frustrated, downtrodden, or protesting preteens and young teens who transitioned earlier in life and have been living consistently in their affirmed gender for several years. Many of them are on puberty blockers; some have just started hormones. What they have in common: They hate, and I mean hate, the word *trans*. As far as I can tell, this is not internalized transphobia. It is a loud objection to a word that just doesn't feel like a fit—"Trans is not me." In other words, they were always the gender they know themselves to be; they were never anything else. In conscious memory, this may actually be true. They can no longer remember their youngest years living in another gender. That loss of memory is exactly why the "watchful waiting" folks get nervous about early transitions, worried that such early switches might create a delusional mind-set in the children about their bodied self. But let's see it from the youth's perspective. They insist that they never transferred over into another gender. Instead, by their own narrative, they just made it clear to everyone else, once they got it clear in themselves, that they are "just a boy" or "just a girl," and always have been. They resent being seen as the transgender girl or the transgender boy in town. They just want to be left alone to live as the girl or the boy they are.

I'm thinking of Larkin, a child I have been working with for several years. Larkin socially transitioned at age eight, but for all practical purposes she was 99 percent transitioned many years before that. She was twelve when she came into my office furious

that her mother had dragged her to the Gender Spectrum conference (Note: In years past she loved going to that conference and
couldn't wait until the day came for it to start). Larkin sat curled up
on my couch, her toenails painted a beautiful shade of blue, her
long blond hair cascading down the front of her plaid flannel shirt,
and blurted out, "I just want to be home with my girlfriends, the
ones I especially chose because they don't like to do girly things.
And all the girls at the conference—well, they were just frou-frou.
Stupid, stupid conference."

I can almost hear the red flags going up—Are Larkin and her
cohort in denial about their history and about their early life living as the other gender? Maybe, and we definitely need to pay
attention to any fault lines of delusional thinking or poor reality testing on the part of our early (or even later) transitioning
youth. But that's me talking as a developmental psychologist
and an old fogy. Now let's consider it from their point of view. If
we are going to do a shake-up of sex and gender so that we can
have penis-bodied girls and vagina-bodied boys, or just vagina-
or penis-bodied people, why shouldn't these children, who enter
their affirmed gender early in life, protest against being pegged as
a girl who becomes a boy or a boy who becomes a girl? They are
a girl, they are a boy, or they are some other gender creative identity of their own making not by our standards but by theirs, standards created soon after we offered them the possibility that girl
does not equal vagina and boy does not equal penis. So, in their
eyes—down with *trans*. From our own adult view, we understand
that, no matter how they define themselves, the outside world
may still see these youth as trans and treat them accordingly.
To that end, we must balance hearing their call for "trans tran-
scendence" while promoting the gender resilience these youth
will continue to need as they meet with a world that will still see
them as trans, rather than just as a boy or girl. And as we listen
to their declarations, we must also make sure that this trans tran-
scendence is not a thinly veiled defense against the aspersion of

being trans in a transphobic world, for pride in gender in all its iterations is what we are about.

I've said that if we want to know the children's gender, we should listen to them, rather than tell them. We also need to listen to them when they tell us we're passé, behind the times, or oppressing them with what to them is experienced as our outmoded sensibilities about gender. My epiphany: You never graduate from gender school.

EPIPHANY #6: THE RISE OF THE FRUIT SALADS

It was in the last weeks of writing *The Gender Creative Child* that the film *Three to Infinity* was released. The content was about as fruit-salady and gender creative as you could get—gender revolutionaries of all ages challenging the concept of masculine-feminine dualities and constructing lives and selves that are truly gender mosaics, often leaving others wondering about their gender. They do this with their clothes, their own creative use of medical interventions, and their insistence on being referred to in gender-neutral terms. To say that they live in the middle would be adhering to a binary model—point a, point b, and the space in between. Better to say that they live in the space between finite and infinite, if we can get our head around that.

Soon after the release of *Three to Infinity*, *The Gender Quest Workbook* by Rylan Testa, Deborah Coolhart, and Jayme Peta came out.[90] The workbook follows in the same vein as the film—gender lies within an infinite space. The authors invite teens and young adults to explore the full range of who they are and how they like to be that person—in both their gender identity and expressions—with plenty of room for apples, oranges, and fruit salads.

But what about the younger folks? Recently I met with a mother whose six-year-old child, an assigned male at birth, wears dresses, asks everyone to use the child's given name as a pronoun, and explains, "I'm not a boy, I'm not a girl." As we talked, this mother expressed frustration that there were no books for a child like hers. She's right. And that got me to thinking—given the rise of the fruit salads, why aren't they showing up in books so that our youngest fruit salads can find themselves reflected? We have books, films, and videos about boys who want to wear dresses or be princesses, girls who are boys and boys who are girls, but what about the gender-ambidextrous, gender fluid, gender-hybrid child, the one who lets us know, in word and action, "I'm neither one nor the other, but both, and maybe something else altogether"? My epiphany here is that we talk a good line about gender expansiveness, but we have to get the rubber to hit the road and do better in highlighting the pathways for our children who enter their gender journeys early as our fruit salads. Who knows, maybe that will be my next volume on gender.

EPIPHANY #7: I WANT IT NOW: SPOILING CHILDHOOD AND THE GENDER CREATIVE CHILD

For weeks I mulled over the story of the parents who appeared at a gender clinic announcing that their transgender daughter had proclaimed that if she didn't get a vagina by the time she was nine, she was going to kill herself. Following this announcement, the father leaned toward the medical director with a piercing look understood to mean, "So-o-o, what are you going to do about it?" It brought me back to the years writing my book *Spoiling Childhood*, in which I investigated the tremors modern-day parents felt when they had to say no to their child and the entitlement children felt to demand what they wanted and get it *now*—or else. So, why wouldn't that pattern extend to children's feelings about gender—a sense that everything happens instantaneously, waiting is an obsolete concept, and if no immediate gratification is forthcoming, threaten death by suicide or homicide? Now I am exaggerating, but the trend has been in that direction since the late twentieth century, and it is not unheard of to see this sensibility, which I labeled "Your Majesty, the Baby," embedded in children's expressions of gender dysphoria, when such dysphoria exists: "I want boobs now!" "I absolutely refuse to wait until I'm older to start hormones. I have to be like everyone else and have my puberty *now*. So what if I'm only eleven?" I think you get the gist. For some children and youth, there indeed is an impending crisis that requires immediate attention to avoid gender trauma and possible self-harm. But for other children, crisis is not the operating variable. Instead, patience and reflection are foreign concepts, and, for their parents, keeping their children happy by acceding to all their wishes becomes the dominating force in child rearing, particularly when they imagine the stresses their child may have to face within an unaccepting genderist world.

When my own children were growing up, we called on the unsavory character of Veruca Salt from *Charlie and the Chocolate Factory*—"Daddy, I want it *now*"—to remind them (and us) that we were veering in the direction of Your Majesty, the Baby. Those five words were typically enough to stop Jesse or Rebecca short. (Who would ever want to become Veruca Salt, the most unpleasant of children?) Since gender is not an area exempt from the Veruca Salt syndrome, I have learned the necessity of sorting out true gender urgency from indulgent parents/child royalty conundrums, where *no* and *stop* become verboten words.

Eurocentric Western culture does not receive high scores for helping our children build frustration tolerance and accept delayed rather than immediate gratification. Now couple that with an electronic world in which if you want to order something online, you can have it by tomorrow. That's where the gender path can become a speed raceway. I've emphasized repeatedly that we need to listen to the children. My epiphany, which sounds so basic, is that our gender creative children also need a guiding hand. For example, in growing up, cross-sex-hormone-induced puberty through the administration of estrogen or testosterone is really not that different from naturally induced puberty—it doesn't always come exactly when you would want it to (ask any late bloomer), and sometimes you just have to wait. You, the parents of the gender creative children, may never want to be a gate-keeper, but you will sometimes need to be the engineer driving that train, pulling on the brakes or slowing things down along the gender journey when need be.

EPIPHANY #8: THE NEW LOVE AFFAIR WITH ADOPTION

For many, many years I have worked in the areas of foster care, adoption, and assisted reproductive technology. I have witnessed so many parents exploring alternative means of building their families, adoption being one of them, and I have sat with them through their journeys, experiences sometimes filled with joy, sometimes laden with pain. Those among them who have embraced adoption as the means to become parents now have a young cohort joining them—transgender teens. Never have I experienced a group of people as positive about having a child through adoption. They don't come to this through support groups. They don't come to it by direct instruction. Instead, one by one, as we have sat with youth at our gender clinic and explained to them the reproductive outcomes of the various gender paths they might choose, we hear a repeated story: "Oh, I'll just adopt. There's too many children in the world anyway, so that's the best way to go." This is typically in response to learning that if they should go directly from taking puberty blockers (starting them before they begin producing viable eggs or sperm) to taking hormones, they will not be able to have a genetically related child of their own (at least at this moment in history).

We already know that parents may carry a lot of angst about signing off on these interventions at an age when their children couldn't possibly know exactly how they'll feel about being a parent when they're twenty-five, thirty, or thirty-five. The youth are clearly feeling something very different. They have no worries about being infertile. Could it be that they're all riffing off the same Internet site about transgender parenting (or not-parenting)? I don't think so. Could it be that their impressively altruistic sentiments about adoption are really a psychological defense against the opposite feeling that they will forever be robbed of childbearing choices because someone dealt them the wrong hand a long time ago? Potentially, but I would say not likely. My epiphany is that this expressed love affair with adoption, repeated by one child after another in the privacy of the clinic meeting room, is an authentic individual psychological response telling us a social story. And the story goes like this: "More important than anything in the world is getting the opportunity to live the gender that is me. If medical supports can help me do that, that's front and center for me. How I become a parent, if I become a parent at all, is back seat, if in the car at all." What am I learning? That gender authenticity trumps desires for genetic parenthood. Epiphany #8.

SO, WHERE ARE WE GOING?

From the beginning to the end of writing *The Gender Creative Child*, I have watched the continuing transformation of gender from bedrock to moving boulders. As a hiker, I know full well that trekking across bedrock is far less of a challenge than traversing moving boulders, but never as exciting. So, I exit *The Gender Creative Child* balanced on the moving boulders of gender, wondering where they are taking us and whether they will ever stop moving so fast. Periodically I ask myself, "In one hundred years, will people be looking back and saying, 'Really, they got hung up on all that stuff about gender and genders. That's just so quaint. I wonder what it was like to be not beyond gender'?" Forget about the next century. What about our gender creative children today? Where will they be at age fifty? The early transitioners—will they look back at their lives with gratitude, the gratitude that their older cohort of transgender adults imagined they would have felt if only their own elders had known enough to let these transgender people live their authentic gender lives as young children, when they already knew but couldn't say? The children who chose to use puberty blockers—will they indeed be healthier as adults, or will we discover some yet unknown health risks to these interventions that might have made us pause rather than confidently pressing the pause button on their puberty? Youth who chose cross-sex hormones/hormone replacement therapy—will hormones fortify their gender resilience over the course of their life? How will these youth feel later if they bump into medical side-effects or life-threatening conditions that might be related to their very long-term use of hormone therapy? The children who go straight from puberty blockers to hormones—despite their love affair with adoption, could I be wrong and will they later regret having given up the opportunity to have their own genetic offspring? Was it worth the trade-off—to live a life that feels authentic and real and find alternative means to build a family? The gender fluid youth who may change their self-affirmations of gender over time—do we want to try to discourage too many turns in the road, or do we want to make room for all-terrain gender vehicles that can go forward, back, and sideways over the course of the life journey?

I embrace the concept of gender infinity, but let's get real. Complexity is rarely easier than simplicity, and ever-growing iterations of gender definitely count for being complex. With gender expansiveness, might we possibly suffer from gender overload, or will we bathe ourselves in the sparkling waters of never-ending gender flow? So, I leave us all with two questions: "Where are our gender creative children taking us?" and "Are we ready for the ride?"

And I leave us with an answer as well. The gift of the gender creative child is this: Because of them, we know so much more about gender than we ever knew before. Because of them, gender still remains a mystery. That is what makes the gender journey, with all its pathways, so exciting. So, where *do* we go from here? Dial back to 2003. Picture my granddaughter, Satya, then age three, elatedly dressed from head to toe as her favorite character, Buzz Lightyear. Listen to her as she raises her hand to the sky, and calls out, in her loudest voice, "To infinity and beyond."

Notes

CHAPTER ONE

1   Cheryl Kilodavis, *My Princess Boy* (New York: Aladdin, 2010); Sarah and
    Ian Hoffman, *Jacob's New Dress* (Park Ridge, IL: Albert Whitman, 2014);
    Lori Duron, *Raising My Rainbow* (New York: Broadway Books, 2013).

2   Jayme Poisson, "Parents Keep Child's Gender Secret," *Toronto Star*, May
    21, 2011.

3   Part of the gender revolution initiated by the young is the insistence
    on using gender neutral pronouns, rather than the binary "he/she."
    Although we diehard feminists of the 1960s thought we had made great
    inroads in gender equality by insisting on desisting with the use of "he"
    to refer to everyone, male or female, and substituting "he or she" to be
    gender-inclusive, we now find ourselves outmoded. The preferred gender
    neutral pronoun requested by many of the young people in the commu-
    nity is "they" rather than he or she. Although it sounds discordant and
    grammatically incorrect by adults schooled in American English, it was
    pointed out to me by an astute, if not brilliant, self-identified agender
    patient that Shakespeare's work is replete with the use of "they" in the
    singular, as this particular youth was asking to be referred to. "Their"
    message to me and others: "Get over it." So, in the spirit of letting our
    young lead the gender revolution, I will be using the pronoun "they"
    throughout *The Gender Creative Child* to refer to a singular gender creative
    child, unless they have indicated that they would like to be referred to as
    "he" or "she." This will be part of my effort in getting over it.

4   Katy Steinmetz, "America's Transition," *Time*, June 9, 2014, 38–46.

5   Piper Weiss, "Dad Protects Son from Bullies by Wearing a Skirt. Guess
    What? It Works," *Shine* from Yahoo! Canada, August 31, 2012, ca.shine.
    yahoo.com.

6   Seth Menachem, "My Son Wears Dresses, and That's OK with Me," *Huff-
    ington Post*, July 14, 2014, huffingtonpost.com

7   *The O'Reilly Factor*, May 24, 2012.

8   *Laura Ingraham Show*, May 30, 2013.

9   *Laura Ingraham Show*, August 8, 2014.

10 *Laura Ingraham Show*, August 6, 2014.

11　For a thorough, scientific description of the gender affirmative model, I would refer you to M. Hidalgo et al., "The Gender Affirmative Model: What We Know and What We Aim to Learn," *Human Development* 56 (2013): 285–90.

12　The term *cross-sex hormones* is commonly used to refer to the estrogen or testosterone that transgender youth take to align their bodies to their affirmed gender. Some people prefer to use the medical term *hormone replacement therapy*, which in no way implies that anyone has crossed any sex lines but instead indicates that this person just needs an addition of hormones to solidify their affirmed gender. *HRT* as a term has its own set of problems, since so many of us—particularly ciswomen of a certain age—associate hormone replacement therapy with the plight of menopausal women in the early twenty-first century, who were told for many years of the benefits of such treatment and then warned that those very treatments might be causing them physical harm. To avoid this terminology conundrum, I have opted to simply use the term *hormones* whenever possible to refer to the treatment that allows a youth to receive hormones in alignment with their affirmed gender identity.

CHAPTER TWO

13　Nanette Asimov, "Mills College Spells Out What It Means to Be Female," *San Francisco Chronicle*, August 20, 2014, A1, A10.

14　Michelle Goldberg, "What Is a Woman?," American Chronicles, *The New Yorker*, August 4, 2014, 24–28.

15　Ruth Padawer, "Sisterhood Is Complicated," *The New York Times Magazine*, October 19, 2014, 34–39, 48, 50.

16　See Stephanie Brill and Rachel Pepper, *The Transgender Child* (San Francisco: Cleis Press, 2008); Diane Ehrensaft, *Gender Born, Gender Made* (New York: The Experiment, 2011); and Jake Pyne, Rainbow Health Ontario Fact Sheet, 2012.

17　BBC News India, "India Court Recognises Transgender People as Third Gender," April 15, 2014, bbc.com.

18　D. W. Winnicott, *Playing and Reality* (London: Tavistock, 1971).

19　See Genny Beemyn and Susan Rankin, *The Lives of Transgender People* (New York: Columbia University Press, 2011).

20　V. Pasterski et al., "Increased Cross-Gender Identification Independent of Gender Role Behavior in Girls with Congenital Adrenal Hyperplasia: Results from a Standardized Assessment of 4- to 11-Year-Old Children," *Archives of Sexual Behavior*, published online September 20, 2014.

21　Two major articles about androgens and gender: P. T. Cohen-Kettenis, "Gender Change in 46,XY Persons with 5alphareductase-2 Deficiency and 17beta-hydroxysteroid dehydrogenase-3 Deficiency," *Archives of Sexual Behavior* 34 (2005): 399–410; H. F. Meyer-Bahlburg, "Gender Identity Outcome in Female-Raised 46,XY Persons with Penile Agenesis, Cloacal Exstrophy of the Bladder, or Penile Ablation," *Archives of Sexual Behavior* 34 (2005): 423–38.

22 Stephen M. Rosenthal, "Approach to the Patient: Transgender Youth: Endocrine Considerations," *Journal of Clinical Endocrinology and Metabolism* (2014), 1–11, jcem.endojournals.org. See p. 3 for the cited quote.

23 As a sample of my perusal, one might take a look at Jerome Kagan, *The Growth of the Child* (New York: W. W. Norton, 1978); Herbert Ginsburg and Sylvia Offer, *Piaget's Theory of Intellectual Development: An Introduction* (Englewood Cliffs, NJ: Prentice-Hall, Inc., 1969); Jean Piaget, *Plays, Dreams, and Imitation in Childhood* (New York: W. W. Norton, 1962); Erik Erikson, *Identity, Youth, and Crisis* (New York: W. W. Norton, 1968).

CHAPTER THREE

24 The World Professional Association for Transgender Health (WPATH), *Standards of Care for the Health of Transsexual, Transgender, and Gender Nonconforming People, Version 7* (2011), 17, wpath.org.

25 The Brothers Grimm, "The Frog Prince," in *Grimms Fairy Tales* (New York: Crown Publishers, 1973), 17.

26 Candace Waldron, *My Daughter, He: Transitioning with Our Transgender Children* (Rockport, MA: Stone Circle Press, 2014), 47.

27 E. B. White, *Stuart Little* (New York: Harper Trophy, 1945), 9.

28 Genny Beemyn and Susan Rankin, *The Lives of Transgender People* (New York: Columbia University Press, 2011).

29 Thomas D. Steensma et al., "Factors Associated with Desistence and Persistence of Childhood Gender Dysphoria: A Quantitative Follow-up Study," *Journal of the American Academy of Child and Adolescent Psychiatry* 52, no. 6 (2013): 582–90.

30 Hoffman and Hoffman, *Jacob's New Dress.*

31 Richard Green, *The "Sissy Boy" Syndrome and the Development of Homosexuality* (New Haven, CT: Yale University Press, 1987).

32 GenderQueer Revolution, "About," facebook.com.

33 Some people may recall *fruit* being used as pejorative term for any boy or man who appeared effeminate. This is, of course, not what I am referring to here. In the spirit of the queer movement, I am appropriating the word *fruit* with pride, as our own gender affirmative term, in relation to apples and oranges, to acknowledge and celebrate the mélange of gender that defies gender boxes in both identity and expressions.

34 Wikipedia, "Genderqueer," en.wikipedia.org, January 5, 2015.

35 Suzanne Leigh, "Getting Beyond Male and Female," *San Francisco Chronicle*, February 12, 2014, D1, D2.

36 GenderQueer Revolution.

37 Eric Erikson, *Childhood and Society* (New York: W. W. Norton, 1963).

38 Jennifer Carr, *Be Who You Are* (Bloomington, IN: AuthorHouse, 2010).

CHAPTER FOUR

39 Mx. Nathan Tamar Pautz, "On Not Judging a Book by Its Cover," in *Trans Bodies, Trans Selves: A Resource for the Transgender Community*, ed. Laura Erickson-Schroth (New York: Oxford University Press, 2014), 97.

40 WPATH, *Standards of Care*, 26.

41 For more information, see Alexander Thomas, Stella Chess, and Herbert G. Birch, *Temperament and Behavior Disorders in Children* (New York: New York University Press, 1968); and Stella Chess and Alexander Thomas, *Temperament* (New York: Routledge, 1996).

42 See Annelou L. C. de Vries et al., "Autism Spectrum Disorders in Gender Dysphoric Children and Adolescents," *Journal of Autism and Developmental Disorders* 40 (2010): 930–36, published online January 22, 2010; Doug P. VanderLaan et al., "Do Children with Gender Dysphoria Have Intense/ Obsessional Interests?," *Journal of Sex Research* 52, no. 2 (2015), 213–19; and a review by Kyle Simon, cofounder of the Autism Family Center, "Is There a Link Between Autism and Gender Dysphoria?," *Huffington Post Gay Voices*, September 13, 2013, huffingtonpost.com.

43 See Avgi Saketopoulou, "Minding the Gap: Intersections Between Gender, Race, and Class in Work with Gender Variant Children," *Psychoanalytic Dialogues* 21 (2011): 192–209; and Mark Gevisser, "Self-Made Man," *Granta* 129: Fate, Autumn 2014, granta.com, for further discussion of the need to hold the tension between the old and the new.

CHAPTER FIVE

44 As quoted in Julia Prodis Sulek, "Transgender Grandchild: Rep. Mike Honda Says 8-Year-Old's Gender Change Not a Phase," *San Jose Mercury News*, February 19, 2015, mercurynews.com.

45 As quoted in Anne Saker, "Raising Zay: A Family's Journey with a Transgender Child," *Enquirer*, February 21, 2015, cincinnati.com.

46 Colleen Schrappen, "Max Was Born a Girl, but Always Felt Like a Boy," *St. Louis Post-Dispatch*, October 5, 2014, stltoday.com.

47 As quoted in Hayden Manders, "Angelina Jolie and Brad Pitt Support Shiloh's Wish to Be Called 'John,'" *Refinery 29*, December 22, 2014, refinery29.com.

48 As quoted in KC Baker, "Cher: I Admire Chaz's Courage," *People*, May 1, 2011, people.com.

49 White, *Stuart Little*, 9.

50 For a complete discussion of expectable parental narcissism, see Diane Ehrensaft, *Spoiling Childhood: How Well-Meaning Parents Are Giving Children Too Much—But Not What They Need*, Chapter 2 (New York: Guilford Press, 1997).

51 Andrew Solomon, *Far from the Tree: Parents, Children and the Search for Identity* (New York: Scribner, 2012). Quote is taken from p. 6.

52 Waldron, *My Daughter, He*, 204 and 218.

53 See Derald Wing Sue, *Microaggressions in Everyday Life* (New York: Wiley, 2010), for a further discussion of microaggressions.

54 Leelah Alcorn's mother's statement was quoted in Mikey Prizmich, "Accept Trans Youth and Value Their Diverse Experiences," *San Francisco Chronicle*, February 25, 2015, sfchronicle.com.

55 See Anna Freud and Dorothy Burlingham, *Infants Without Families: The Case For and Against Residential Nurseries* (New York: International University Press, 1944), for a discussion of the wartime nurseries and effects on the children.

56 Even though India has given legal recognition to third genders, in everyday life those individuals are often perceived (not always so kindly) as an adult enclave all their own, and the social mores and expectations of clearly differentiated gender behaviors and presentations for girls and boys remain firmly in place.

57 See Abraham H. Maslow, "A Theory of Human Motivation," *Psychological Review* 50, no. 4 (1943): 370–96; A. H. Maslow, *Toward a Psychology of Being* (New York: D. Van Nostrand Company, 1968); A. H. Maslow, *Motivation and Personality* (New York: Harper & Row, 1970).

CHAPTER SIX

58 Sheryl Ubelacker, "CAMH to 'Wind Down' Controversial Gender Identity Clinic Services," *Globe and Mail*, December 15, 2015, theglobeandmail .com.

59 See Kenneth Zucker and Susan J. Bradley, *Gender Identity Disorder and Psychosexual Problems in Children and Adolescents* (New York: Guilford Press, 1995), and Kenneth J. Zucker et al., "A Developmental, Biopsychosocial Model for the Treatment of Children with Gender Identity Disorder," *Journal of Homosexuality* 59, no. 3 (2012): 369–97, for a full description of this model.

60 As reported in Jessica Smith Cross, "Outcry Prompts CAMH to Review Its Controversial Treatment of Trans Youth," *Metro News*, Toronto, March 18, 2015, metronews.ca.

61 Robert Wallace and Hershel Russell, "Attachment and Shame in Gender-Nonconforming Children and Their Families: Toward a Theoretical Framework for Evaluating Clinical Interventions," *International Journal of Transgenderism* 14, no. 3 (2013): 113–26, 119.

62 See T. D. Steensma et al., "Factors Associated with Desistence and Persistence of Childhood Gender Dysphoria: A Quantitative Follow-up Study," *Journal of the American Academy of Child and Adolescent Psychiatry* 52, no. 6 (2013): 582–90.

63 The Child and Adolescent Gender Center mental health group has created a gender affirmative assessment packet available to clinicians working with children and youth, provided they are first trained as gender specialists. The subcommittee preparing the packet—myself, Dr. Shane Hill, Dr. Joy Johnson, and Lisette Lahana—worked as best we could to develop nonbinary assessment tools to encompass children and youth of all genders within a health rather than pathology model.

CHAPTER SEVEN

64 Robert Stoller, *Presentations of Gender* (New Haven, CT: Yale University Press, 1985), 200.

65 See S. R. Vance, D. Ehrensaft, and S. M. Rosenthal, "Psychological and Medical Care of Gender Nonconforming Youth," *Pediatrics* 134, no. 6 (2014), 1184–92; I. Sherer et al., "Gender Nonconforming/Gender Expansive and Transgender Children and Teens," *Contemporary Pediatrics*, 2014, contemporarypediatrics.modernmedicine.com; I. Sherer et al., "Child and Adolescent Gender Center: A Multidisciplinary Collaboration to Improve the Lives of Gender Nonconforming Children and Teens," *Pediatric Review* 33 (2012): 273–75.

66 As quoted in Sherer et al., "Gender Nonconforming/Gender Expansive and Transgender Children and Teens."

67 P. T. Cohen-Kettenis et al., "Puberty Suppression in a Gender-Dysphoric Adolescent: A 22-Year Follow-up," *Archives of Sexual Behavior* 40 (2011): 843–47.

68 See Vance et al., "Psychological and Medical Care of Gender Nonconforming Youth" for a fuller discussion of medical interventions.

69 Anemona Hartocollis, "The New Girl in School: Transgender Surgery at 18," *The New York Times*, June 17, 2015, A1 and A20.

70 Quoted in Hartocollis, "The New Girl in School," A20.

71 I would refer the reader to an article written by the medical director of our Child and Adolescent Gender Center, Dr. Stephen Rosenthal, for a discussion of the biologic aspects of gender, Stephen M. Rosenthal, "Approach to the Patient: Transgender Youth: Endocrine Considerations," *Journal of Clinical Endocrinology & Metabolism* 99, no. 12 (2014): 4379–89.

72 Norman P. Spack et al., "Children and Adolescents with Gender Identity Disorder Referred to a Pediatric Medical Center," *Pediatrics* 129, no. 3 (2012): 418–25; Annelou L.C. de Vries et al., "Young Adult Psychological Outcome After Puberty Suppression and Gender Reassignment," *Pediatrics* 134, no. 4 (2014): 696–704.

CHAPTER EIGHT

73 John Donne, "No Man Is an Island," Meditation XVII, Devotions upon Emergent Occasions, 1624, from Henry Alford (ed.), *The Works of John Donne*, Vol. 3 (London: John W. Parker, 1839), pp. 574–75.

74 Solomon, *Far from the Tree*, 26.

75 genderspectrum.org.

76 See R. B. Toomey et al., "Gender-Nonconforming Lesbian, Gay, Bisexual, and Transgender Youth: School Victimization and Young Adult Psychosocial Adjustment," *Developmental Psychology* 46, no. 6 (2010): 1580–89.

77 Asaf Orr and Joel Baum, *Schools in Transition: A Guide for Supporting Transgender Students in K–12 Schools* (2015), genderspectrum.org.

78 Foreword by Janice Adams, in Orr and Baum, *Schools in Transition*, ii.

79 Orr and Baum, *Schools in Transition*, 4.

80 E. Menvielle and D. B. Hill, "An Affirmative Intervention for Families with Gender-Variant Children: A Process Evaluation," *Journal of Gay and Lesbian Mental Health* 15 (2011): 94–123.

81 Laura Erickson-Schroth, ed., *Trans Bodies, Trans Selves: A Resource for the Transgender Community* (New York: Oxford University Press, 2014).

82 American Psychological Association, *Guidelines for Psychological Practice with Transgender and Gender Nonconforming People* (2015), apa.org, 25.

83 Transgender Law Center, "Creating a Safe and Fair Climate to Learn and Thrive: Trans Youth Leading Change," *Authentic Lives*, Summer 2015, 10.

84 CeCe McDonald, "On Fashion, Fierceness, and Fighting Revolutions," *Authentic Lives*, Transgender Law Center, Summer 2015, 22.

85 Eric Vilain and J. Michael Bailey, "What Should You Do If Your Son Says He's a Girl?," Opinion Op-Ed, *Los Angeles Times*, May 21, 2015, latimes .com.

86 See T. D. Steensma et al., "Factors Associated with Desistence and Persistence of Childhood Gender Dysphoria: A Quantitative Follow-Up Study," *Journal of the American Academy of Child and Adolescent Psychiatry* 52, no. 6 (2013), 582–90.

87 Elizabeth Povoledo, "Book Ban in Venice Ignites Gay Rights Battle," *The New York Times*, August 19, 2015, A4, A8.

88 Personal communication from Ronald Elson, MD.

89 Jody Norton, "The Boy Who Grew Up to Be a Woman," in *Sissies and Tomboys: Gender Noncomformity and Homosexual Childhood*, ed. M. Rottnek (New York: NYU Publications, 1999), 273.

90 Rylan Jay Testa, Deborah Coolhart, and Jayme Peta, *The Gender Quest Workbook: A Guide for Teens and Young Adults Exploring Gender Identity* (Oakland, CA: New Harbinger Publications, 2015).

References

American Psychological Association. 2015. *Guidelines for Psychological Practice with Transgender and Gender Nonconforming People*. apa.org.

Asimov, N. 2014. "Mills College Spells Out What It Means to Be Female." *San Francisco Chronicle*, August 20, A1, A10.

Baker, KC. 2011. "Cher: I Admire Chaz's Courage," *People*, May 1, people.com.

Beemyn, G., and S. Rankin. 2011. *The Lives of Transgender People*. New York: Columbia University Press.

Brill, S., and R. Pepper. 2008. *The Transgender Child*. San Francisco: Cleis Press.

Carr, J. *Be Who You Are*. 2010. Bloomington, IN: AuthorHouse.

Chess, S., and A. Thomas. 1996. *Temperament*. New York: Routledge.

Chiland, C. 2003. *Transsexualism: Illusion and Reality*. Middletown, CT: Wesleyan University Press.

Cohen-Kettenis, P. T., S. E. Schagen, T. D. Steensma, A. L. de Vries, and H. A. Delemarre-van de Waal. 2011. "Puberty Suppression in a Gender-Dysphoric Adolescent: A 22-Year Follow-up." *Archives of Sexual Behavior* 40: 843–47.

de Vries, A. L. C., I. L. J. Noens, P. T. Cohen-Kettenis, I. A. van Berckelaer-Onnes, and T. A. Doreleijers. 2010. "Autism Spectrum Disorders in Gender Dysphoric Children and Adolescents." *Journal of Autism and Developmental Disorders* 40: 930–36. Published online January 22, 2010.

de Vries, A. L. C., J. K. McGuire, T. D. Steensma, E. C. F. Wagenaar, T. A. Doreleijers, and P. T. Cohen-Kettenis. 2014. "Young Adult Psychological Outcome After Puberty Suppression and Gender Reassignment." *Pediatrics* 134 (4): 696–704.

Duron, L. 2013. *Raising My Rainbow*. New York: Broadway Books.

Ehrensaft, D. 1997. *Spoiling Childhood: How Well-Meaning Parents Are Giving Children Too Much—But Not What They Need*. New York: Guilford Press.

_____. 2011. *Gender Born, Gender Made*. New York: The Experiment.

Erickson-Schroth, L., ed. 2014. *Trans Bodies, Trans Selves: A Resource for the Transgender Community*. New York: Oxford University Press.

Erikson, E. 1963. *Childhood and Society*. New York: W. W. Norton.

Freud, A., and D. Burlingham. 1944. *Infants Without Families: The Case For and Against Residential Nurseries*. New York: International University Press.

GenderQueer Revolution. 2015. Facebook page, facebook.com.

Gevisser, G. 2014. "Self-Made Man." *Granta* 129: Fate, Autumn, granta.com.

Goldberg, M. 2014. "What Is a Woman?" American Chronicles, *The New Yorker*, August 4, 24–28.

Green, F. J., and M. Friedman, eds. 2013. *Chasing Rainbows: Exploring Gender Fluid Parenting Practices*. Bradford, Ontario: Demeter Press.

Green, R. 1987. *The "Sissy Boy" Syndrome and the Development of Homosexuality*. New Haven, CT: Yale University Press.

Hartocollis, H. 2015. "The New Girl in School: Transgender Surgery at 18." *The New York Times*, June 17, A1 and A20.

Herthel, J., and J. Jenning. 2014. *I Am Jazz*. New York: Dial Books.

Hidalgo, M. A., D. Ehrensaft, A. C. Tishelman, L. Clark, R. Garofalo, S. M. Rosenthal, N. P. Spack, and J. Olson. 2013. "The Gender Affirmative Model: What We Know and What We Aim to Learn." *Human Development* 56: 285–90.

Hoffman, S. and I. 2014. *Jacob's New Dress*. Park Ridge, IL: Albert Whitman.

Kilodavis, C. 2010. *My Princess Boy*. New York: Aladdin.

Leigh, S. 2014. "Getting Beyond Male and Female." *San Francisco Chronicle*, February 12, D1, D2.

Manders, M. 2014. "Angelina Jolie and Brad Pitt Support Shiloh's Wish to Be Called 'John.'" *Refinery 29*, December 22, refinery29.com.

Maslow, A. H. 1943. "A Theory of Human Motivation." *Psychological Review* 50 (4): 370–96.

_____. 1968. *Toward a Psychology of Being*. New York: D. Van Nostrand.

_____. 1970. *Motivation and Personality*. New York: Harper & Row.

McDonald, C. 2015. "On Fashion, Fierceness, and Fighting Revolutions." *Authentic Lives*, Transgender Law Center, Summer, 20–22.

Menachem, S. 2014. "My Son Wears Dresses, and That's OK with Me." *Huffington Post*, July 14, huffingtonpost.com.

Menvielle, E., and D. B. Hill. 2011. "An Affirmative Intervention for Families with Gender-Variant Children: A Process Evaluation." *Journal of Gay and Lesbian Mental Health* 15: 94–123.

Mock, J. 2014. *Redefining Realness: My Path to Womanhood, Identity, Love and So Much More*. New York: Atria.

Norton, J. 1999. "The Boy Who Grew Up to Be a Woman," in *Sissies and Tomboys: Gender Noncomformity and Homosexual Childhood*. Edited by M. Rottnek, 263–73. New York: NYU Publications.

Orr, A., and J. Baum. 2015. *Schools in Transition: A Guide for Supporting Transgender Students in K–12 Schools*. genderspectrum.org.

Padawer, R. 2014. "Sisterhood Is Complicated." *The New York Times Magazine*, October 19, 34–39, 48, 50.

Pasterski, V., K. J. Zucker, P. C. Hindmarsh, I. A. Hughes, C. Acerini, D. Spencer, S. Neufeld, and M. Hines. 2014. "Increased Cross-Gender Identification Independent of Gender Role Behavior in Girls with Congenital Adrenal Hyperplasia: Results from a Standardized Assessment of 4- to 11-Year-Old Children." *Archives of Sexual Behavior*. Published online September 20.

Poisson, J. 2011. "Parents Keep Child's Gender Secret." *Toronto Star*, May 21, thestar.com.

Povoledo, E. 2015. "Book Ban in Venice Ignites Gay Rights Battle." *The New York Times*, August 19, A4, A8.

Prizmich, M. 2015. "Accept Trans Youth and Value Their Diverse Experiences." *San Francisco Chronicle,* February 25, sfchronicle.com.

Pyne, J. 2012. Rainbow Health Ontario Fact Sheet.

Rosenthal, S. M. 2014. "Approach to the Patient: Transgender Youth: Endocrine Considerations." *Journal of Clinical Endocrinology and Metabolism* 99 (12): 4379–89.

Rudacille, D. 2006. *The Riddle of Gender: Science, Activism, and Transgender Rights*. New York: Anchor Books.

Saker, A. 2015. "Raising Zay: A Family's Journey with a Transgender Child." *Enquirer*, February 21, cincinnati.com.

Saketopoulou, A. 2011. "Minding the Gap: Intersections Between Gender, Race, and Class in Work with Gender Variant Children." *Psychoanalytic Dialogues* 21: 192–209.

Schrappen, C. 2014. "Max Was Born a Girl, but Always Felt like a Boy." *St. Louis Post-Dispatch*, October 5, stltoday.com.

Sherer, I., S. M. Rosenthal, D. Ehrensaft, and J. Baum. 2012. "Child and Adolescent Gender Center: A Multidisciplinary Collaboration to Improve the Lives of Gender Nonconforming Children and Teens." *Pediatric Review* 33: 273–75.

Sherer, I., J. Baum, D. Ehrensaft, and S. M. Rosenthal. 2014. "Gender Nonconforming/Gender Expansive and Transgender Children and Teens." *Contemporary Pediatrics*, contemporarypediatrics.modernmedicine.com.

Simon, K. 2013. "Is There a Link Between Autism and Gender Dysphoria?" *Huffington Post Gay Voices*, September 13, huffingtonpost.com.

Singer, I. B. 1983. *Yentl the Yeshiva Boy*. New York: Farrar, Straus and Giroux.

Smith Cross, J. 2015. "Outcry Prompts CAMH to Review Its Controversial Treatment of Trans Youth." *Metro News*, Toronto, March 18, metronews .ca.

Solomon, A. 2013. *Far from the Tree: Parents, Children and the Search for Identity*. New York: Scribner.

Spack, N. P., L. Edwards-Leeper, H. A. Feldman, S. Leibowitz, F. Mandel, D. A. Diamond, and S. R. Vance. 2012. "Children and Adolescents with Gender Identity Disorder Referred to a Pediatric Medical Center." *Pediatrics* 129 (3): 418–25.

Spiegel, A. 2008. "Two Families Grapple with Sons' Gender Preferences." National Public Radio, *All Things Considered*, May 7.

Steensma, T. D., and P. T. Cohen-Kettenis. 2015. "More than Two Developmental Pathways in Children with Gender Dyshporia": Letter to the Editor. *Journal of the American Academy of Child and Adolescent Psychiatry* 54 (2) (February): 147–48.

Steensma, T. D., J. K. McGuire, B. P. C. Kreukels, A. J. Beekman, and P. T. Cohen-Kettenis. 2013. "Factors Associated with Desistence and Persistence of Childhood Gender Dysphoria: A Quantitative Follow-Up Study." *Journal of the American Academy of Child and Adolescent Psychiatry* 52 (6): 582–90.

Steinmetz, K. 2014. "America's Transition." *Time*, June 9, 38–46.

Stoller, R. 1985. *Presentations of Gender*. New Haven, CT: Yale University Press.

Sulek, J. P. 2015. "Transgender Grandchild: Rep. Mike Honda Says 8-Year-Old's Gender Change Not a Phase." *San Jose Mercury News*, February 19, mercurynews.com.

Testa, R. J., R. Coolhart, and J. Peta. 2015. *The Gender Quest Workbook: A Guide for Teens and Young Adults Exploring Gender Identity*. Oakland, CA: New Harbinger Publications.

The Brothers Grimm. 1973. "The Frog Prince," *Grimms Fairy Tales*. New York: Crown, 14–18.

The Whittington Family Story: Ryland. 2014. YouTube, May 27, youtube.com.

Thomas, A., S. Chess, and H. G. Birch. 1968. *Temperament and Behavior Disorders in Children*. New York: New York University Press.

Toomey, R. B., C. Ryan, R. M. Diaz, N. A. Card, and S. T. Russell. 2010. "Gender-Nonconforming Lesbian, Gay, Bisexual, and Transgender Youth: School Victimization and Young Adult Psychosocial Adjustment." *Developmental Psychology* 46 (6): 1580–89.

Transgender Law Center. 2015. "Creating a Safe and Fair Climate to Learn and Thrive: Trans Youth Leading Change." *Authentic Lives*, Summer, 9–12.

Ubelacker, S. 2015. "CAMH to 'Wind Down' Controversial Gender Identity Clinic Services." *Globe and Mail*, December 15, theglobeandmail.com.

Vance, S. R., D. Ehrensaft, and S. M. Rosenthal. 2014. "Psychological and Medical Care of Gender Nonconforming Youth." *Pediatrics* 134 (6): 1184–92.

VanderLaan, D. P., L. Lori Postema, H. Wood, D. Singh, S. Fantus, J. Hyun, J. Leef, S. J. Bradley, and K. J. Zucker. 2015. "Do Children with Gender Dysphoria Have Intense/Obsessional Interests?" *Journal of Sex Research* 52 (2), 213–19.

Vilain, E., and J. M. Bailey. 2015. "What Should You Do If Your Son Says He's a Girl?" *Los Angeles Times* Opinion Op-Ed, May 21, latimes.com.

Waldron, C. 2014. *My Daughter, He*. Rockport, MA: Stone Circle Press.

Wallace, R., and H. Russell. 2014. "Attachment and Shame in Gender-Nonconforming Children and Their Families: Toward a Theoretical Framework for Evaluating Clinical Interventions." *International Journal of Transgenderism* 14 (3): 113–26, 119.

Weiss, P. 2012. "Dad Protects Son from Bullies by Wearing a Skirt. Guess What? It Works." *Shine* from Yahoo! Canada, August 31, ca.shine.yahoo .com.

White, E. B. 1945. *Stuart Little*. New York: Harper Trophy.

Wikipedia. 2015. "Genderqueer." en.wikipedia.org, January 5.

Wing Sue, D. 2010. *Microaggressions in Everyday Life: Race, Gender, and Sexual Orientation*. New York: Wiley.

Winnicott, D. W. 1971. *Playing and Reality*. London: Tavistock.

World Professional Association for Transgender Health. 2011. *Standards of Care for the Health of Transsexual, Transgender, and Gender Nonconforming People*. wpath.org.

Zucker, K., and S. J. Bradley. 1995. *Gender Identity Disorder and Psychosexual Problems in Children and Adolescents*. New York: Guilford Press.

Zucker, K. J., H. Wood, D. Singh, and S. J. Bradley. 2012. "A Developmental, Biopsychosocial Model for the Treatment of Children with Gender Identity Disorder." *Journal of Homosexuality* 59: 3, 369–97.

ACKNOWLEDGMENTS

First and foremost, I want to thank all of the gender creative children and families who have entered my life over these many years—in my private practice, at the UCSF Benioff Children's Hospital Child and Adolescent Gender Center Clinic, at workshops and conferences throughout the world, and in my personal life. You have been my guiding light and my mentors in helping me understand just exactly what it means to be a gender creative child, sibling, parent, caregiver, grandparent, aunt, uncle, or cousin.

And next come the people at The Experiment, who have made this book a reality. A very special thanks to Matthew Lore, cofounder and president of The Experiment, for meeting with me for coffee one day in 2008 at Oliveto's Café in Oakland, California, and putting his faith in me to morph into print my ideas and my passion about gender creative children. And without the incredible support of Allie Bochicchio, editor; Jeanne Tao, managing editor; Iris Bass, external editor; Jennifer Hergenroeder, publicity and marketing manager; and Elizabeth Johnson, events manager, those ideas would have remained just that.

I now come to my village of gender specialist colleagues, my midwives in giving birth to *The Gender Creative Child*. Without a doubt, Stephen Rosenthal has been my closest colleague, friend, and muse in founding the Child and Adolescent Gender Center, making our pediatric gender clinic at UCSF Benioff Children's Hospital a reality, and just being there. Right alongside him are my other team members at CAGC and the clinic—Asaf Orr,

Joel Baum, Meredith Russell, Molly Koren, Stanley Vance, Ilana Sherer. And then there is each and every member of Mind the Gap, the ever-growing mental health subgroup of the Child and Adolescent Gender Center. Without you and our monthly Sunday meetings at my house, I would never know what I know today. To Lisa Kenney and Pam Wool at Gender Spectrum, deep gratitude for all that you do and all the support you have given me. And special thanks to some particular colleagues who have come along with me on this gender journey for many years, if not decades—Herb Schreier, Stephanie Brill, Caitlin Ryan, Karisa Barrow, Susanna Moore, Susan Bernstein, Dan Karasic, Jamison Green, Lin Fraser, Susanne Watson, Shawn Giammattei, Lisette Lahana, Joy Johnson, Michelle Jurkewicz. And reaching across the continent: to my close friends and colleagues in the South, that would be Santa Cruz, California—Jennifer Hastings, Shane Hill, and Ben Geilhufe; Los Angeles—Joanna Olson and Aydin Kennedy; Texas—Colt Meier; New Mexico—Nate Sharon. In the Midwest—Marco Hidalgo, Diane Chen, Scott Leibowitz, Rob Garafolo. In the East—Amy Tishelman, Norm Spack, Randi Kaufman, Francie Mandel, Edgardo Menvielle, Catherine Tuerk, Jean Malpas, Aron Janssen, Cathy Renna. North of the border— Jake Pyne. And across the globe—Sam Winter, Thomas Steensma, Annelou de Vries, and Simon Pickstone-Taylor.

A few people, close friends and colleagues, have simply been grounding poles for my whole professional life, not just for my gender explorations, and to them I want to express my deepest gratitude for helping me be the best psychologist, writer, and feminist I could be. That would be Gloria Lawrence, with special thanks for every one of our Thursday lunches for almost twenty-five years now; Toni Heineman for reading, writing, thinking, working, and playing with me and for her endless dedication to children in foster care; my decades-running child consultation group—Eileen Keller, Bonnie Rottier, and Stephen Walrod—

without which I could never be the therapist I am today; Marcy Whitebook, for her dedication to the lives of young children and keeping me on track with mine; Nancy Chodorow, for thinking, walking, sharing her mind with me; Barbara Waterman, who has showed undying enthusiasm for my work and has always generously lent me her critical and insightful eye as both a thinker and commenter on my writing.

A person does not live by work alone, and this book could have died on the vine if I had not had the warmth and love of close friends around me. From far away—Elli and Robby Meeropol, Mindy Werner-Crohn and Joel Crohn, Stephanie Riger and Dan Lewis, and Cathey Billian. Closer to home—Alan Heineman, Matt Ross. To my communal eating group, I would like to extend the heartiest of thanks, not just for the food we eat but for the years of friendship, intellectual sharing, talking politics, raising families together, and offering the love that feed both my mind and my soul—Joanna Levine and Marc Stickgold, Joan Skolnick and Randy Reiter, Nancy Hollander and Stephen Portuges, Anne Bernstein and Ringo Hallinan, Noree Lee and Ron Elson, Yana and Len Goldfine. Everyone should be as lucky as I am to have a chosen family like you.

And last, I want to acknowledge my family, both close in and miles away: my mother and father, Edith and Morris Ehrensaft, for being my role models for living a very long and full life and giving me all the educational opportunities they did not have so I could be here writing these acknowledgements right now; to my brothers, Phil and Rick Ehrensaft, for lovingly showing me about gender across the aisle—that would be the world of boys and their toys; to my children, Rebecca Hawley and Jesse Ehrensaft-Hawley—words can't even begin to describe the depth of my gratitude to them for all they have taught me and all they give me; the same goes for my granddaughter, Satya Hawley, who could sing her way into anybody's heart. And always, and forever, I will thank my husband, Jim Hawley, for being the wonderful husband, father, and grandfather he is, for putting up with a sometimes write-aholic partner, for giving me the bandwidth to talk endlessly about gender, and for helping me come up for air, with a glass of wine and a smile on his face.

INDEX

nature, in gender web, 25, 27
needle phobia, 109, 110, 111, 113,
    177, 192
needs, hierarchy of, 143
Netherlands, 63, 161–62
"New Girl in School: Transgender
    Surgery at 18," 198
New Yorker, The, 22–23
New York Times, The, 198, 243
New York Times Magazine, The,
    23–24
Norton, Jody, 246
NPR (National Public Radio),
    14–15, 228
nurture, in gender web, 25, 27

onset, early, 56–57, 66–67
oranges
    about, 64–65
    confusion about, 65–66
    early onset of, 66–67
    example, 68
    gender expressions, 67–68
    gender maze and, 122
    as "gender offensive," 66
    "I wish I were a …"
        statements, 67
    protogay children as, 65
    See also desisters
outing, 236

parental acceptance
    about, 139–41
    as form of protection, 142–46
    hyperactive, 141–42

parental support, 137–39
parents
    as ally, advocate, ambassador,
        146–51
    apples and, 57–58, 63–64
    in conflict, 171–72
    guilty feelings, 213–14
    medical interventions and,
        211–16
    motivations and psychological
        issues, 100–101
    support networks for, 231–32
pediatricians, 185–90
persisters, 49, 53, 61–62
    See also apples
Peta, Jayme, 252
"phase," gender exploration
    described as, 134–35, 187–88
Pickert, Nils, 8–9
pink boys, 2–3
Pitt, Brad, 117
possibility, 83, 84
Priuses, gender, 36
pronouns, gender-neutral, 259n3
protection, acceptance as form of,
    142–46
protogay children, 41, 65
prototransgender youth, 41–42
psychiatric conditions, comorbid,
    84–85
psychiatric gender fixers, doctors
    as, 185
psychiatrists, referral to, 188–89
puberty, delayed, 200–201, 203

About the Author

DIANE EHRENSAFT, PhD, is a developmental and clinical psychologist who for over thirty years has worked with gender-nonconforming children and their families. Dr. Ehrensaft is the author of numerous books and articles on child development, gender, and parenting. Her previous books include *Gender Born, Gender Made*; *Parenting Together*; *Spoiling Childhood*; *Mommies, Daddies, Donors, Surrogates*; and *Building a Home Within* (with Toni Vaughn Heineman). Dr. Ehrensaft is an associate professor of pediatrics at the University of California, San Francisco, and the attending psychologist at the UCSF Benioff Children's Hospital Child and Adolescent Gender Center Clinic. She is a founding member of the Child and Adolescent Gender Center and serves as its director of mental health. She speaks in the United States and abroad on the subject of gender-nonconforming children at both community and professional conferences and is cited frequently in the media. She has appeared in *The New York Times* and many other media outlets and was featured in National Public Radio's landmark 2008 two-part series on gender-nonconforming children. Dr. Ehrensaft is a founding member of A Home Within, a national project focused on the emotional needs of children and youth in foster care, and holds leadership positions with Gender Spectrum, a national organization offering education, training, and advocacy services to promote gender acceptance. She is a mother, a grandmother, and a proud member of PFLAG. Dr. Ehrensaft lives and practices in Oakland, California.
dianeehrensaft.com